CINDER GIRL

Growing Up on America's Fringe
A Memoir

HOLLY THOMPSON REHDER

BOMBARDIER
BOOKS

Published by Bombardier Books
An Imprint of Post Hill Press
ISBN: 978-1-63758-120-9
ISBN (eBook): 978-1-63758-121-6

Cover Design by Tiffani Shea

All people, locations, events, and situations are portrayed to the best of the author's memory. While all of the events described are true, many names and identifying details have been changed to protect the privacy of the people involved.

Scripture quotations taken from The Holy Bible, New International Version® NIV® Copyright © 1973 1978 1984 2011 by Biblica, Inc.™ Used by permission. All rights reserved worldwide.

Scripture quotations marked HCSB are taken from the Holman Christian Standard Bible®, Used by Permission HCSB ©1999, 2000, 2002, 2003, 2009 Holman Bible Publishers. Holman Christian Standard Bible®, Holman CSB®, and HCSB® are federally registered trademarks of Holman Bible Publishers.

Scripture quotations taken from the Amplified® Bible (AMP), Copyright © 2015 by The Lockman Foundation. Used by permission. www.lockman.org.

Post Hill Press
New York • Nashville
posthillpress.com

Published in the United States of America
1 2 3 4 5 6 7 8 9 10

~~~~~~

To my true ride or die.

I never realized how much you were there,

until you were gone.

Peace out DD,

Your Little Sister

~~~~~~

TABLE OF CONTENTS

Cinder Girl

When I thought of a name for this memoir, a line from my favorite movie, *Ever After* (1998), immediately came to mind. The elderly woman telling the story speaks of the "little cinder girl," a young woman whose childhood was filled with struggles and tragedies. Her story contained numerous villains, but a couple of giants as well. Not giants in our normal sense of the word, but giants when it came to wisdom and love. Unlike the traditional Cinderella story, the little cinder girl was not protected or saved by a male hero. She figured life out for herself, made mistakes along the way, and worked her way out of her bad situation. Her remarkable resilience and compassion for others were direct products of her harsh upbringing.

As I thought back to the scenes of that familiar movie, I quickly looked for the definition of "cinder."

Cinder
| `sinder |

a small piece of partly burned coal or wood that has stopped giving off flames but still has combustible matter in it.

Exactly. A life that has been partly charred, isn't in flames any longer, but has a fire burning deep, deep within.

I can totally relate. "Partly charred," most definitely. I have scars and bruises from life, and no matter how ugly or painful, they've only served to make me stronger. So, I don't hide them. Thinking of cinders reminds me of something often underestimated. To the eye, they may not look like much, but you can't always see the fire they have burning inside. Throughout my life and career, many have underestimated me. But trust me, I don't give up. When I'm fighting for something, I'm tenacious. You can't pat me on the head in hopes of shutting me up or shutting me down. I will not go quietly into that good night—just like a fire smoldering inside a cinder does not go out when it's told to.

I instantly knew it was a perfect title.

Girls like me do not typically grow up with the ability to look back and see a crazy but extraordinary, journey. I grew up on welfare and food stamps. No actual father around. My mother struggled with mental illness her whole life. Her struggles translated into five marriages and too many men to count—in and out of our lives over a span of a few years. Some would live with us; some would be in and out. We traveled frequently across the country via Greyhound bus. When her love of choice became a problem for Mama, we boxed up our belongings and headed out. These years were also riddled with sexual abuse, domestic violence, and drug abuse.

For me, this lifestyle meant that I was the new kid at school multiple times each year. It also meant that I had to save my mother at times from the bad choices she seemed to constantly make and to save myself and my sisters sometimes from the danger around us. I was the responsible one, or at least I felt responsible for everyone. Finally, as it happens with so many, this way of life then equated to me cycling back around and making many of those same bad choices at an early age myself. Welcome to the poverty cycle.

The poverty cycle is something we hear people talk about a lot in politics. I am a product of it. Soon after I turned fifteen, we were in a terrible car accident, and I needed to quit school to take care of my mother and little sister. Which I did. I also married my twenty-one-year-old boyfriend, who had already been living with us on and off for over a year. I then became a mother myself a little more than a year after the accident. Living like gypsies in and out of trailer parks for most of my childhood, becoming a high-school dropout and a pregnant teenager, I was smack on the path to continue the life that my first education had taught me: the poverty cycle, government reliance, broken will, and broken soul.

Let's pause for a moment. It's important that I clearly state that me getting out of this dysfunction and poverty is nothing to pat myself on the back about. I know me. I was never the kid who stood out. I was always incredibly shy. A skinny little redhead with a long nose. A good student because I cared to do well, but I definitely had to work for it. I was diagnosed with dyslexia early on in my childhood, so I was certainly not the kid that got tested for the gifted classes. Our moving around during the school year also made it difficult to keep up. We moved over thirty times from my last month of third grade to my first month of tenth grade. My success is unequivocally because God honors hard work, obedience, and dedication—regardless of where you have come from.

So that's me. Going from a high school dropout at just fifteen, married, pregnant, and homeless at times, to a business owner with a college degree, a state representative, and now a state senator—I don't just talk about the American dream. With every inhale, with every exhale, I *know* the American dream.

What I have learned, though, from my upbringing, is that our current welfare system too often hinders people's ability to rise to their potential—like it has for many of the women in my family. As a new state legislator, I quickly realized that those trying to make policies to bring people out of poverty have never seen it from the inside. They have never experienced it, much less gotten themselves out of it. I don't want to hear the number of people that were cut off of welfare this year; tell me the number of *those* individuals that are now working full time or have received a degree or training certificate. That's the number that helps to ensure that generations to come experience upward mobility, and that our tax dollars are not just feeding the cycle.

My desire is for this book to provide a little hope, insight, and understanding with a little less judgement tied to it. I feel that each can be seen through the mountains and valleys of many of my life experiences. I am not a trained writer or researcher. That is why this is a memoir; these are my personal memories. Those of you trapped in the poverty cycle need to see that there is hope, that your upbringing and/or your previous bad choices do not have to define you. Those who have never been in the poverty cycle truly need to understand that many of us are raised very differently. *Life* has trained us differently. We are jaded. We start from a different lane. Our obstacle course is very different, so, many times, our paths to success simply cannot be the same as those of mainstream America. Government programs that begin by attempting to mash us into that "normal" box do not work well.

On top of what's passed down generation to generation, we struggle with higher percentages of mental illness and drug abuse—for many different reasons. All of the "crazy" in my life that you will see in the coming pages, actually made the choices that I made—like getting married at fifteen—seem incredibly normal to me. In the trailer parks where we grew up in, this was normal. As you read this memoir, I only ask one thing—please save all judgments until the end. As my mother would always say to us girls, "Until you've walked a mile in their moccasins"—we really have no idea. We must step outside the vacuum that we live in and learn about others if we are truly going to make substantial changes that help people; specifically, Americans who are living in the margins.

Many growing up in this same culture are incredibly affected by the opioid crisis. Understanding substance abuse is something I try to give a little insight to. Not because I have the solution. I do not. There is no silver bullet to fix this crisis. What I have found, though, through my years as a legislator fighting for myself and others in the bowels of this hell, is that most with the power to help simply do not get it. Many still think of addiction as a moral failing. Many have never faced addiction as a child living through it. I have. Many have never seen it through the hollow and dark eyes of their own child. I have. The understanding that so many in politics simply do not have on this public health crisis unfortunately only serves to feed the stigma. It doesn't have to be that way; education and understanding can, and do, make way for faster and better outcomes.

Until the opioid epidemic, you didn't hear this group being spoken of often. Poor, rural, uneducated, and mostly white, "trailer trash," "white trash," and "redneck" are a few of the names that we're called. I have learned that many have made it out like me. They are just silent about their raising. Many are purposefully hiding their past in the shadows because that past holds shame and guilt. Many know that speaking about it would only serve to rip open scars and penetrate portions of their soul that they simply need to remain in darkness. They've gotten out and refuse to look back. I respect that; survival comes in many forms.

But in this book, I choose to write about it. I tell those embarrassing and shameful stories of my past because God has given me the ability to look back, laugh, and be thankful. He has given me the ability to let it go and use the agony of years past to become the person that I want to be. I am simply writing about my life. What I have lived. I am not writing for sympathy. There are countless numbers of people who have been raised with much less, who have survived abuses beyond compare. For whatever reason, God allowed me to get out. As a state legislator, he has also given me a microphone at this moment in time, so I'm going to use it.

This book is not meant to be academic or scientific. It is simply real. I have chosen to change the names of the innocent, and some of the guilty, because blaming is not what this book is about. It's about hope. For the policymaker, the community leader, the mother struggling to understand what went wrong, I pray it offers thoughtful insight into an epidemic that is hard to comprehend. I truly believe that by seeing through the prism of my eyes, you can have a glimpse into so many Americans' reality. For those who love tragedy and drama mixed with a little comedy, this book is for you. If you love to read nonfiction struggles, pain, and triumph, this is also a good book for you. A gut-honest, modern-day Cinderella story.

When some see cinders, they see a pile of worthless, dirty ashes and a fire that's almost out. That's not what I see. I see coals that, although their color is different because of their intense journey, smolder too hot to touch or manipulate. Coals with a fire inside that unmistakably says that they, and they alone, will decide when to burn out.

I will never forget where I have come from, or who brought me out.

"For I know the plans I have for you," declares
the Lord, "plans to prosper you and not to harm
you, plans to give you hope and a future."

—*Jeremiah 29:11*

CHAPTER I

TEXAS

I still remember that night as if it were yesterday, not over forty years ago. Remembering childhood events can be foggy sometimes, especially as we get older, but not this memory. Not this night. I was only eight years old, but this night changed the landscape of my days. It changed the safeness of my nights. It literally changed how I saw people, and how I read situations around me. Family. Truth. Justice.

Sometime in the middle of the night, I was awoken by my mother's sad and distressed voice, "Holly Bells, I need you to wake up." I was sound asleep on my waterbed in my bedroom in Garland, Texas, and this was not completely abnormal. My mother struggled with mental illness; of course, at that time in my life I didn't have a name for it. We just knew that sometimes Mama was really sad and sometimes she had some off-the-wall emotional outbursts.

We had a four-bedroom Mexican modern–style house. Each of us girls had our own bedroom, but my sisters always insisted on sleeping together. Not me. I had my own thing going. A waterbed with satin sheets, a black drum set, a record player, and my own albums—KISS and Leif Garrett were my favorites. *Tiger Beat* posters filled my walls, and my room was always clean. I didn't want, or need, a roommate.

As Mama came to wake us, my sisters were asleep in my little sister, Lisa's, room. Dawn was ten and Lisa only five years old. Lisa's room was down the hall from mine. My mother woke me first and I followed her to wake my sisters. Daddy was upset and I could sense the tension, once again, in the house. He wasn't home much because he was a long-haul truck driver, but it seemed like when he was home, they were fighting. I sat quietly on the edge of Lisa's bed while Mama woke my sisters. I always tried to stay out of the way, not wanting to add to her drama.

Mama's midnight-hour "happenings" were actually pretty normal when Daddy was on the road. Most of the time, however, they didn't include us. Not intentionally at least. I knew her signals, excuses like she would be up late reading so none of us could sleep with her. On those nights, I would watch and sneak on her to find out which guy was parked down the road this time or whose clothes were strewn throughout the living room. I never wanted my sisters to know that Mama had company so I would make sure they were asleep and that Lisa's bedroom door was closed. I would lay awake in the room with them until I heard the car start and then I would watch him leave from Lisa's big window. Then, and only then, would I go to bed.

But not this night. This night was all wrong. There was something eerie in the air, something dark. Daddy was home and Mama was an emotional mess getting us out of bed in the middle of the night. It was also during the school week, and she was saying we needed to hurry and get in the car because we were leaving for Grandma's house. Now let me say, going to Grandma's house was always a reason for celebration. The woman was a saint and she not only walked on water, but she helped hang the moon as well. So those words were always "game on" to me. But we didn't go to Grandma's in the middle of school time. Grandma's house was 600 miles away in Sikeston, a sleepy little town in the flatlands of southeast Missouri. We talked about it and planned for weeks before leaving for Grandma's. Something was very wrong, and I needed answers. All I got were tears and hugs from Mama. She told me to hurry up and gather a few of my favorite clothes and two toys; Daddy would have to come back for the rest of our things when it's safe.

Safe? What is not safe? My young mind was reeling. I went straight to the living room where Daddy sat sadly and quietly on the couch. I knew I would get answers from him. He and I were close. He was not my biological father, but I was closest to him. They married on my second birthday, so he was the one living in our home and raising me. My biological father didn't have that opportunity. He lived hours away in southeast Missouri. So, my stepdad, John, was whom I called Daddy. He and I weathered my mother's mood storms together. We had a language just between us, and yes, I told him things. Things that happened when he was away on the road working. Apparently, that is what triggered this awful night. Daddy explained only that we could talk later and that it would all be okay. He sternly told me to go and do as she said; we had to get on the road.

Daddy John always had time for me to climb in his lap. He always had time to talk through my quiet questions that I trusted only to him. None of this added up but I did as he said, knowing that he would be with us. I could ask again once we had another minute alone. I threw my favorite clothes in my tiny suitcase. I grabbed my Baby Crissy first, as she was my most favorite toy. Baby Crissy, you have to understand, is a real-life-size baby doll with auburn hair. She looked like I could be her mama. I got her for Christmas when I was four years old. I was never a Barbie kind of girl. I'm a realist. My entire doll collection consisted of Baby Crissy and the Bionic Woman. Again, because I'm a realist. I forwent my Bionic Woman; she could handle herself until I got back. I grabbed my red tabby cat, Sunshine, and we climbed into the back of my mama's new maroon Thunderbird. I wanted to get in before anyone else and get settled in case someone had a problem with Sunshine going. I was prepared for the oncoming fight.

As we pulled out of town, I listened to my parents' sad voices arguing as I laid my head back and stared at the raindrops hitting the car window. Sunshine was asleep in my lap, and Baby Crissy was tucked safely under my arm. My sisters were already sound asleep as if they didn't have a care in the world. I listened intently. I did not understand it all, but much of what I was hearing them say made me want to cover my face with my pillow and disappear. As the streetlights became fewer and fewer, I fell asleep trying to piece together the awful story their words to each other were describing.

Maybe I should start from the beginning.

Me and Sunshine in our Texas life.

My mother was beautiful. She was top of her high school class and was an aspiring artist. She and my biological daddy, Steve, ran off and got married when she was only seventeen. She was far from being ready, but she was in love, and she needed to get out of a sexually abusive home situation. Her plans were to finish high school elsewhere and start college. Instead, she got pregnant with my sister Dawn. Then pregnant with me only two years later. They divorced after four years when I was one and Dawn was three. My mother seemed to fall in love quite quickly. She soon married John, my stepdad, and we moved to Dallas, Texas.

We had a small two-bedroom house on a quiet street with sidewalks, driveways, and backyards. Plenty of trees to climb and plenty of kids to play with. My earliest memories start there, on Wasina Drive. I was three when my little sister Lisa was born. I honestly don't remember her being brought home from the hospital. What I do remember though is this wild child that seemed to be walking, climbing, and jumping off of things in no time. Dora Lisa Jeannette Coyne. She was daring and beautiful. Long, silky, dark brown hair and big brown eyes like my mother. As soon as she could pull herself up, she was climbing on anything and everything, touching all my stuff and playing with things that were not hers. She would slam doors, scream in the house, and play in the dirt while wearing nothing but her sandals and panties. I'm talking out of control. Lisa was happiest when she was running and screaming and laughing. It was exhausting trying to get her to act right. Clearly that was not my job as a sibling only three years older than her, but I seemed to take on that responsibility. Someone needed to. And that was me, the responsible one.

Dawn, Lisa, Holly—Wasina Drive, Dallas, TX.

I was Lisa's opposite. Long, strawberry-blonde, shiny hair, fair skin, freckles, and light green eyes. On top of that, I'm the only one of us that is left-handed and dyslexic. All of this combined makes me look like the child who must have actually been the mailman's, which wasn't a far stretch of thought with my mama. My smile has always been too big for my face and back then, showed more gums than teeth. I was quiet, very shy, and a watcher. A light sleeper too. Nothing went on in our house that I didn't know about. It hurt my feelings if anyone got into trouble, though, so I made sure to keep all information gathered on others to myself. Most of the time, at least.

My older sister Dawn looked like our biological father, Steve. He was a drummer—good looking and super cool—so she was very proud to look like him. Blond hair, blue eyes, and fair skin. Dawn Marie Thompson, as she preferred to be called. Or Delta Dawn, like the Tanya Tucker song. She switched it up often and I went along with whatever she decided. Dawn was different. While Lisa and I were both extra thin, Dawn was a little thicker. Not big at all, but she was always worried about her weight.

Two years older than me to the day, Dawn was always interesting and colorful. When we played dress-up, she would go straight for the blue eye shadow, no lie. All over her eyelids like she didn't have a care in the world and dared anyone to not like it. As the timid one, I will have to admit that her extraordinary use of such a bold color freaked me out a bit. I could never be so daring, not even playing dress-up at home with just my sisters. But Dawn could and did. I loved that about her.

Dawn's hair didn't feel like mine and Lisa's. Her hair was thick and coarse to the touch, and very dry. She was born, however, with silky Shirley Temple curls. All the old people in the family talked about it when we were around them. Mama would tell us the story of how Dawn would throw fits and not let her comb through the rats (that's what we called tangles), so she chopped off all the curls in the front yard one day and it grew back into "this," meaning coarse, thick, and dry. I always felt bad for her over that story. But honestly, her hair most likely ended up being the least of Mama's offenses that Dawn held against her before it was all over with.

Daddy John was a construction worker at the time, but he soon went off to truck-driving school. He was gone two weeks and I very much remember that, even though I was so young. I didn't like him being gone and I felt as if he would never return. It was the longest two weeks of my so-far short life. Things were different when Daddy wasn't home. Mama slept a lot and seemed really sad most of the time. As I got older, I came to understand that she struggled with manic depression. What we knew then was that we could never guess what the next day would bring.

I very much blame my first spanking on this—Mama's manic depression. As I have already noted, I was a quiet and shy child and tried to stay out of the way. I remember only two real spankings in my life. Side note here—in the South, there is a difference between a "spanking" and getting the fire slapped out of your mouth.

Back to my first spanking.

Mama was asleep and it was already late morning. I was really tired of being inside the dark house and knew there was no telling when she would be getting up. Daddy was at truck-driving school and my sisters played well together, but not so much with me—the middle child. I decided to take the chance and wake her up to ask if I could go out to play with my friends. I quietly went into her dark bedroom. During these times, Mama kept the window shades drawn and the entire house dark. It was too dark for me. Too dark for my inner being. I hated it. Standing by her bed, I gently woke her while I stroked her soft hair. "Mama," I said, speaking softly, "would it be okay for me to go across the street to Karen's house to play?"

In her groggy voice, she said, "Okay."

"Thank you, Mama," I whispered then reached over and kissed her cheek softly before quietly exiting her bedroom. Free at last.

I was already dressed as I never wasted time in the mornings. I took off out of the house, looked both ways, and crossed the road to Karen's house. I knocked on the door and was happily invited inside, where we played with whatever Karen wanted to that day. Board games, jacks, whatever. It didn't matter to me. Her mother was older, kind of crabby actually, but was always up cleaning and cooking with the shades up and the sunlight coming in. Life was good at Karen's.

Good until sometime later, that is. I am not sure how long I had been there playing when a frantic knock came at the screen door. I looked up from the living room floor where I was sitting and saw my mother, sheer nightgown, bare feet, and all, standing on the porch with the angriest face I have ever seen. She locked eyes with me, and she immediately started screaming. The embarrassment, and her disappointment in me, brought instant tears to my eyes. Tears even before she was able to reach in, snatch me up, and drag my skinny butt out of there, all while beating me all the way back across that street home. She screamed the entire time about not crossing the road and how I could be dead. Which, honestly, I kinda wanted to be at that moment.

Once we got to our porch, she broke down crying and apologized. She cried all over me while smothering me with hugs and kisses, holding me too tight and telling me how it would be the death of her if anything happened to me. All I wanted was for her to go inside and put some clothes on.

That was my mother. A beautiful mess.

The truck-driving school went well. Once Daddy was finished and back home, we celebrated his new job and the cool big rig he got to drive. My sisters and I could not believe the size of his truck! And man was it awesome to scale the side like a monkey, climb up into the cab, and stretch out on the bed. It had a bed!

Wait, why does it have a bed?

I was quickly informed that Daddy would be gone for a few days at a time. Or forever, as my mind calculated it. I was promised that I could go with him sometimes on his runs. Now the thought of that did excite me. Me and Daddy on the open road. No sisters, Mama, or drama. We could listen to "Satin Sheets" by Jeanne Pruett and sing as loud as we wanted without my sisters interrupting.

Maybe this would be a good thing after all.

It was not. As I said, my mother was beautiful. Striking even. She was tall. Busty. And had legs that went on forever. She had no shortage of suitors, and she wore her sexuality like Bambi wore innocence. Her being left alone for days at a time was not good for us girls, it was not good for her depression, and it was not good for their marriage. She was about twenty-five or twenty-six years old and there was not a trip to the grocery store that didn't end up with some strange guy talking to her too long already. Without Daddy around, her attention was far from the three of us girls. She was never abusive, but her protectiveness was hit or miss at best.

Mama—twenty-three years old, Dallas, TX.

My first concussion happened during this time. I was six years old, and Mama went next door for a Tupperware party. She took my little sister, thank the good Lord, and left me and Dawn at home. She was just next door so we could come find her if we had to, but it was after dark, so we were not allowed to be out milling around in the yard. I mean, what could happen?

As I have explained, I was a scrawny little thing and Dawn was, well, not. She asked me if I wanted to play helicopter and for whatever reason, I thought it sounded like a great idea. Dawn had me lay down flat on the floor with my face in the carpet. She reached down and grabbed me by my ankles, and she said she was going to lift my legs and spin me around as fast as she could. And she did. She really did. I am pretty certain we didn't make it around more than two or three times before gravity pulled me from her grip. I went flying, more like a rocket than a helicopter, across the living room and headfirst into our wooden rocking chair. I blacked out. Dawn ran and got Mama and we were on our way to the hospital before I realized what had happened. They kept me overnight, which was totally fine by me. It was my first trip to the hospital, and they treated me like a queen. I had no idea hospitals could be so fun. The next day they decided I could go home, but I had to take it easy because of my concussion. *Heck yes!* I was happy to milk that for as long as possible.

I've often wondered why my mother left a six- and an eight-year-old alone in a house. Even if just next door for a couple of hours. It was a different time, I guess. But there were many things back then that simply were not normal.

My aunt, my mother's older sister, came from Missouri to visit us during one of my daddy's long runs. My mother was adopted at about ten years of age by distant relatives who became Grandma and Papa to my sisters and me; this was Mama's biological sister that came to visit. My aunt's new boyfriend drove her the entire way in what I considered a pretty cool van. It had shag carpet inside—ceiling included. He was only seventeen years old. I know this because Dawn got all the details for me. We both had an issue with them being at our house and pretty much didn't like any of what we were seeing or hearing around us. My aunt's boyfriend also brought his best friend Grant. Grant was only fifteen years old, and he ended up sharing the bedroom with Mama. From night number one, I couldn't stand him. Clearly a lot to unpack there.

Mama was certainly in a better mood with Grant around fawning over her but even at my very young age, I knew what this meant to Daddy. My heart hurt for him, and I missed him terribly. We seemed to have a lot of weird people coming around at this time. A couple of times, we went to house parties, where I learned the smell of pot. My mother never smoked, drank, or took illegal drugs. She may have had us in these places, but she was totally sober the entire time. Other than her prescribed medications, and she had a few, she honestly did not mess with drugs. I heard her say "No, thank you" a thousand times.

I have no recollection of how all that ended, but it ended soon thereafter. My aunt, her boyfriend, and Grant loaded up in the shag carpet van and went back to Missouri. Daddy moved back home, and Mama got to pick out a brand-new home in Garland, a suburb of Dallas. We were now getting to move from a two-bedroom ranch-style house into a four-bedroom home on a street that was so new it only had four houses! Our house had a stucco exterior, and all I know is that it felt like a palace to me. Life was turning around.

It was the summer of 1976. I was six years old and had just passed the first grade. I could read now with the tools I had learned, and I was getting to enroll in the public school with my sister. This was a really big deal for me because I had skipped kindergarten to be put into a special school for first grade due to my early dyslexia diagnosis. New home, new neighborhood, new school. I was not afraid. With Grant and the others in the rearview mirror, things were going to be good again. Riding in the front seat of that U-Haul, just me and Daddy driving to Garland, I remember the song "Afternoon Delight" by the Starland Vocal Band coming on. In my thick Texan drawl, I said, "Turn it up, Daddy! It's time to sing!"

Some moments in time feel so good you can hold onto them forever. No matter how small they may have been.

Garland seemed like a good change. Mama loved the house and the community. She enrolled us in school, and she enrolled in art classes. I believe the art classes must have given her back some of herself that she felt had been lost. She had given up so much opportunity when she quit school, got married, and became a mother. I know this because she talked about it a lot. Not that I understood much of what she was talking about then, but the older I got, the more I understood those earlier years.

Her depression seemed much less in Garland, although there were still days that we came home to curtains drawn and her still in bed. Most days, however, we would come home to the curtains open across our big picture window in the living room facing our beautiful backyard full of shrubs, flowers, and a massive jungle gym. The sun would be shining through that huge window while music seemed to be playing from the rafters—Marty Robbins, the Bee Gees, Elvis, The

Beatles; she loved to sing, and her taste was very eclectic. I get that from her.

The men, however, did not change. They were everywhere, it seemed. A very young grocery bagger at the Safeway. An artist that she and I would meet at Dunkin Donuts; they would drink coffee and talk while I ate minestrone soup a few stools down. Daddy's boss's son at the trucking company. Even some random guy at the YMCA while I was enrolled in karate classes. Classes that I finally had to quit because I couldn't focus, seeing her out the window sitting next to some strange guy and laughing on the park bench. I would rather us just not be there. My stomach got so upset one evening watching through the window that I walked out in the middle of class, grabbed my bag, went straight to her, and said I needed to leave now and wasn't coming back—and I didn't.

At times, Dawn and I would find ourselves entertaining Lisa in the stairwell of an apartment complex while Mama was inside with someone. Sometimes even at night. I don't remember ever meeting him face-to-face. I remember, however, those cold concrete stairs and the echo it caused when we spoke louder than a whisper. You can imagine how well all of this worked out with my little sister being the wild child that she was. Lisa would use that cold, iron stairwell banister for her monkey bars. I just knew she would fall and crack her skull open on our watch. Gosh, that made me a nervous wreck. Foreseeing anything bad that can happen has always been my brain's specialty—even as young as six or seven years old.

One guy Mama was seeing still lived with his mother. I remember sitting quietly on the couch while this older lady sat in the chair watching TV, my mama in the bedroom with her son. He may have been an adult, I honestly don't know, but it was still all too weird and felt wrong. Even I knew that. Through a large air vent toward the bottom of the wall between his room and the living room, I could see their clothes hitting the floor. Pants coming off legs—one at a time. I was so embarrassed. I stared into space praying that old lady wouldn't talk or look at me. Mama was about twenty-seven or twenty-eight years old then.

And to those midnight hour "happenings" I mentioned earlier...

The clothing trail would typically go from the living room of our house to her bedroom door. Of course, only on the nights we did not get to sleep with her and when Daddy wasn't home. My excellent investigative work, consisting of light walking and holding my breath, showed me that the majority of the time those clothes belonged to Daddy's boss's son. He was handsome for sure. He reminded me of Barry Gibb of the Bee Gees, who was mine and Mama's favorite Bee Gee. I would watch him walk up the sidewalk after parking down the street in front of the empty lots. As I said before, we lived on a street with only four houses, so looking back now, the parking-down-the-street strategy seems pretty pointless.

Now we are close to caught up in the story, so back to that strange and life-changing night.

What I have not told you yet is that a few nights before our middle-of-the-night escape, Daddy had called. He was still out on the road, and I answered the phone. He asked me if anyone had been at the house. I told him "yes." He asked if it was his boss's son, and to that, I also said "yes." He told me he loved me and to give the phone to Mama.

Screaming and crying came next. While Mama was losing it on this side of the phone, I slipped off to my bedroom. A bit later, she came in to let me know that Daddy said he was going to kill her and that it was pretty much my fault. I should not have told him those things. In my heart, I was so very sorry. I honestly wished that I had not, but he asked me, and I answered. I didn't like how she was treating him, and at the moment of being asked those questions, the gravity of my response wasn't something I had thought through. I've often wondered how our lives could have been different if I would have thought before I spoke. If I could have walked through in my mind how negative things could turn with me telling the things that I saw. Proverbs 18:21 (Holman Christian Standard Bible) says, "Life and death are in the power of the tongue." Our words matter and oftentimes put things into motion. I learned this crucial life lesson at the tender age of eight.

Daddy made it home the next night, still angry, and he did hit her. He grabbed her and told her he was going to throw her through the big picture window so her face would be cut up and no one would want to look at her again. I begged for him to let her go. He sent us girls to our rooms and after a bit, things seemed to calm down. We walked to school the next morning and they both seemed okay when we left. At some point, late that night, however, is when things were no longer okay and she was waking us up to leave our home, our school, our lives, like bandits in the dark of night.

As I lay back in the car listening to my parents argue quietly while we pulled out of town, I heard them fighting over things I could not put together. The judge—if only Mama hadn't gone to the judge today and told him the things she told him. The video camera—Daddy should not have made her do the camera things. The police—they are coming for Daddy or taking us kids.

My little head was spinning.

What had Mama told them? What had my Daddy done?

CHAPTER II

You're Not in
~~Kansas~~ Texas Anymore

This is where life gets weird. We made it to Grandma's sometime in the early morning. I was happy to get away from all of the grown-up talk and decided to busy myself with showing Sunshine and Baby Crissy around. Baby Crissy had been to Grandma's before, but Sunshine had not. I found out quickly that Papa didn't like cats and he was sure not happy about me bringing mine. But it was Papa, so I figured he would be okay with it after all the fuss. I was very wrong. First, Papa grumbled something about Sunshine making good fertilizer for his garden as he walked into his concrete shop that sat next to the house. I didn't understand but didn't want to ask either. Papa came back out of the shop with a rope he had found and said Sunshine would have to stay tied up outside. "Tied up outside?" I protested. "That's not even possible, he's a cat!" With very little effort, Papa showed me otherwise. Even today, I still do not have words for this.

I have no idea what Mama and Daddy told Grandma and Papa about why we were there, or how long we would be staying. Daddy slept for a while and then kissed me goodbye. He told me he would be back with more of our stuff as soon as he could. Other than that, I really had no clue what was going on and didn't plan to talk to Mama about it. This was one of those times that I knew talking to her could easily make matters worse, so I left it alone and decided to make a vacation of it until Daddy returned.

But Daddy didn't return. Not soon anyway, and not for good ever. Mama enrolled us in an elementary school on the same block as Grandma's house, Matthews Elementary. The school sat down the street about half a block and across the road. As the scrawny new kid with red hair and a slow Texas drawl, making friends did not come easy. Most of the kids only spoke to me when they were making fun of the way I talked. I was certain Daddy would be back to get me soon, so I tried to keep my chin up like he would always tell me.

When we got home from school each day, Mama was in bed sleeping. The three of us girls were familiar with this when Mama was sad, so we tenderly checked in on her and then went about our homework each day. Grandma, however, was not someone to put up with "laziness." And that's exactly how she saw it. We were only there a week or so before things blew up altogether and Mama said we were leaving. I sat in the living room listening to them argue thinking how in the world could we go anywhere? *We don't even have our car and Daddy hasn't made it back yet!* I thought. Mama proved me wrong. Soon, my aunt, the one who had come to stay with us in Dallas, arrived to pick us up.

We moved to a small town outside of Sikeston named Salcedo, with my aunt and her three kids. Her boyfriend with the cool van lived there too. I silently prayed that his friend Grant had dropped off the face of the earth. I soon found out I was half right. Grant had gotten a steady girlfriend, so he wasn't there much. Salcedo seemed more like a pit stop than a town. It was a few dirt roads and a small gas station/grocery store. Dirt roads, rickety houses with worn-out, lop-sided porches and patched-up roofs, weather-beaten trailers, and animals running wild. Or wild animals running—both are accurate descriptions.

Mama promptly enrolled us in the grade school where the kids from Salcedo went. It was in a town nearby so we would have to catch a school bus down the road that ran in front of the house. Morehouse Elementary was its name and it was like no other school I had ever seen. Some of the kids didn't even wear their shoes all the time. One of my cousins, Lori, was five months younger than me and in the grade below me. She was in the second, and I was in the third. Morehouse Elementary, however, was such a small school they put multiple classes together. This little oddity put me and my cousin in the same classroom. I was excited about knowing someone this time, even though she and I had only been around each other a few days at this point.

Lori was a little bigger than me, with long blonde hair and beautiful glass-blue eyes. She was the only girl among her siblings. With two brothers to contend with daily, Lori didn't mind a good fight and everyone at Morehouse Elementary knew that. That was a big plus for me—no one teased me about the way I talked, and no one teased me about the color of my hair. At least not when Lori was around. We were family, and being family matters in rural Missouri. I learned fast that having three cousins in the same school doubled mine and my sisters' fight power—unless we were fighting each other, of course. From the looks of this ole shantytown, I knew that was going to come in handy.

No one seemed to have air conditioning in Salcedo, nor did Morehouse Elementary. The playground was basically on dirt. With the kids taking their shoes off so much, in class and during recess, filthy feet and floors were something I had to learn to accept. Grass didn't seem to have a fighting chance in this part of southeast Missouri. Gosh, I missed the thick Texas grass in our backyard that you could lay down and roll in. The other kids didn't seem to mind. They appeared to wear the dirt purposefully all over their faces, clothes, and bodies. "Dirt necklaces" even seemed to be worn proudly.

None of this was okay to me. I loved my aunt, and she was very good to take us in, but life here was so different. I was a nervous wreck with so many strangers in and out. Bad words and cigarette smoke filled the air, then stuck to the walls in the form of yellow dingy film. Not only was this incredibly uncomfortable for kids who had never been around cussing or smoking, but Lisa was also allergic to cigarette smoke so being around it daily increased her asthma attacks. The three of us girls slept on a pallet on the floor next to the bed Mama slept on unless Lisa was having trouble breathing; if that happened, she would sleep with Mama. This was fine with me because with all the activity in that bed, I didn't want to lie in it.

Our bedroom door opening was covered by a sheet because for some unknown reason, the door was missing. This tattered sheet door guaranteed no privacy, ever. So gross. I sure missed my quiet, clean, and very private bedroom where I could read my *Tiger Beat* magazine alone, turn on some music to sing to, or spend time drawing, all completely undisturbed. I missed our beautiful home that always smelled good and, regardless of Mama's ups or downs, mostly had an air of peace. And with all my heart, I missed my daddy. I quietly cried myself to sleep each night wondering when he would come back to get me.

I started missing my mama too.

Of course, she was there with us, but, at the same time, she wasn't. She seemed to have left us emotionally, I guess you could say. Mama enjoyed her new freedom and new friends. This setup gave her the go-ahead to pursue other relationships in the open. Unfortunately for us girls, it happened to be *very* open at times.

When we moved into my aunt's, we didn't have much left of the school year. Getting off the school bus in the afternoons and racing to the house was a new daily ritual that we all enjoyed. A ritual that ended quite abruptly with a very unfortunate event, to say the least. I wasn't the fastest of us kids, so I was never first or second to make it through the door. That day, however, I bet I was a close third. As my hands hit the tattered screen door and my feet landed proudly in the living room, the excitement of my good run dropped like a cannonball straight to the floor. The clanky old box fan sitting on the floor just happened to be blowing at the perfect angle to hit the sheet hanging across the door frame to our bedroom. As everyone screeched to a full stop with eyes as big as golf balls, there my mama was, naked and uncovered on the bed in the middle of the day with some butt-naked man. I felt like

I had been punched right in my stomach, my mama having sex right there for all the world to see. That stupid fan was so loud that they never even heard the screen door slamming. Never even looked up.

I guess she technically was in the bedroom. But without a real door and with the fan blowing the sheet out of the way, she may as well have been in the front yard. We all stared in horror. *For the love of Jesus*, I thought, *let this be a dream.* I snapped out of it as I felt my little sister touch my back as she ran in behind me. Turning quickly, I grabbed Lisa's hand and walked us right back out of the house. "Come on," I said. We walked down the dirt road to my hiding spot, a quiet ditch at the end of the road with a large flat rock nestled inside. I could sit on the rock and see a good distance, mainly because of the open lots where several houses had been torn down. The true beauty of this flat rock, however, was that someone had to be close up to see me sitting there. I would go there most days to sit and hide from the dirty neighborhood kids while I watched for my daddy to come back to get me. On this day though, I gladly brought Lisa along. We sat together in silence.

Words could not explain what I knew she had seen. I had seen it all before, but not this brazen. Not in the light of day, and certainly not in front of others. Others who I was now afraid would laugh and talk about it. My stomach hurt with the shame of it all and my heart ached with sadness for what Lisa was feeling. I certainly remembered my first time walking in on Mama, and it was the worst. As we sat there quietly, I waited for Lisa to bring it up. She didn't. She didn't say a word. We both just stared down the street. I was praying Daddy's big rig would round that corner any minute. I figured Lisa was praying that too.

Some things are better if you refuse to give them life with words. It's best to bury them—deep, deep within—then pray like heck that the memory decomposes quickly. Sometimes, if you're lucky, it will.

My older sister, Dawn, was finding her own path at this point too. She fell in love with a sixteen-year-old that lived down the street from us with his grandma. His name was Quinton, and he wasn't bad looking at all. Quinton had already quit school, so he would just hang out at his grandma's all day. Dawn was only ten years old, but she no longer looked it. She dropped weight fast in Salcedo and man, did she have boobs! This realization surprised us all, but they were certainly a welcome sight for Dawn as she was trying to get Quinton to notice her. Notice he did. Dawn would disappear at Quinton's quite often, where they would make out until she heard Mama yelling for us kids to get home. All of their face-sucking was so gross. However, it worked out well for me because Dawn couldn't care less about being up in my business all day any longer.

Dawn was as fearless as you could get. She loved to push the limits and didn't seem to mind whatever punishment came with it. One evening, Dawn didn't come running home when Mama yelled for us, so I was sent back out to find her. Lori decided to tag along; after all, it's always fun to be a part of telling your sibling or cousin how much trouble they're in. Lori and I walked straight to Quinton's house. As we knocked on his door, it slowly opened on its own. I looked at Lori and we both shrugged our shoulders and walked on in; his grandma didn't seem to be home. We heard noises coming from the back, so we started down the hall quietly; sneaking up on Dawn was a well-honed craft of mine. I figured busting her in the middle of a make-out session and scaring them both was well deserved since I had to come back out to find her.

As Lori and I got to the bedroom door with the noise behind it, we listened a few seconds before quietly turning the doorknob, yelling "surprise" as we opened it as fast as possible.

"Holy shit!" Lori screeched.

I stood big-eyed and frozen. They were not just making out with the disgusting tongue kisses that we had been busting them at for weeks. They were under the covers, and I was sure, in my few-second glimpse, that I saw Dawn's bra on the floor.

"Get the hell out of here!" Dawn yelled while simultaneously throwing something that barely missed us both.

We took off out of there, down the hall and out the front door like our butts were on fire. I stopped in the front yard. "I have to wait for her," I said. I wasn't about to go home and be the one to answer all Mama's questions, which would start with "Where is she?" Lying was basically impossible for me. I was horrible at it, so it was better that I wait on her. Lori wasn't about to wait; she ran on home.

Dawn finally came strolling out of the house as if nothing had happened.

"You're gonna get beat," I said. "No way Lori hasn't already told on you."

"Let her tell," Dawn quipped back showing zero concern. "I also had sex, so I'll let Mama know that too." I froze in my steps, turning to look her straight in the face.

"I wish you wouldn't tease like that," I said, knowing her having sex would for sure be one gigantic sin. She assured me it was no joke and continued walking toward the house. Dawn was in love and for the first time, she felt that someone loved her back. I guess to her, who had seen two years more of life with Mama than me, having sex was just a part of it. We certainly were no strangers to what it was by this point, and you get calloused to the magnitude of the things you're around a lot. Even when they are wrong. But to me, there was no question. I may have only been eight years old, but I was a true believer in Jesus and all I could think about was how God was not happy about this. It was shamefully wrong and most definitely something she could burn in hell for.

"You're a kid," I continued. "You're not supposed to do that, Dawn; he saw you naked?"

Unmoved, Dawn responded "I saw him naked too! And stop being such a baby; you're not supposed to have sex if you're not married but Mama does that *all* the time."

Oh God. It's all true, I thought to myself. I wanted so much to be pleasing to God, but these women in my family seemed like they couldn't care less. Thoughts ran through my mind: *Dawn is only ten years old, almost eleven, though. She doesn't look ten or eleven—thirteen, maybe?* I don't know if I was more concerned about her eternal soul or what Mama was going to do to her when she found out, but Dawn didn't care about any of my concerns. She was over the moon for Quinton and would take whatever consequences came with it.

As you can imagine, that love affair didn't last long.

As the dog days of summer rolled on in Salcedo, my constant positive was that we would get to go visit Grandma and Papa on the weekends. I loved going and would be ready for hours in advance. We would get to go to church, watch *The Dukes of Hazzard*, and have root beer floats at their house. Grandma showered us with warm hugs and meals. Being there was so much like being home in Texas, I never wanted to leave. Dawn was a little different. She hated going. Being at Grandma's cut into her time with Quinton. So once we returned, she would take off out of the car and head straight down the street to see her man.

One Sunday, as Papa dropped us back off in front of the house, things went south fast. Reluctantly getting out of the car as always, I climbed our rickety steps and quietly sneaked to the opposite end of the porch. I figured I could play with my new set of jacks a little bit before I would have to tell anyone that I was home. Playing alone was my preference. Dawn, never one to ask permission, got out of the car and went straight to Quinton's. This evening, however, she was headed back to the house within minutes it seemed. Walking through the dirt yard, kicking at the family of ducks who constantly tried to eat us, she looked at me and asked, "Have you seen Quinton?" His grandmother had told her she thought he was at our house. "Nope, but I've not been inside yet," I said in a leave-me-alone kind of way. With that, she hopped onto the old, wood plank porch and walked past me.

As she headed into the house to find Quinton, I heard the screen door slam behind her. I didn't bother looking up and went back to my game.

Dawn, inside the house, started screaming "I hate you!" which was pretty normal. The uncontrollable crying that immediately followed was not. I jumped up to see what was happening just as Dawn stormed out of the house, passed by me, and ran straight into the yard, still screaming.

Next came Mama flying out of the door, screaming back at her, "Get inside!" It was at that moment that I turned and saw Quinton through the dirty screen, shirt open, buckling his pants. I didn't need an explanation. I knew what Dawn must have walked in on. Honestly, I don't remember what happened next, but what I can tell you is that at that very moment in time a war started within our house that never really ended.

It wasn't long after that awful day between Dawn and Mama that Mama started dating Terry. Terence was his actual name, but everyone called him Terry. This was utterly confusing because he also had a younger brother named Terry. Terry/Terence was certainly too young for my mother to be dating; he was eighteen or nineteen at the time. Mama was twenty-nine. He did have a job, though, so this instantly made him the catch of the group. Terry/Terence still lived with his mother in a small upstairs apartment in Sikeston on Handy Street. Handy Street, as we quickly learned, was also known as the wrong side of the tracks, sitting just on the west side of the train tracks going through Sikeston. Terry, the younger brother, lived there too. Maybe a couple of sisters as well. Hard to remember because the apartment was always full of people and I'm not sure who was related and who wasn't. It was a shotgun-style apartment that was all but falling apart.

Shotgun-style means that all rooms are in a straight row. In the Handy Street apartment, you walked in from the back door after climbing the worn, half-broken, dangerous stairs. When you entered, you were in the kitchen; you walked through and you were in the bedroom; you kept walking and you were in the living room. Attached to the living room was a front porch facing the street. It was a screened-in porch with lots of holes in the screens. Terry and Mama became fond of each other quickly, so we soon moved in with them. All of them. Terry's family and the four of us, in a very small, one-bedroom upstairs apartment. Still no air conditioning, and it was blazing hot that summer.

I didn't care for Terry's mother, and I wasn't sure about him. I was beginning to realize this may be our life for a while, so I wanted to like him. If for no other reason, simply because Mama wasn't dating multiple men when Terry was around. She seemed focused on just him. His mother was a different story. She seemed to pick at my mama all the time and never had a kind word to say. I'm sure it was a strain on her to have us move in as we did, but to be honest, the apartment seemed to be a place where people just flopped anyways. All I saw was someone being very mean to my mama and my mama refusing to stand up for herself. Even at only eight, this drove me crazy and kept me in trouble because of my mouth.

Living on Handy Street was even more of a difference from the lifestyle we had lived in Texas. At my aunt's house in Salcedo, we were family. Sure, the living conditions were off-the-charts different from our Texas home, but there was still a strong sense of love and protecting each other. Handy Street was like the jungle. You're either the hunter or the hunted. You really didn't know if someone was a friend or only being nice to get something from you. I picked up on that early and I knew we didn't belong. I guess I felt that way everywhere we moved, but gosh, this was the top of the worst. What few nice things we had from our lives in Texas all but disappeared on Handy Street. Some actually did disappear.

Mama had the most beautiful rings. She used to wear one on almost every finger. My daddy always bought her pretty things like that. I loved all of her rings, but my favorite was an emerald-cut ruby that sat atop a thin gold band. It was magnificent. So classy and bold with its deep dark red color. I was planning for that ruby ring to be mine one day. I had already asked Mama if I could have it once I was a grown-up lady. I knew for certain that I would wear sparkling rings on all my fingers one day too.

Apparently, I wasn't the only one that admired Mama's rings.

At some point in our stay on Handy Street, they all came up missing. Every last one of them. I couldn't figure out why she would have taken them off to start with. "Look at where we are living, Mama!" I fumed. Everyone around us seemed shady. I didn't have much, but what I had pretty much stayed with me at all times. Mama was trusting, though. Way too trusting. The morning Mama woke and realized her rings were gone, she cried and cried. But not me. I was hell-bent on finding out where they were and who was responsible. To me, it was time to go through everyone's things and confront Terry's family. Someone was gonna cough up my ruby ring.

Mama didn't agree.

She got dressed and drug us girls down the street to a place called Pawn Shop. Pawn Shop had bars on the windows and doors, and all of the windows had black paper covering them so you couldn't see inside. "Don't touch anything," Mama said as we walked in. *Huh*, I thought, rolling my eyes behind her and looking over at Dawn, *No worries here*. Looking around, I took it all in. My guess was that people got killed here. Guns on the walls, lots of pretty jewelry in brightly lit glass cases, and no sun coming in from the outside—I decided fast it was a den of death. I wasn't about to touch a thing. A big, burly guy standing in the back with a fat cigar hanging from his mouth looked my mama up and down then gave her an approving head nod and sly smile. She flashed her come-get-me look and I knew we were in. Man, she was good. But I still watched my back the entire time we were in there and gave Lisa the evil eye every time she got close to touching anything.

"Pawn shops," Mama explained on our walk over, "are where some people take stuff they steal from others to sell for money." Makes sense. If Terry's mother would have worn Mama's rings after stealing them, we would know she had them. Cigar Man was obviously happy to see my mother sashay into his place. Her smile had a way of making men drop their guard—or whatever—quickly. She explained the situation with just the right amount of pouty and asked if he had happened to come across her rings the day before. The guy really didn't seem to know anything about them, but my mama continued to flirt and tease him along until he finally remembered. *She is so smart*, I thought. He disappeared into the back through a hanging-curtain door and then returned with an envelope. Opening the envelope, he shook the contents out and, lo and behold, Mama's rings.

Cigar Man explained to Mama that the person who brought them in had thirty days to pay and pick them up before he put them out for sale. He also said he wasn't allowed to tell us who the person was, but that didn't last long either. My mama sure had a way of getting this guy to talk. We caught her, Terry's mom. We said our goodbyes and walked out. "Call the cops, Mama!" I said, itching for us to break this down for them, get her rings back, and watch Terry's mama drive away in the back seat of a cop car. But she wouldn't do it. Mama wouldn't call the cops on Terry's mother. "Then tell her we know she's a thief and make her come pay and get them back!" I pressed further. No. She wouldn't do that either. Sadly, Mama explained that we were staying in her house, and if we confronted her, we would all be living in the street by nightfall. *Life lesson number two at eight years old: When you depend on other people for your livelihood, you always pay a price, but you don't always get to choose what that price is.*

The nights on Handy Street were especially painful. It was seriously hot. No one used blankets or sheets, except me. I had to have a sheet or something to crawl under and hide before I could fall asleep. We were all in the same room with beds next to, and across from, each other. Me and my sisters slept in one, and Mama and Terry slept in the one at the foot of ours. Others were in the beds beside us. One night I woke up sometime after everyone was asleep hearing some very strange noises in the pitch-black night. Creaking, squeaking, and something sounding wounded. I couldn't see what it was, and I wasn't really sure that I was even awake. I raised up as I tried to get my eyes to focus in the dark. The noises seemed to be coming from a white, bald, oversized, fat head, with a thick, black mohawk. *What the heck?*

I blinked...and I squinted...then I rubbed my eyes some more hoping to make them come into focus; about that same time my brain kicked in and I realized what was going on. I knew those sounds all too well, and then I saw it: No more than a body length from me was the hairiest naked butt-crack I had ever seen! I gasped and stared in horror. *EWW!* I quickly pulled the covers back over my head. I knew right then that my eyes could never unsee that. My stomach turned and chills ran down my spine as I fought off a gagging reflex. *For the love of Jesus...*

Typically, once she and Terry would start in at night I would slide out of the bed and sneak through the living room and onto the front porch. Once there, I couldn't hear them because of the fans. This night, however, I made my exit a bit grander and more obvious. Standing up, I wrapped my sheet around me and stomped out of the room hoping she would have some form of embarrassment. The front porch consisted of a couple more mattresses on box springs filled with more people, but at least they were asleep and not having sex. I found the best open spot to curl up in and tried to fall back asleep as the mosquitoes feasted on my small frame.

Good grief.

Just like in Salcedo, every Friday night or Saturday morning, my grandparents would come to pick me up. It didn't matter if we lived in Salcedo or Sikeston or wherever, as long as it was within driving distance, they were there to save me. I remember my final Saturday morning on Handy Street well. I didn't know at the time that it would be my last. I woke up as the sun came up, and got dressed to await my grandparents' arrival. Everyone was still asleep, so I sneaked down the stairs of death and sat on the curb in front of our apartment. I planned to just holler up to my mama once they pulled up and then get the heck out of there. Sometimes my sisters would join me at Grandma's and sometimes they wouldn't. Either way, it didn't make much difference to me. I went to my grandparents' house every single opportunity that I had.

While I was sitting on the curb waiting for my grandparents, a friend of mine came out of his house to sit with me. His name was Gene, and his house sat right next door to the apartments we lived in. Gene also wanted to go play at my grandparents' house; I made sure everyone knew my grandma was the best cook in the entire world and that we got to have root beer floats after bath time. As Gene and I sat there tossing rocks across the street waiting for my ride, we noticed a cable TV line hanging down low as if it had been knocked loose from the pole. It was right in front of Gene's house. Across the street from us was some sort of trucking company that diesel trucks came in and out of daily. As Gene and I discussed how we could maybe climb up the rusty gaffs coming out of that pole and tie that cable line up higher, a diesel truck turned off the main road and started down Handy Street toward us. As the truck progressed, gaining speed and switching gears, we realized he must not see the low cable line. Gene and I looked at each other, and with catlike reflexes, we both sprang into action. Gene and I were the only ones on the block that could see the oncoming disaster. In our young and dramatic minds, there was no way that truck could possibly fit under that low-hanging cable—*poles will be ripped out of the ground for blocks!*

As I jumped up, I quickly grabbed the cable and pulled it tight and as high above my head as I could reach. I wasn't sure what brave action Gene was taking at the moment, but I didn't have time to formulate a plan for us both. As I stretched that cable line high over my head, holding on tightly, I looked up and saw the flat face of that Mack Truck just as it hit the cable. That's the last thing I remember before waking up in the middle of the street with my half-naked mama screaming and crying standing over me.

Her nightgown was pale blue that morning with her signature see-through sheer material. It was a shorter one it seemed, but it may have just appeared that way because as I first opened my eyes to her screams, all I saw was her nakedness under that dang gown. "Mama!" I screamed. My head felt like it was going to split open. "Clothes! Please!" But Mama couldn't care less; her baby was alive. The paramedics arrived and took me away in the ambulance. Some kind soul must have grabbed a shirt for her because I remember she had a plaid button-up on over her gown in the ambulance. I lay my head back on the bed and wondered: *What the heck just happened?*

It was a very interesting chain of events that I later found out about from Gene, the eyewitness. As I said, my memories stop when the truck hit the cable line. That's when Gene's began. "When the rig hit that cable wire, Holly, you held on like a man," Gene explained. "So tight," he continued in great excitement. "It flung you, and then jerked you down to the ground!" Then Gene's face grimaced as he recounted the worst part, "Your head slammed down on the concrete curb. I thought you were dead!"

But my near-death experience didn't end there. Just as I hit the curb, Gene said, Ole Man Jamerson from the corner gas station came through driving his pickup truck, and the broken cable wire got wrapped up in his tires. But he didn't know the cables were caught in his tires, nor that the other end of the cable wires had wrapped around my body when it flung me. So, with one end of the wire caught in Mr. Jamerson's tires and the other end around me, Gene said, "He drug you into those nasty trash cans and on down the road before he saw me running and screaming 'Stop!'" So, there I was. Out cold, in the middle of the street, with broken cable wire wrapped around my body, most tightly around my bare knees. Had to be a scary sight for a mother to come upon. Guess that's why she didn't bother to put some dang clothes on.

Another hospital stay. Another concussion. However, this time, I had a fractured skull as well. That was fine by me. I got to stay in the hospital for what seemed like weeks. Air conditioning, fresh sheets, a nice pillow, no bugs, and basically being treated like a queen. Me and Baby Crissy soaked it up and wished our hospital stay would never end. The good news was that Mama moved us out of Handy Street and down to New Madrid while I was still in the hospital. New Madrid is a town about twenty miles south of Sikeston. We moved back in with my aunt. She had moved there from Salcedo and welcomed us in once again. When I left the hospital, we went straight home to my aunt's apartment. I was pretty excited at this point because I had remembered that New Madrid was where my real daddy, Steve, was from. This accident was a big win all around in my opinion.

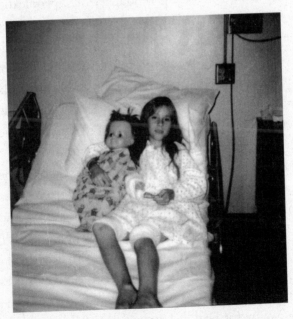

Me & Baby Crissy—hospital stay, Sikeston, MO

New Madrid was a nice enough place. Living conditions were about the same, and Mama was still dating Terry. He drank a lot, and they fought a lot, so it was on and off. My aunt worked at the local honky-tonk, Rosie's, and it was fun riding our bikes there sometimes in the afternoon to get cooled off in the air conditioning and listen to jukebox music. Sometimes she'd let us all share a soda before the evening crowd came in.

I did some research on the location of my real daddy, Steve, once I was settled in. This "research" consisted of me asking every adult I met if they knew him and then proclaiming to the ones that did that I was his daughter, newly moved here from Texas. Surprisingly enough a lot of people did know my daddy Steve. New Madrid is a town with a population of only around 3,000. People know each other and each other's business pretty well. He wasn't living there at the time, but it sure made me feel good to have people say things like "You look just like a Thompson!" or "I've known your daddy since we were knee-high to a grasshopper!" That one never gets old—just picturing it in my mind makes me giggle.

Mama got us enrolled in New Madrid school as the summer came to a close. We had only been away from Texas a few months, but with all that had happened, it sure seemed like years. I asked my mama constantly if she knew when Daddy would be back for us. I stayed so worried that with all of our moving, he wouldn't even know where to find us. She assured me that he would. It was obvious, though, that Mama didn't like me asking for Daddy. I guess I silently blamed her for us losing the life that we had, and she wasn't about to let Daddy off the hook. She made certain to tell me he wasn't perfect like I thought. Then she would allude to some of the things I had overheard that night in the car. In my mind, I knew she just didn't know. I knew my daddy. He said he was coming back, so I waited.

New Madrid Elementary turned out to be a tough little school. Dawn got into a fistfight with a boy on the school bus within the first couple of weeks. It was really scary. I heard them arguing, then cussing each other, but I was near the front and she was in the back. I turned around and peeked over my seat to see what was happening, but kids were up and down yelling in the aisle, blocking my view. I pushed my way through to the back and he had her by the hair of her head and was punching her right in the face over and over! I started screaming for the bus driver to stop. He pulled over and emptied us all out of that bus right onto the side of the road.

Once it was over, Dawn really looked bad. That boy was sure strong and even though I knew firsthand how tough my sister was, he got the best of her. She had to go to the doctor's to get checked out to make sure she didn't have a concussion. I guess after my two, Mama started worrying about our heads a little bit more. The police station visit came next; we all had to go down to the station and tell them what happened on the bus. I was the eyewitness and I knew exactly what had happened and I wasn't holding back. *No one treats my sister like that and gets away with it.* Mama filed charges because Dawn had just turned eleven and this boy was a teenager. I made sure to let the officer know that we were Steve Thompson's children, just in case it helped us out.

Mama was given a lawyer-man for us to talk to. He was probably the prosecutor of the county, but all I knew at that time was that we had to speak to him about all of the things that happened, and he kept asking us the same questions over and over. So I didn't think he believed us. Mama told me to stop worrying over it. She explained that they had to be tough on us because the boy who beat her up had a lawyer too. She said they were going to say I'm lying once they get me on the witness stand, so it's very important that our lawyer-man had us ready.

Witness stand?

I was such an incredibly shy child. I wouldn't even raise my hand and ask a question in class; how could I possibly survive something of this magnitude? This entire mess had me twisted in knots. All I wanted was to go home. For real home. Back to Texas. Back to Dawn being chubby and mean to me, not having sex and fighting big boys on school busses full of kids we didn't even know. This was just awful.

Then it happened.

As I sat in class trying to focus on my teacher, my mind was constantly drifting off. I visualized being called a liar with the instant scream of a "gotcha" moment coming from the boy's attorney, just like in the movies. Gazing out of the big windows that lined our classroom's wall, I could see far into the clear summer sky. But nothing could get my mind off the dreadful court day that was coming, not even a beautiful day. The sky was so blue and the trees green and full, a sanctuary I thought, for the sweet little birds flying all about. I wondered if they ever treated each other badly. I wondered if the little birds ever got into fights. I wondered if their daddies left and never came back? *But mine would be back; he said he would.* I lifted my head to try to refocus on the teacher once more when I heard diesel air brakes in the faint distance. My heart started beating hard and fast like it had so many times before. Then I heard it again, a little closer this time. I thought my heart may beat out of my chest. I looked back out the windows. Nothing. I couldn't see it, but I certainly heard a diesel engine getting closer. My hands instantly beaded with sweat as I heard it once more. Grabbing both edges of my desk, I looked down to pray. *That sounds just like my daddy's truck,* I thought. Taking a deep breath, I looked up and out the window again—*it was my daddy's truck! He came back for me!*

I saw his face and shoulders in the windshield of his big rig as he rounded the school building into the parking lot. I wasted no time, and I wasn't about to ask permission. I jumped up and ran straight out of that classroom like my clothes were on fire. When I got to the hallway, I stopped for a millisecond, looking to the right toward the double doors that led outside to the back parking lot. Driving his big truck, I figured he would have to park there so I ran as fast as I could toward those doors. Before I got to them, they both opened and there was my daddy, standing with the sunlight shining in all around him. He may as well have been an angel sent straight from heaven. I ran even faster and jumped into his arms, burying my tear-soaked face in his neck. I begged him to never leave me again.

Sadly, Daddy explained, he was only passing through.

Late September or early October, Mama was growing tired of New Madrid. We moved back to Sikeston for a month or so, and then into a trailer with Terry outside of Benton, a town about sixteen miles north of Sikeston. Another trailer, another school—it was kinda like switching horses on the same merry-go-round. Mama and Terry didn't get married or anything; she may still have been married to Daddy at this point, I'm not sure. She supported us on welfare so she couldn't get married even if she wanted to. When you are on welfare, you lose your benefits if you get married. We had food stamps each month and a welfare check to pay the rent and light bill. In addition to that, we had a free medical card to cover doctor expenses. Grandma said all the free help was why Mama could "laze" around all day in her nightgown. But Mama would say that if our dads would bother paying child support, she wouldn't have to live off the government. Either way, it wasn't a bad gig for a woman who had kids and really wasn't interested in working.

Mama sued a bunch of people over my Handy Street accident: the cable company, the trucking company, and even Ole Man Jamerson. By February, the money came in and I got to pick out one toy to buy with it. At nine years old I knew enough about our traveling habits to know that it needed to be portable. I picked a stereo so I could play my music. It was everything in one box and could be carried with a handle. Its proper name was a boombox, and it was fantastic. I couldn't have been more excited until I realized getting the accident money meant it was time to move again. The state wouldn't be giving Mama welfare for us for a while, because now that money would be factored in.

Mama and Terry bought an old station wagon with the money, packed up the trailer and us girls, and we headed to California. My aunt had moved there a few weeks back. We were getting good at this gypsy routine and didn't have much in the way of belongings anyhow, so we were on the road in no time. The problem, however, was that it was the winter of '79 and a once-in-a-lifetime blizzard was coming in. The kind where the weatherman warns you that you may be trapped in your home for a while. We pulled up to Papa and Grandma's to break the news to them. It was dark, the snow was falling harder and harder, and from the conversations between Mama and Terry, I was sure this was a terrible idea.

Saying bye to Grandma was always hard on me. We ran inside the house and down the hall into the kitchen. Grandma had her apron on and was washing up the supper dishes while Papa sat listening to the weather report coming out of the radio. By their faces, I knew they were surprised and confused to see us come running in. I blurted out, "We're moving to California so we're here to say goodbye." Papa looked like he had been punched in the stomach, but he didn't speak a word. Grandma wrapped her arms around me, and I laid my head on her chest. I was not happy about this move; I didn't have a clue where California was, but overhearing Mama, it sounded like it would take us days to get there. Days of travel away from Sikeston meant not seeing my Grandma and Papa. Dawn and Lisa were excited and talking a mile a minute, ready for the next adventure. Mama walked in and my grandma asked, "Is this true, Lynn?" Her voice was angry; I could tell. With her arms still around me, she continued, "You're driving these babies through a blizzard in a used car you just bought and know nothing about?" Her voice was low and slow at first but it got louder as she questioned Mama. I moved to the side. I hated arguing. Papa stood up, took his coat and hat off the rack, looked over at my mama with his icy blue eyes, and said, "You need your ass whipped," then opened the back door and slammed it on his way out.

That was a first for me. Papa never said much to Mama while angry, at least not in front of me. He sure never used cuss words! It was usually Mama and Grandma if fussing was happening. Mama started laying out her case. "Jan has a place for us to stay until we get on our feet," but Grandma had heard that all before. "What does that mean, Lynn? Are you getting a job?" We all knew that getting on our feet just meant settling into the next place to live. Grandma then pointed out the kitchen window where my Papa was now shoveling snow with fury and said, "Are you trying to kill your father? He's going to have a heart attack over this!"

My mama was upset at this point and was done. "These are my kids and I'll take them where and when I want to!" With that, she stormed down the hall.

Grandma wrapped her arms around us all and tears were rolling down her face and mine.

"Get in the car, girls!" Mama yelled, then slammed the door behind her. Terry never even bothered coming in the house.

I walked out of the front door and saw Papa shoveling snow. I walked over and gave him hugs and kisses. "Papa, please don't keep shoveling; you could have a heart attack." Papa hugged each of us girls goodbye, "My heart will be broken missing you girls, but I bet your mother won't have you there too long." He walked to the end of the driveway and looked at Terry and Mama with some serious hate, "You're gonna get these girls killed in this storm."

With that, my mama told us to get in and we drove away. I watched Papa go back to shoveling through the back glass of the station wagon and wondered if he would fall over dead of a heart attack. My mama sure didn't seem to care one bit.

I'll admit, the trip to California was a scary one. The station wagon back seat was folded down so the three of us girls could have a pallet in the car, which was super cool. Dawn and Lisa slept while I watched cars and trucks skid off the road around us. It was terrifying. *What in the world are we doing?* I wasn't sure if we would make it there alive.

As we pulled into El Cajon Valley, I was thankful we made it in one piece. Us girls marveled through the station wagon windows at the very tall and odd-looking trees. The streets had steep hills and it was so nice to see the sun shining again. Mama and her trusted Rand McNally atlas came through once more for us. All we needed now was a phone booth to call Aunt Jan for directions to her house. Well, it wasn't exactly my aunt's house. It was my aunt's boyfriend's sister's house. I guess it wasn't actually hers, either; it was her boyfriend's. Anyway, he was a wealthy businessman and was out of town working so it was okay for us to stay for a couple of nights. The house had a swimming pool and everything! *Finally, we are getting back to civilization.*

That night, drinks were flowing and a couple of people were smoking pot. I knew the smell well by now. Not Mama, of course, but Terry was sure enjoying himself with the beers. I sat cuddled up on the couch with a blanket around me and Baby Crissy, just watching it all. The other kids were playing outside but I didn't like leaving Mama in these types of situations. I had seen this scene before—drinking, smoking pot, and loud music—and it never turns out okay.

Mama and Terry were dancing and laughing. He had a beer in one hand and was very awkwardly using the other to spin her, touch her, or balance his drunken self. Then, out of nowhere, he reached down and wrapped his free arm around the bottom of my mother's thighs and lifted her up high, all while laughing. I wasn't. She wasn't either.

Mama started in: "Put me down!" When he didn't, she started squirming trying to get loose to get down herself. "You're gonna drop me!" Her voice sounded frightened, but the whole time Terry was swaying and laughing with a cigarette hanging from his mouth. He was so unsteady. I just knew he would topple over with her at any time.

"Terry, put her down!" I screamed.

I could tell she was scared and upset, but he was too drunk to realize it. Then the music stopped—and Terry dropped her. Accidentally of course. I mean, he blamed her for wiggling and kicking. But there she lay, crying on the floor, holding her back, with a sloppy drunk leaning over her explaining how it was all her fault.

I loathe drunks.

They got Mama to the emergency room, and she had a fractured tailbone. She was in tremendous pain, and mad as hell at Terry. The doctors gave her some pain relievers and sent her home with a donut pillow for sitting. Even with her being so sore, within a couple of days, Mama had us an apartment to move into. It was two bedrooms and beat the heck out of the trailers we had been staying in. I loved having sheetrock walls again instead of paneling and windows that you just push up to open.

Mama got us enrolled in an elementary school that was walking distance to our apartment. The temperature was perfect in California, not too hot and not too cold. I could see why Mama always wanted to live here. It really was beautiful. We made friends with a boy named Chopper who lived in our apartment complex, and he taught us how to skateboard. Terry got us each our own skateboards, so we now had an even faster way to get to school. I almost started liking him for moving Mama to the place where she always wanted to live and that she had always wanted to paint. Unfortunately, on top of breaking Mama's tailbone, Terry also stopped coming home after work. So, my attempt at kindness toward him was short-lived, and Mama's mood started taking a downward spin.

With alcohol on his breath and a clumsy walk, Terry would eventually find his way home each night. Mama always waited up to fight with him, and with slurred speech, he always had some lame excuse he knew she wouldn't believe. The straw that broke the camel's back arrived on a Friday night. He got paid on Fridays, so my sisters and I were expecting him not to make it home until very late. We could tell by Mama's mood that she didn't expect him to do right by her that night either. We ate supper and cleaned up the dishes.

Mama got quieter and quieter as the night wore on until she had tears on her face while she sat on the couch reading. We had been on Terry's drinking roller coaster for a few months now and we knew what the look in her eyes meant. He made it home long after us girls had fallen asleep. I woke up when I heard the door. Right after she peppered him with, "Where have you been?" she demanded to know how much money he had spent. He deflected by pushing her around and then passed out.

The next morning early, while Terry was still in his drunken stupor, we all went down to the corner 7-Eleven. Mama asked the manager if they had some empty boxes, and we were in luck. With three good-size boxes, we went back home and packed up. Mama got some cash out of Terry's wallet and then left a note telling him where he could find his "piece of crap station wagon." Mama never cussed. With that, we loaded up our boxes and drove to the Greyhound station. We left the keys under the floor mat; Mama was done.

The bus trip from California took several days but we finally arrived back in Sikeston. Moving and new schools had quickly become our normal.

Mama's life growing up had been different, but not different like the gypsy life she gave us. When she quit school her senior year to run off and marry my dad, she said she did that because her father, Papa, had sexually abused her for years and she wanted out. I thought on this a few times as a kid growing up, and always decided it must not be true. My papa was wonderful, and he protected me. Plus, it also didn't make sense to me because Grandma loved him, and he was a good man. My mind just couldn't reconcile what I saw and knew with what I heard from Mama.

For a woman who valued education and enjoyed learning, Mama's lack of a college degree really bothered her. With Terry ousted again, we moved to Cape Girardeau before the next school year began. Cape is a large college town thirty miles north of Sikeston. Mama enrolled at Southeast Missouri State University, and she couldn't have been prouder. She was an art major and thought teaching art would be a good path for a single mother of three.

We liked Cape. We had an apartment instead of a trailer, which I loved, of course. We didn't have a car, but we were close enough to Grandma and Papa's that they came to get me every weekend. We even had a laundry facility in the basement of the apartment complex, so we didn't have to hitch a ride to the laundromat once a week. Life in Cape was really good. We had a dishwasher, lived within walking distance from the school, and we even had a telephone! Mama seemed to have a purpose for the first time that didn't have anything to do with attention from men. Oh, Mama had plenty of men around, most certainly, but none had her single focus. She really cared about making good grades, and the three of us were old enough to manage ourselves, so it was a comfortable time for us. Lisa was seven, I was ten, and Dawn was twelve.

In Cape, we had a good schedule down. Every day, we came home from school and did our homework first. If it was still daylight out once we finished, we played outside for a bit before coming in, starting supper, and setting the table. Mama would be home at some point around supper, or if she was home already studying, she would come out from her bedroom. We would all eat together and then Dawn and I would clean up while Mama went back to the books. Dawn still had her rebellious streak in Cape, but it was nothing over the top, and she and Mama seemed to be doing okay in this new routine. Mama and Grandma still had issues but I managed to keep Mama happy so she wouldn't stop my weekend visits. Mama was fast to tell me how Grandma would hit her in the mouth with the back of the wooden hairbrush if she smarted off like I did. I never believed her, but I tried my best to keep that to myself. If I ran my mouth or messed up in any way, Mama wasted no time telling me I couldn't go to Grandma's the coming weekend. She knew how to keep me in line—that was for sure.

I found a best friend for the first time since Dallas; her name was Sarah. Sarah had a super normal home life and I loved hearing her tell me about their Sunday family nights: They played board games and were not allowed to watch TV or have friends over. Just family time for the entire evening. It sounded so wonderful, just like *The Waltons* on TV. I knew one day when I had a family of my own, we would have family night every Sunday night too.

Sarah and I were very competitive with most things: our grades, our art, our hair, even in PE! Having her as a friend challenged me to try harder at just about everything. She beat me that Christmas at the Santa-drawing contest for the entire fifth grade. Mine was better. I could look at a photo and draw it almost identical. My Santa looked just like the one they posted for us to draw. All the kids talked about how I was going to win. Sarah's drawing was really good too, but it was a skinny-head Santa with a longer beard. I was surprised when she won but I decided they must have given points for originality, so I didn't let it bother me...much.

Then came the drawing and slogan contest for Fire Safety Week. I won that one with a pretty solid win. As our posters hung in the hallway at school everyone was talking about mine. I was certain it would be chosen, and I was right! But what few triumphs I had on Sarah in art, she had me hands down in grades. She was so smart. Back and forth, Sarah and I competed as best friends. I loved having a best friend once again. Even though I had sisters, the constant moving made life pretty lonely when it came to friends.

The end of the school year came around, which meant awards and certificates. This was the first time we had been in the same school for several months in a row and I was so excited about my possibilities. On the second to the last day of school, our PE teacher let me in on a little secret: I was the winner of the Most Athletic Girl Award for the fifth grade! Oh my gosh. I was elated, then nervous, knowing my name was going to be called out in front of everyone at the assembly. I could hardly sleep, wondering if I might trip in front of everyone. I had managed more sit-ups than the other girls, more push-ups too; I had increased my chin-ups, increased my time for the mile run, and no one, I mean no one—boy or girl—could shimmy up the gymnasium rope as fast as me. I had earned this prestigious award fair and square. I refused to let the fear of a school assembly get me down.

Sleeping that night was hard but the sun finally came up. I quickly got up and put a nice dress on, since I knew I was going in front of the school and wanted to look my best. I brushed my long, silky hair and pinned back my bangs with colored plastic barrettes that matched my dress. I was ready. "Why are you looking so fancy today?" Dawn smirked, gobbling down her cereal. "It's the last day of school," I said. I wasn't planning to tell anyone about my award. I knew they would find something stupid about it and ruin it for me.

"I want to wear a dress too!" Lisa said.

Good grief, I thought. "We don't have time to change; we can't be late," I reasoned.

Lisa, never one to accept no, started screaming, "If you're wearing a dress I get to too!"

I was ready to explode.

Dawn stepped in. "Fine, wear a dress," she said while rolling her eyes but quickly defusing the situation before we woke Mama up.

Dear Jesus, she is going to make us late, and what if I don't get my award because I have a tardy?! I ran into our room and found Lisa a dress. We got her changed and out the door before she realized she was still wearing tennis shoes and I had my dress shoes on.

All morning, I watched the clock and waited for 2 p.m. I held my secret just like the coach told me to. My superstitious mind knew that if I spoke a word of it, it wouldn't come true. Lunchtime rolled around and I couldn't eat anything. My stomach was so nervous knowing that in just a couple of hours, my name would be called out in front of the entire school. When we got back to class, I watched the clock get closer and closer to two o'clock. Suddenly, the two-way speaker system buzzed and the office lady broke in: "Mrs. Wilson, please send Holly Thompson down to check out."

No! Please, no! This can't be happening! My mind was screaming inside me. I looked around the class, and then slowly gathered my things. Leaving school impromptu-like was our specialty. I hugged my teacher goodbye, left the classroom, and walked down the long hall where so many of my drawings had hung over the past few months. *Maybe she will let me stay; it's only a couple more hours. I have to try at least. Even if she tells me I can't see Grandma this weekend. I have to try. I can't miss this moment; I've worked for it.*

I got to the office and saw my mama through the glass windows. She looked a mess and had been crying. The range of problems this could be due to was so vast I didn't even try to figure it out. I opened the office door and said "Mama, please. Please let me stay through—"

Before I could finish my sentence, she was crying and hugging me saying my grandma was dying.

"What?" I peeled her off of me. "What, Mama? What did you say?" I wasn't hearing right; I prayed that this was her overdramatization of something, anything but this.

She sat down, grabbed me by both of my arms, and looked me straight in the face, "She's dying, Holly, my mama is dying!"

In my head, I started screaming, *Your mama? You mean my blessed grandmother that you hate?!* I felt as though I had been stabbed in the heart. I could only hear a loud ringing in my ears. I broke from her grip and ran from the office and out the front doors. I needed air and a place that she wasn't. I needed to breathe. Once outside, I saw Papa sitting in the car with Dawn. I ran down the stairs and to the car. Papa had tears settled in his eyes, so I knew it was true. Mama came out the door still crying, holding Lisa's hand. Papa sat emotionless and so did I. I stared out the car window as we drove to Sikeston, listening closely to Mama's questions.

Grandma had been having some pains in her side for a month or so now. I knew about them, but she didn't seem worried. She had even accidentally used the bathroom on herself a few weeks before while we were cracking and shelling pecans in the front yard. I felt so bad for her and never spoke of it to anyone. Just like she never spoke of it when I accidentally wet the bed. She blamed things like that on my home life, but I wasn't sure what to blame her accident on. Regardless, it was our secret. Listening to Mama and Papa, I now knew how serious it was. She had cancer in her pancreas, whatever that was; they said she would die a "fast but painful death." I remembered that Grandma first thought her pains had been from me kicking her in my sleep, something else that stemmed from my home life, so she didn't get them checked out right away. *Had my kicks brought the cancer on?* I wondered, keeping my eyes on the cars passing by as I thought through it all. I was pretty sure I wouldn't make it in this world without her. All the things that I love go away—our home in Texas, Sunshine, Daddy, and now my Grandma. My protector. My defender. My most special person in this whole entire world.

A fast but painful death.

Mama vowed to take care of her mother on her deathbed, so we moved quickly back to Sikeston, then a few more places, before landing in a trailer a few miles out in the country down Crooked Creek Road. I had just turned eleven, Dawn thirteen, and Lisa was only eight. Papa would pick Mama up to sit with Grandma during the day while we were in school. After school, I would get to go sit with Grandma too. She was so frail. I would take my kitchen stool and set it next to her bed and hold her hand. When her sisters or friends came in, I would go out quietly so no one would think I was in the way. I knew Grandma wanted me there, and I wanted to be there, so I didn't want to give anyone a reason to shoo me away. My heart was so angry with Mama. Doting over Grandma the way she was, trying to act like the perfect daughter. I didn't understand people. Life. Death. Or why this all had to happen.

My grandma seemed to be slipping away more with each day. On a cold December morning I remember well, we woke up to the heat in the trailer barely working. I drug my cover with me and sat over the floor vent with my clothes inside like a teepee as I tried to warm them before getting dressed. I knew in my heart that something was wrong, and I asked Mama if I could miss school and come with her to Grandma's. She said that would be fine. I sat with Grandma most of the morning, listening to the ladies in the kitchen. When some guests came in, I slid to the kitchen out of the way as always. I took down my little china teacup from the cupboard and made me some hot tea. As I put a teaspoon of honey in it, like Grandma had always done for me, I wondered if it would always be my teacup. I wasn't sure how these things worked when someone dies but I knew enough to wonder if Mama was nice to Grandma because she planned to get something out of it. I just didn't know.

I had been their baby, Grandma and Papa's. Grandma always told me the story of how Dawn was born far away in Michigan, so even though she was technically the first baby—as Mama was adopted and Grandma didn't have any biological children—I was born in Memphis, so Grandma got to be there. She got to hold me as a brand-new baby. Mama lived close to her and Papa, so I was their baby. Once we moved back from Texas, Grandma felt she had to protect me from Mama's parenting. She taught me about the Bible and how important it is to read it for yourself. She taught me about tithing and being a part of a church family. She had me read the mission report in front of the church every Sabbath to teach me to be confident. She taught me how to cook and sew, and how you can show love through kindness. When others made fun of me, acting like I was so different because I had red hair—calling me Carrot Top and other not-so-nice things—Grandma told me how special I was and that my hair looked just "like spun gold." Grandma asked me one day what I wanted of hers when she passed away and I told her I wanted her wedding ring. It was white gold with a box of small diamonds on top. Three rows of seven diamonds each and it's the only ring she wore. I knew it was special to her, and I knew I was special to her. So that's what I wanted.

Me and my lovely Grandma, a few months before she passed.

I sat down at the kitchen table with my tea and stared out the window as people were coming in and out visiting quietly. I sat in silence, holding the cup up to my lips, letting the steam from the tea warm my face. Taking small sips, I gazed out the kitchen window across the front yard thinking, knowing, I'd never see her sitting in her lawn chair snapping beans in a bowl again. I sipped my tea once more, wondering what I would have to look forward to when she wasn't here each weekend. As I sat in silence pondering my fate, my grandmother's sister appeared from the hall.

Frail and tired, she rested her hand on the back of the kitchen chair as if to steady herself. "Holly Bells, she's gone," she said softly as she tried to fight back her tears. The moment had come.

I held my breath as I felt my heart being ripped slowly from my chest, like the pain and pressure were just here to stay. I swallowed the burning knot in my throat and looked out the window once more, but this time through the haze of tear-filled eyes; heavy snow began to fall.

A few hours after she had passed, my aunt took a trip to Walmart to pick up some things for the kitchen and I opted to ride along. While we were shopping, I ran into a girl from school who was shopping with her mom.

Jana, looking me up and down curiously, said, "What happened to you? You look like you've seen a ghost!"

I blankly stared at her, not really knowing how to respond, "My grandma's dead," I said flatly, after what I'm sure was a very long pause.

Jana looked down at her feet. "I'm really sorry," she said, then gave me a big hug. As Jana walked away with her mom, I realized things were different. I felt different. Life no longer held color. Only black and white—life and death. It felt meaningless.

The following days were painful and dark. My heart hurt so badly for my grandma that at moments I didn't know if I could breathe. Thankfully, there was still work to be done for her. Papa and Mama worked together on the funeral service, and I got to help because I knew what Grandma wanted. At the church service, I made sure her favorite hymn, "The Old Rugged Cross," was on the list to be played. Our pastor at the Seventh-day Adventist church made sure the piano lady took her time with it during her service, just like my grandma always liked.

I sat up straight on the front pew and I forced myself to sing the hymns just as Grandma would have wanted. I listened to the cries and sniffles behind me throughout the sanctuary. But I sat lifeless. *No one here has lost what I've lost*, I thought to myself. *No one could possibly understand.* My sisters were crying and having trouble making sense of it all. Our first death of a loved one. Typically, either of my sisters' sadness would have trumped mine and would have been my primary concern. Not today.

Today, my grandma is dead.

As the service ended, the pallbearers approached and closed the casket lid. They then moved Grandma to the church foyer and reopened the lid. The funeral man started dismissing the pews, from the back to the front. One by one, friends and family paid their final respects to my beautiful grandmother before walking out the double doors into the cold winter air. Our turn came last. Mama and my sisters walked ahead of me, Papa behind me at the end of the line. As we moved closer, the cold air from the doors opening and closing chilled me to my bones. Mama walked slower and slower as we moved down the aisle toward the casket. Her gait was unsteady, and she was crying as she approached Grandma lying in her forever bed. Suddenly, my mother's arms flew up in the air and she let out a bloodcurdling scream—the scream then turned into loud, uncontrollable sobbing. Mama's arms seemed everywhere as she threw her upper body over

Grandma and into that casket as she wailed, "Don't leave me, Mama, don't leave me!"

Unbelievable.

I took a couple of steps back and watched quietly in disbelief. Or maybe disgust. This woman, who had spent years telling me every single bad thing she could think of about my lovely grandmother, had now decided that she couldn't live without her. My blood boiled. I was so angry. Angry for all the years that she made me walk a tightrope just to get to see my grandma. Angry because even now, on the one day that was only my grandmother's, she still found a way to make it about her. Her dramatic breakdown was happening right between me and the now-open double church doors. I looked past her and saw all the people looking at her with pity etched across their faces. For a split second, I dreamt of running and pushing her as hard as I could so she would fly out of those double doors, down the steps, and into the onlookers. They could have her for all I cared. I heard my mama say my name and I snapped out of it. She was looking back at me with her tear- and mascara-stained face. I wondered if she somehow heard my thoughts.

"H-O-L-L-Y," she bellowed again, reaching for me to join her. *No. Not this time. Not this moment.* I stood very still, refusing to allow her to drag me into her scene. I didn't care if she passed out cold on the floor or if she had to be carried away in a straitjacket; she wasn't going to take away my last few minutes—alone—with my grandma.

Our pastor, along with Papa and the nice funeral man, got Mama moved to a chair; without the commotion, the doors found their way closed again. While they held her, calmed her, and basically made a fuss over her, I walked quietly to my grandma's side for the last time. I stood alone, looking at her beautiful face. I reached in and touched the hands that had held mine so many times. I thanked Jesus for giving her to me, the most perfect grandmother ever made. Tears began to stream down my face. Without warning, the double doors burst open again and a cold, fierce wind howled through like a freight train coming straight for me. My backbone stiffened like steel as the frozen air cut through my thin coat and dress. I wrapped my coat and arms around my small frame tightly. *Just breathe.*

Some painful moments get tucked deep inside in the hopes that they will never be remembered. But occasionally, sometimes, it's those painful moments that define you.

I wiped my eyes, lifted my chin, and, reminiscent of this moment, reminiscent of my life, I stepped out to face the cold *alone.*

CHAPTER III

When the Kaleidoscope Comes into Focus

In the book of Ecclesiastes, King Solomon talks about seasons in our lives. I can clearly look back and see where the seasons changed in my life. My grandmother's death was a major one. No longer was there someone I could always rely on for protection, a kind word, or a hug for no reason at all. That season was over. Even at my young age of eleven, I intuitively knew it was time to grow up. Time to stop waiting for Daddy. Time to stop waiting for my Texas life to come back. Those were a child's dreams. It was time to accept my obvious station in life.

Even as an adult, I always enjoy kaleidoscopes. The endless new images with their beautiful, bold colors. With every twist, a new fascinating picture comes to life as the mirrors inside do their work. Usually, it's brilliant colors bursting with life. But occasionally, the dark colors fall together—the grays and blacks and deep blues. When this happens, the imagery appears more like demons dancing to music that only they enjoy. Sneaking. Lurking. Always there, just not always seen.

That's how I describe the bridge between my childhood and becoming an adult. One painful, clarifying turn of the kaleidoscope brought everything, past, present, and future, into focus for me. A frightening glimpse of what had always been in the shadows, just patiently awaiting its turn to be seen. As life-shattering as my grandmother's death was, that was not my clarifying moment. But it was most certainly those winds of change that began to lift the fog of innocence for me.

After her death, time moved through like molasses. We all seemed to be dealing with some heavy facts of life. Me, the loss of my grandmother, of course. Dawn, dating and trying drugs—two major things at a time when we basically had zero supervision. And then there was Mama. She was dealing with the loss of her mother; regardless of the love-hate relationship they shared, and regardless of the fact that this was her adopted mother, it was her mother. I tried to realize and understand that. She was also dealing with the loss of her purpose. She had quit school, which she loved, to care for my grandmother. Now that my grandmother had passed, she found herself in the middle of the winter, in the middle of the country, living in a trailer with little heat, three daughters, and no man to distract her. No car, no phone, no laundry facilities, no grocery store. Without any purpose or distraction, her depression hit hard.

But one cold, snowy Saturday morning, Mama took a deeper emotional dip, before the following chain of events pulled her out.

Waking us up early, she told us to get dressed and said we were going into town. I figured Papa must be coming to get us to take us to the laundromat, but Mama was never up early so that didn't make sense. Down the gravel road from us in one of the neighboring trailers lived a teenager that had a pretty cool souped-up Charger painted like the General Lee—the famous *Dukes of Hazzard* car. He was really nerdy and quiet. I don't remember his name, but he wore black, horn-rimmed glasses and 100 percent did not fit the coolness of his car. Mama must have known what time he would be leaving for work because she had all three of us girls standing in the front yard with our coats on when he pulled out that morning. Flagging him down, she asked if we could catch a ride into town to Sambo's.

Sambo's was located just as you pulled into Sikeston. I believe it was still a Sambo's at this time. Regardless, Sambo's was a restaurant similar to a Denny's and always seemed to have a full parking lot. Inside Sambo's, they had a long bar-style counter with stools for customers to sit on. The stools faced the backs of the cooks who were cooking on big, steaming, silver grills. They also had booths all along the perimeter of the café next to a big picture window that ran fully across the front and side of the building. The booths were covered in bright orange pleather seats that would make a noise as you scooted your butt across them. Once we were dropped at the door, Dawn, curiously or suspiciously, asked Mama if we were meeting someone. We knew her patterns, so we were all wondering which man was coming back into our lives. Surprisingly, she said "No." Confused, and not fully convinced, we followed her inside and were quickly seated by a smiling hostess.

The café was bustling with activity as the heavy snow continued to fall outside. It was such a nice feeling, sitting in a warm and bright atmosphere while being able to watch the snowfall through the windows. Our trailer windows had foil on them to deflect the sun in the summer and thick plastic stapled around them in the winter to keep the cold air out. Sitting inside while watching outside wasn't an option, so this was a treat for sure. A waitress came to take our order and Mama ordered a cup of coffee with cream and sugar and a small hot chocolate for each of us girls. The waitress left menus on the table for us as she left to get our drinks. The three of us girls silently looked at each other and then down at the menus. No one reached for one. We all watched Mama quietly. She let them lay, so we did too.

The air was filled with the thick smell of bacon and ham cooking on the grill. My mouth watered as I watched the cooks flip pancakes and fry eggs from across the room. A constant "order up" was being yelled as waitress after waitress grabbed a ticket and the accompanying food plates and then hustled back out to their customers. As much as I loved sitting there in so much life and activity, it felt wrong. Our trailer felt dark and lonely at this time in our lives. Having happy people around was nice, but I knew we couldn't buy a meal, so humiliation seemed inevitable. *Why are we here torturing ourselves like this?* I wondered as I watched. To be honest, I wasn't even sure how we were going to pay for the coffee and hot chocolate, but I, along with my sisters, remained silent. Dawn and

I made occasional glances at each other with the unspoken knowing that this may not end well.

Once our hot chocolates were finished the waitress asked if we needed anything else. My mother ordered each of us refills on our water, and a coffee refill for herself. My little sister asked for more hot chocolate and Mama quickly said, "You've had enough chocolate." Once the waitress walked off, she explained that her coffee refills were free but the hot chocolates were not, so we would have to sip on water. Dawn and I remained silent, but that was difficult for Lisa, the child who couldn't sit still. Lisa soon realized that bathroom trips would get her the entertainment she needed, so I offered to do the taking. I couldn't handle just sitting there while people stared at us—the family sitting forever in a booth with one person drinking free coffee refills.

Mama seemed to long for conversation. To make a connection with another adult. Between losing Grandma and living so far out from human existence, she wasn't doing well. Mama never said it, but I felt like she was waiting for someone in particular that just never came. It was sad and I was sad for her. As mad as she would make me over her choice of men, I wanted desperately for her to have a nice man. Someone who would love her and make her laugh. But more than anything at this moment in time, if we were going to be endlessly sad, I just wanted us to please do it in the privacy of our dark, morose trailer, and not in the middle of a busy restaurant. The shame of that Sambo's booth was so intense I can still feel it forty years later.

After several refills and many trips taking my sister to the bathroom, I could tell our waitress was no longer happy with us. I watched her walk to the manager and nod toward us as she spoke to him. Mortified, I whispered to Mama, "I think we better go." I was good at reading people, and our time was definitely up. Before I could get her to listen to me, the manager came over and told Mama we needed to pay our bill and go. He said they were a place of business, and if we needed a homeless shelter, he would be happy to make a call for us. *Jiminy Christmas*. He could have had a bit more tact. Straight to the homeless shelter line. *What a d-bag*. Mama's face was flush with embarrassment and honestly, desperation. I really don't think the morning had gone the way she intended. Now she had three girls, and herself, with thin coats, facing miles of walking in freezing temperatures and falling snow. She paid our tab with some change from the bottom of her purse, and we bundled up and walked outside.

The icy wind stung my face instantly. I pulled my coat hood over my head and plunged my hands deep into my thin pockets praying for a way out of this. As we started walking across the parking lot toward the highway, I knew we wouldn't make it home. Freezing to death was about to be our reality.

"Mama," I started, knowing full well she was in a pretty delicate form, "Want me to call Papa for a ride?"

"No," she responded sternly without even turning to look at me.

Walking against the blistering wind gusts, I pressed further: "I will tell him we wanted to come for hot chocolate really bad and the neighbor must have forgotten to pick us back up." *Blame me, I don't care—I want to live,* screamed the voice in my head.

She stopped walking and turned to me, "I don't have any money for the payphone now," she said in a low voice. I could tell she was holding back tears.

"It's ok. I'll run back and ask that manager to let me use their phone." With that, I turned and took off for the door before she had time to stop me.

They all ran back as well and waited for me inside the first set of glass doors into the café. I watched them through the glass as the hostess got the manager for me. The manager, who was way past agitated, suggested to me that maybe he should just call the police. Like that would help. Using the most sweetness that an eleven-year-old could conjure up, I explained that our ride simply never came back for us. "Sir, we live miles outside of town, my little sister has asthma so there's no way she can make the walk in this weather, without dying of course." I was certain he wouldn't want that on his head—and although I didn't say it, I made sure the implication was clearly there. I already knew how to deal with men like him, men who think so much of themselves that it's okay to treat women and children in need as if they are far above them, so he didn't scare me. He allowed me to use the phone, but he insisted on dialing the number to make sure I wasn't calling long distance. Just in case *that's* what the little homeless-looking girl had up her sleeve all along, to run up some long-distance phone charges at the Sambo's. Unreal.

On the phone with Papa, I knew I had to sell the storyline I told Mama I would. Otherwise, he would show up and be mean to her for endangering us girls. I knew she wasn't in the frame of mind to handle it. Mama threatened to kill herself from time to time, and unfortunately, we had just found out how long it takes to call for help and get an ambulance out to us if you overdose. Odds weren't great in my opinion. We needed a ride and it needed to be my fault. I did an excellent job selling the story to Papa. I could tell he was irritated, but he said he would be right there to get us. I thanked the manager profusely to feed his ego, and then joined Mama and my sisters in the weather-protected breezeway while we watched for Papa.

"Is he mad?" Mama asked.

"Nope," I responded definitively. "He was about to be out and about anyways and said he's been missing us."

Mama was relieved; however, that all changed once we climbed into the car with Papa. His stern face spoke volumes and I knew he didn't blame me as I had hoped. I talked all the way home to keep the conversation off of Mama. But once we pulled up to the trailer, Papa lit into her as us girls climbed out of the car. Thankfully, she didn't reach for a bottle of pills. She didn't scream and cry for hours on end. She pulled the boxes out of the closet and simply said, "Pack up."

After Sambo's, life evolved at rapid pace. Climbing on the Greyhound, we all knew it was time for a change of scenery, and we all needed it. A new spot in Texas was our destination. Terry was back in the game and had a new job living in a town outside of Houston called Pearland. This is where I finished my last few months of the sixth grade.

Pearland and Terry lasted about as long as you can imagine. By midsummer, we moved back to southeast Missouri to Morehouse, a town of fewer than 2,000 people. Morehouse sits only six miles west of Sikeston—six miles away from Papa. If you're following the geography of my gypsy story, this is the town we ended up finishing our school year in when we initially moved to Missouri from Texas. My aunt was now living there, so it was our next location to "get back on our feet." I had hit puberty fast, had boobs overnight, and for an eleven-year-old, I passed easily for thirteen or fourteen. Not only in body shape—my mouth and backbone as well. Without Grandma's protection, I found I stood on my own pretty well. Allowing Mama's emotions to dictate our every move was becoming too much for me to go along with quietly anymore.

Dawn was thirteen years old and could pass for eighteen—*all. day. long.* She ran with a pretty rough crowd, in my book. Smoking and selling pot filled her days while she and her friends hung out at the park in the middle of town. Mama had new boyfriends to attend to, so me and Lisa were either at home or running the streets. Our emergency food stamps were having trouble getting to us since we made two moves in such a short period of time, but we didn't go hungry. Props to my mama for sure because no matter what crazy situation she had us in, we never went hungry. She taught us how to make bread patties out of flour and water. She bought a tub of butter and a jar of grape jelly. This kept us fine until the stamps came through. It was like dessert every day as the main meal.

We knew other kids who didn't have moms that made sure they had food, so we didn't complain.

We were also blessed with the DAEOC summer lunch program. DAEOC—the Delta Area Economic Opportunity Corporation—was an agency that did things for poor kids; that's all we knew. They were located in a downtown building in Morehouse, right next to the park. They opened every day right before lunch. Inside the door they had a check-in table to the right, with two clipboard ladies checking your names off as you came through. Straight ahead was a long table with the lunch items placed in groups—sandwiches, fruit, then a tub of ice full of small milk cartons. The rest of the room held several long tables with folding chairs open all around them and that was about it. I made sure Lisa and I were in that line every day come hell or high water. It was a simple procedure anyone could follow—line up out front with the rest of the kids, go in, give them your name. If you missed out on that daily free lunch, you were just plain lazy in my opinion. Or on drugs. Lisa and I loved getting to sit in the air conditioning and eat our cold sandwich, piece of fruit, and drink that cute carton of milk. My three cousins were always with us too. Dawn, not so much. She had outgrown us and was busy with her new friends in the park.

The DAEOC program had a drawing going on that summer. Every time you came to eat, your name got put in for the drawing. Two winners would be chosen to go on a trip to Six Flags in St. Louis at the end of the summer with the winners from the other DAEOC programs near us. The only thing you had to have was a ride to the bus and a ride picking you up from the bus. I figured we would worry about that problem if we got to it. I made sure our names were in that bucket every day.

Drawing day came and I was ready. We sat patiently waiting for the lunch ladies to call out the winners. They went through some speech no one even cared about and then finally did the drawing.

"Holly Thompson!"

I won! I won! Unbelievable! Immediately turning to share my excitement with everyone, I found that the jealousy from the other kids was pretty palpable—diminishing my joy quite a bit. I came to realize when you're poor, not many are happy for you when good flows your way. Unless it's your family, and they were excited for me. But I won fair and square. Next came the questions from the clipboard ladies. Not to worry, I assured them with a strange amount of confidence, my ride would be no problem. They gave me the date, time, and told me the location to catch the bus—New Madrid, at 6 a.m., on a date a couple of weeks away. My heart dropped a little. *New Madrid makes things more difficult*, I thought to myself while maintaining a solid poker face. New Madrid was over thirty miles away. I had hoped it would be Sikeston so if I needed to, I could spend the night with Papa and then just walk to the bus stop. Regardless, I knew I would figure it out.

A *free* trip to Six Flags!

I called Papa. I told him all of the particulars and he said no problem. I could stay the night before and then we would get up early, drive to New Madrid, and I could catch the bus. He would then come back to pick me up at 11 p.m. I could spend that night at the house again, then he would take me back to Morehouse the next day. Perfect. I even asked to be picked up early the day before so that I could mow his yard to make some spending money for my trip. All plans were tied up like a fantastic, magical bow. It was going to be perfect.

But then there was Mama.

The trip wasn't scheduled right away. It was a couple of weeks off and in my childhood, a lot could happen in a couple of weeks. And did. Some very horrendous things happened to Dawn one night at the hands of one of Mama's boyfriends. After the police weren't much help, it only took Mama a day or so to decide we were leaving. Don't get me wrong, I'm thankful Mama got us out of Morehouse, I just didn't feel we needed to run from it all. We needed to be close enough to fight back.

If my memory serves me right, I believe it was Grant that she turned to after this. He was living in Indiana, so moving to him would put distance between Mama and all that had happened in Morehouse. I understood her wanting out of Morehouse, but there were many reasons she needed to stay at least in Sikeston and follow things through with the police. Dawn wanted out too, the sooner the better. Which I absolutely understood. But I still felt just moving out of Morehouse would fix the problem. We didn't have to move to another state.

My anger ran white-hot and all I knew was that I wasn't doing this again. To run, and not push, to make him pay for what he did, made me crazy. I realize now, it isn't that easy. But I also knew that wasn't the only reason Mama was going.

She was done with the new guy, and she was moving on—leaving the negative past behind and heading for a better tomorrow—damn whatever gets crushed in the process, just like always. On top of that, I was dealing with my own injustices as well. I had taken care of my little sister for weeks making sure she got a meal each day. We had stayed out of everyone's way, and I never asked for anything, knowing how tough things were for us. I had won a Six Flags trip fair and square. Mama's impulsiveness and bad choices in men wasn't going to take that away from me. Not this prize. Not this time.

Papa had a cousin I was very close to, Aunt Cindy. Where I'm from, cousins of your parents and grandparents are your aunts and uncles. We live more like clans than single families. Aunt Cindy lived in Sikeston, was in her sixties, and was a former New York City model. She was my favorite. Her stories of life in New York City fascinated me. Aunt Cindy always called me "darling" with a slow, southern, movie star type drawl. It sounded like "*daah*-lin," and she had such a classy aura about her. She had reddish-blonde, perfectly styled, short wavy hair. She also chain-smoked long skinny cigarettes like the glamorous movie stars in the fifties. When Aunt Cindy first moved back from New York, she took her savings from modeling, or maybe from a divorce, and bought a nice little house on the west side of the tracks in Sikeston. The "tracks" basically divided the poor folks up from the rest. But Aunt Cindy's house was kept really nice. She was absolutely fabulous in my eyes.

Aunt Cindy was only about 5'1", but she didn't take crap off anyone, and everyone knew that. She cared about people in a way that was so interesting to me. She didn't just take family in. It seemed like she always had someone living with her that she was helping out for a time. People she just ran across in everyday life. She was inspirational and positive, and I was in awe of her. But, as with us all, she wasn't without her flaws. Aunt Cindy started every day with vodka and orange juice. As much as I hated drunks, I didn't mind Aunt Cindy's drinking. She wasn't a mean or a fall-down drunk. She would pass out late morning, wake back up and drink some more, then pass out about bedtime. She didn't know that I knew. We never discussed it. Aunt Cindy treated everyone like they were important to her. Like she saw them for who they were on the inside only. She didn't see the cuts, the bruises, or the damage that life tends to tattoo on us.

In the wake of the news that we were packing up again, I called Aunt Cindy.

If anyone was going to understand how much I was about to get hosed, it would be her. After all, she left as a teenager and moved to New York City just to get away from her family. I asked Aunt Cindy if I could move in for a few weeks, do my trip, help her around the house, then decide my next move—Indiana or wherever Mama might be by that point. She thought it was a "fabulous" idea. I told my mama I wasn't going; I was going to stay at Aunt Cindy's. I packed up my bag of clothes and they dropped me in Aunt Cindy's yard on their way out of town. I couldn't have been happier waving goodbye.

My plan went off as scheduled. I went to Papa's early the day before and did yard work all afternoon to earn some spending money for my trip. Slept well, woke up early, got ready fast, and then climbed in the car and headed to New Madrid to catch the bus. It was an incredible day. I've never been one for scary rides but getting to hang out with friends at such a happy place, without family to drag me down, was more fun than I had had in a really long time. Exhausted, I slept on and off on the bus ride back home. Pulling into town, the familiar sound of the air brakes and downshifting from the bus woke me. I gathered my goodies from the day—a small papier-mâché rose I had bought for myself, a key chain with "Six Flags" on it that I had bought for Dawn, and a Six Flags pencil I had purchased for Lisa—and then climbed off the bus and into Papa's truck. It had truly been a great day.

We drove the twenty-minute trek back to Papa's house. I kissed him goodnight and told him thank you. I really meant it. It had never been lost on me that I could always count on him to take care of me. He managed the rides that I needed so I didn't miss out on my great day. He also let me work so that I had money to spend on some small gifts for myself and my sisters. He was my rock, and his house was my safe place. I went into my grandma's room and was out like a light.

I'm not sure how long I was asleep before I woke up to something touching me, inside my panties. I've always been such a light sleeper so I can't imagine it being very long, but I was exhausted and the only place I could ever truly sleep was at my grandparents' house, so it's possible that I was in a deep sleep. Maybe even why I didn't hear him coming into the room. I flipped over quickly burying my face in the pillow as I realized this wasn't a dream. Someone's hand was now in my panties and squeezing and rubbing my bottom. I flipped back over with my eyes wide open, and I saw all that I could have never imagined I would see. I kicked and I squirmed as I felt like every ounce of air had been stolen from my lungs. I prayed. I cried. But I couldn't make him stop. Once Papa was finished, he left the room apologizing. I laid there quietly crying into my pillow with my knees pulled to my chest and my eyes fixed on the door. My world had just crashed on top of me. My heart was shattered and laying in a million pieces all around and I was too terrified to move. To gather my pieces. To breathe.

I need to breathe.

As the sun came up and began to poke its light through the bedroom window, I dared to get dressed and sneak down the hall to the bathroom. I quickly locked the door behind me. As I looked in the mirror, the girl I saw was no longer me. Her face was pale white and her eyes distant. They seemed hollow, maybe even cold. There were no more tears to be cried. I took a washcloth from the stack and ran cold water into it. Squeezing it out, I placed the freezing rag onto my face, and I held it there. *I would get through this.* I combed my long, strawberry-blonde hair and brushed my teeth.

I would get through this.

I unlocked the bathroom door, stood up straight, took a deep breath, and opened it with force. *I would get through this.* I walked into the kitchen, looked my Papa straight in the face, and demanded to be taken home right now.

Papa stammered a little and said something about us talking. My brain couldn't make out his words and I couldn't look at him anymore. I again took a deep breath, stood tall with my backbone of steel, and said, "Take me home now, or I'll walk." With that, I climbed into the cab of his truck with my sack of dirty clothes pushed down hard on my lap, protecting myself in a way. The treasures I had found and purchased for me and my sisters the day before seemed meaningless now. Trivial. Stupid even. My chest felt hollow, yet painful at the same time. I stared out the window as we drove. To this day, I remember that as the longest and quietest drive I have ever taken. I still remember the stop signs we stopped at. The turns we took. I remember them all so very well. Once we got to Aunt Cindy's, I quietly got out of the truck and walked inside. I told her that I was tired and asked if I could just sleep. I went into the bedroom, locked the door, turned my music up, and buried my body under the protection of her covers for a really long time.

At some point, Mike, a nineteen-year-old that was staying at Aunt Cindy's too, knocked on my door. He was tall and slender and had blond, moppy hair and very rugged good looks. He roofed with his dad during the day, so his tan was perfect. I had an incredible crush on him. Mike and I had gotten to be really close. He taught me to French kiss, and we shared our crazy family stories with each other. I knew there was no judgment with Mike. His mother had left him as a little kid and his dad was an alcoholic. He tried his best to help his dad keep his roofing business going. I let him in the bedroom, and we sat on bean bag chairs staring into space and just listening to the music. After a bit, he looked at me, knowing something was wrong, and asked, "Are you okay?"

I told him.

It was easier than I guessed it would be. To give it words. I was all cried out. There was a very matter-of-fact coldness in my speech. Looking back, as with other things in my life, I guess my brain built some silos and walled me off from the emotion of it all. The pain was there, and I was dealing with it, but somehow emotion was now removed from me. Mike took it all in. I remember his face. His eyes narrowed as I told him. I'm not sure what I expected his response to be—a hug maybe, a quiet "I'm sorry," possibly?

But with the most out-of-the-blue response, Mike kind of half-laughed, shrugged his shoulders a tad, and said, "Huh, I guess old gramps still has it in him."

I told him to get out.

My eleven-year-old brain couldn't comprehend my incredibly insane reality. A reality where men do these things to the people they know, even love, and other men seem to be okay with it all. My sister was brutally raped only a couple of weeks before by a man we knew. Now my Papa. Right along with what had happened with Papa, all the stories that Mama had told me came flooding into my head. Were they all true? *They must be all true.* I needed out. Out of my head. Out of this messed up, godforsaken family that somehow, someway, I had been born into. The kaleidoscope had turned. Only the deep blues and blacks and grays were visible. I now had an intense clarity of the perversion that had been around me for years. My papa, my uncle, my daddy John...*had all Mama's stories been true?* Our family's demons could no longer hide from me.

As it started to get dark outside, Aunt Cindy came in to ask if my trip had gone alright. Me hiding in the bedroom had her worried my day hadn't gone as planned. I told her everything. She put her arms around me and cussed my Papa's life, birth, and very existence up one side and down the other. *That* was the response I needed. She looked deep into my eyes and said he had done this to her too when they were kids. She and Papa were first cousins, but they grew up in the same house like siblings. He, and other men in the family molested and sexually abused her. Her family didn't seem to care; they all had their own issues. No one tried to stop it. Aunt Cindy described it as just normal, acceptable behavior throughout the family. That's one of the reasons she left, went to New York City, and vowed to never come back. Softly wiping my bangs from my eyes, she promised me she would make him pay for this. But somehow, in my heart of hearts, I knew I had to do this on my own. My stay at Aunt Cindy's was only temporary. I would have to protect myself; it was mine to do.

Papa kept calling the house asking for me. I refused to speak to him. I had nothing to say. Aunt Cindy let him know that I was telling people about what he did. I had nothing to hide. My mama may not have been able to protect me from him, but she had taught me enough to know it wasn't my fault and I didn't need years of psychiatric appointments to tell me that. I watched her be a victim for years. Not me. That wasn't going to be me. I refused to be one more of my family's dirty little secrets. Papa begged Aunt Cindy to get me to stop telling people. She told him no, that he was sick and needed help. He tried to blame it on the fact that he'd been smoking pot and it must have impaired his decision-making, but Aunt Cindy wasn't having it. As hard as it was for her to confront him with it, she brought up what he had done to her as a child. Aunt Cindy didn't stop there; she demanded he get professional help or he's lost us both. He agreed.

My aunt was no one's dummy. She insisted on going to the counselor with him. She may not have been able to go in and make sure he was talking about his sexual perversion and abuses, but she could at least make certain he was truly seeing a counselor. After a couple of weeks, Papa begged to speak with me. He said I could have anything I wanted, but he just couldn't bear losing me. I asked for the only thing I felt might save me—I wanted to be placed in a Christian boarding school. Away from him, away from Mama. I had thought long and hard on how to make a normal life for myself and this was all that I could come up with. I guess you could argue that moving away to a boarding school wasn't exactly in the realm of "normal" for a kid like me. But my desire at this point was simply some stability without drama, and without sexual abuse.

The Seventh-day Adventist boarding school was tucked snugly inside the enormous, towering trees of the Tennessee smoky mountains, somewhere close to Chattanooga. Papa and Grandma had supported the church's missions for many years, which included this school. I knew the religion well and considered myself a Seventh-day Adventist. I knew that what

I didn't know I would learn quickly. It was time for a change of scenery, but this time, just for me. Aunt Cindy and Papa drove me there with what few belongings I was currently traveling with and got me settled in.

The school was co-ed, and all of the girls in the school lived in the same trailer. It was basically our "dorm" for sleeping and bathing. We had a nineteen-year-old from Florida as our house manager, her name was Rachael. Rachael was super cool and had long, thick, dark red hair. She and I got to be good friends fairly fast. I was only eleven, but my life experiences made me much older inside. The way I evaluated people and places. Especially after that night with Papa. Simply put, I wasn't a kid anymore. I grew up that dark night. My kaleidoscope had fully come into focus, even if for just a split second, and that horror could not be unseen. It could not be unfelt. I was fully and solely responsible, from here on out, for my own protection.

The school was over-the-top warm and inviting. The people who ran it were incredibly kind. I remember them as a soft-spoken, quiet bunch that came across as total nerds. Everyone smiled more than normal humans. Especially when they were talking to you. You know the kind.

"Hello, how are you today, Holly?"—then head tilt/smile combo while they stare straight into your eyes and patiently wait for your response. Actually eager to hear what you have to say. So weird. I come from a passionate and dramatic clan who love fiercely, yell often, and thrive on high drama. I knew this would take some getting used to, but I needed bland. I needed this.

Unfortunately, my new chosen way of life didn't last long. These precious people and their school have only a very small, temporary spot in my story. Within a couple of months, the school was closing and I was in Chattanooga being put on a Greyhound bus alone and headed to Houston.

Yes, Houston. No longer happy with Grant, Mama was back with Terry. It never made sense to me; her siren song could reel them back in so easily. But that was just Mama.

The bus ride from Chattanooga to Houston by myself wasn't a concern like you may think. As I racked up the miles on the road, it also felt like racking up miles on my life. I had just turned twelve, but I easily looked sixteen. I knew my way around bus stations, as well as bus-riding protocol, so I was fine. I was no longer a naive child.

Living in Pearland this round was a bit different. Dawn already had a set of friends, so I hung out with them and started dating. Life seemed easier this way. I knew we wouldn't be here long, and the older guys were noticing me, so why not? I had already been taught well how to French kiss and Mama was easy to get around because Dawn had become quite the handful.

However, within a few months, we were back at the Houston bus station headed to Winter Park, Florida, to live with Daddy John.

Oh yes. You read that right, we were headed to Daddy John. My time had finally come. The moment I had waited for. The moment I had begged, pleaded, and cried my eyes out for—for four years—was here. Florida not Texas, but I didn't care. This crazy carousel of clowns and demons was about to stop and let us off.

Or so I thought.

We arrived in Winter Park and moved into Uncle George's house with his family. George was one of Daddy John's brothers. He was a professor of some sort. Daddy's family helped Mama get a job at the dry cleaners and all three of us girls got enrolled in school. I loved Winter Park school; even the kids my age were cool. I got in quick with some skateboarding punk rockers and we spent the afternoons skating around town and stopping to take a dip in a local lake. The kids accepted us with no questions asked. It was an incredible feeling to live in a nice house again, even if it wasn't ours. Mama and Daddy planned to get a house together and we would live as a family and look like a family, but they were both going to date other people. Heck, Mama had already met someone from working at the cleaners. I'll admit that was very disappointing to me, but it was a compromise that I was more than willing to get on board with. I had seen much in the past four years. I traveled to many places and had my eyes opened to more than a twelve-year-old should ever have to mentally process. My parents deciding to make a good home for us was a huge win regardless of who either of them was dating. No more would every Tom, Dick, or Harry be able to move in and try to take over. My daddy was home.

Still a truck driver, Daddy was now taking shorter hauls than he did when we lived in Texas. I knew once school was out, I would get to go too. It had always been our dream. Me and him, on the open road, talking, listening to music, eating at diners with people bustling everywhere. Or maybe...it had just been my dream. A safe place that I had made up in my mind when I needed a way to fall asleep at night. We all do it. Or at least I assume we do. Lay in bed and think of a brighter place. Be the star in a movie in your mind, written by you so all the characters are perfect, except the one you assign as the villain. Mama was always quick to tell me how I put Daddy on a pedestal. She would tell me disgusting stories about him and swapping spouses, perverted sex, drugs, and accusations of incest. Stories a kid should never hear, and stories I certainly didn't want to believe, but now stories that I had to face as possibly being real. Daddy had always been the hero in my movie, and my mama, well Mama had always been my villain.

As happy as I was that my plan, my dream, had finally taken a similar enough form, I had not considered that I was different. My past four years might as well have been a lifetime. Others' demons had been revealed to me—some people that I loved, and some people that I didn't. I was jaded. Trusting men, no matter how much I loved them, was no longer in my ability. Papa had taken that from me. Knowing Mama was right about him made me wonder if all she had told me about my daddy was true also. As a child in Texas, I had seen and heard a lot of things that didn't quite make sense, and those pieces were now fitting eerily together. I had always assumed she was being overdramatic and who knows, maybe she was being over-the-top on some of it. But the clarity I now possessed made me realize that at least a part of it had to be based on truth. That realization certainly hung over my head like a storm cloud ready to break open.

But man was it amazing being with Daddy again.

As soon as school was out that summer, I took my long-awaited road trip with Daddy. Just the two of us, on the road for a few days. I wanted so much for this trip to be all that I had dreamed of. I had high hopes of catching him up on what we had been through in the last four years. It was a great plan, but a pie-in-the-sky dream for sure.

Leaving for my long-awaited trip, I was all smiles and big goodbye waves to my sisters and Mama. I couldn't say "See ya!" fast enough. I was so happy and didn't have an ounce of concern pulling out of that parking lot. The trip, however, proved to be very different from my childish dreams. From day one, it was mentally and emotionally exhausting. Instead of feeling security and happiness, I felt stiff and nervous. My body and mind were on high alert the entire time. My brain deeply evaluating Daddy's every move and every single thing he said to me. Unconsciously scouring his words for any form of sexual innuendo. And sadly, those signs and red flags were undoubtedly there. We had delivered the load we were hauling and were on our way back when Daddy looked at me and said, "The centerfold in Playboy looks just like you this month!" Whether intentional, or just not understanding how to speak to a child any longer, that comment made me realize this had to be my last trip with Daddy. I felt like I was going to throw up. Not only did I not feel safe on that three-day run, but I also felt exposed. My heart was broken once more.

My dream was just a dream after all. I wasn't an innocent child anymore that could just turn up the radio, sing loud with Daddy, and love being in the moment. The colors my mind now colored with were much darker. Much more defined. I knew the kaleidoscope only shows sections of the picture at a time. I knew about the hidden demons now. They had always been there. Peeking out at me from the cracks. Just waiting for the next twist of the scope to come out and dance eerily across my life.

Unsurprisingly, we were headed back to Missouri on a Greyhound in the twinkling of an eye.

CHAPTER IV

Sex, Drugs, and Rock 'n' Roll

That summer seemed to be a turning point for me and Mama. I had finally forced my childhood dreams of Daddy and Texas behind me. Dawn had pretty much decided she was free to be home or not, and I took the position of the second parent in the home. We moved to Agnes Street, right across from Aunt Cindy. It was an actual house! Three small bedrooms, sheetrock walls, and large windows! I found a couch someone threw away and used it as a bed in my bedroom. It was fantastic. All of this, plus being right across the street from Aunt Cindy, meant we had a phone for emergencies and her words of wisdom from time to time. Mike was still staying with her, and I had forgiven him for the stupid remark he made after me telling him about what Papa had done to me. I didn't know what Mike's childhood had been like, or maybe what he had gone through himself, so I didn't feel like it was fair for me to judge his reaction.

Mama took a job serving at the local Eagles Club. Eagles are membership clubs that help improve their communities. Where I come from, they are also super popular for their food, weekend entertainment, and being an all-round fun watering hole. It was only a mile walk from our house, so it worked out well. Mama worked days, made good tips, and was paid in cash so she didn't have to turn it in as wages to the welfare office. If she had turned in her wages, we would have been docked on our monthly check, our Section 8 housing, and our food stamps. Cash-paying daytime jobs were a good find, and Mama loved the attention that she got from the members at the Eagles lounge. She went to work every day just before the lunch shift and walked home a little after the supper crowd.

When Mama worked the day before, Lisa and I would get up early, get four dollars from her tips, and head to the public swimming pool. It was a two-mile walk and it opened at 10 a.m. I didn't want to be home when Mama, and whoever her man of the moment was, woke up. That summer, she mostly dated a guy she called "Hippie." Hippie had long, shiny coal-black hair that went down his back. He looked Indian—very tan, attractive, and in his twenties. Hippie rode a Harley and lived in another state, so he was only around a few days a week. He was nice, but I was way past over it when it came to her men, so I didn't waste time getting to know him. He did buy Finesse brand shampoo and conditioner, though. That definitely endeared me to him more than the others. Once a week I would sneak and use his products while he and Mama were still asleep. I loved the smell of that shampoo and how it made my long hair so much easier to comb through. Much easier than the cheap brand we could afford. We didn't have a blow-dryer, so something small like a great conditioner really mattered. I was cautious not to use his products too often. I knew they must have cost a lot and I didn't want him to stop leaving his bottles in the bathroom. I stayed smart and controlled.

Dawn was fourteen years old and only came home a few nights a week. When she did, she would have friends with her. Mama was always home in the evenings, even on the days she worked, so when Dawn showed up, I could take off with her and her friends for a while. I looked way older than twelve, and acted older, so they didn't mind the little sister hanging around. All of her friends were old enough to drive, some old enough to buy alcohol too. I didn't smoke or drink, though, knowing how God felt about all that. I had no plans to go to hell over trying to act cool.

One of Dawn's boyfriends, or friends, I never knew which they were on any given day, was Lil Kevin. Lil Kevin was only nineteen and had already served a stint in prison. Blond hair, super tan, handsome, and totally cut. Lots of tattoos. He was such a tough guy. When we would all hang out in the park at night or the parking lot uptown, no one even considered messing with us if we were with him. I always felt so protected with Lil Kevin. I had such a crush on him that summer.

Lil Kevin, Dawn, and their other friends would often come to the swimming pool too. All the girls checked Lil Kevin out constantly and he did so right back at them. He knew well how to flirt and get his way. Those girls would buy him sodas and chips and giggle at all his jokes. It irritated the fire out of me. Kevin would look at me often and wink like only he and I knew what he was doing. Then he would whistle at me in front of them like I was the prettiest girl at the pool. I would completely ignore him and try my best not to smile. Lil Kevin clearly knew how to work me too. When the pool closed, he would walk me and Lisa all the way home. Kevin walking us out of there always gave me a nice parting glance and smile to all of the preppy girls who had just wasted their money on him.

Kevin slept at our house from time to time. He didn't really have a solid home, never had a job that I knew of, and just stayed between his family members' and friends' houses. I knew he had a crush on my mama, most of our boyfriends did, but I still enjoyed it when he came around. Kevin had a way of making all the girls feel special, and I blew him off constantly to make sure it was me that got most of his attention.

One of the evenings when it was just me and Lisa walking home from the pool, an old brown car ripped around the corner to our street. It startled and scared us both as it drove very recklessly around us. We were only about half a block from our house. Before I could yell in response to the way it peeled past us, the car screeched to a stop in front of our house. I remember so vividly how the back passenger side door flew open, and I heard my mama scream. Then I saw someone kick her from that back seat into our front yard. She was curled up as she landed on the ground, and a man's arm and some of his body leaned out and pulled the door shut as the driver had already stepped on the gas once more.

I ran as fast as I could toward the house. I don't remember much more than just sitting in the front yard and holding Mama as she screamed and cried. The police came. I vaguely remember them questioning her as I sat in silence feeling miles away from this moment. *Why did they bring her home? I'm so glad they did, but isn't that odd? How terrifying is it that men do this kind of thing and clearly have little or no reason to be afraid of being caught?* Mama filed a report, but she didn't know the men who had done this to her.

Once Mama was calm enough for me to get her inside, we got more of the story. She said that one of them must have put something in her Pepsi before she got off her shift. She had started feeling disoriented as she began the walk home. Some men she had been waiting on that afternoon, pulled up and offered her a ride. Mama appreciated the ride as her head and body were feeling stranger and stranger. The men, however, didn't take her straight home. They took her somewhere else where they all took turns raping her. Then they brought her home.

She said her body was too limp to fight. Mama never drank alcohol or took street drugs so we knew it had to be something slipped into her soda that could make her body and perception so useless. To this day, I would know that car if I saw it. Memories of moments like this never leave. They are burned into your soul.

Lil Kevin showed up sometime after I had calmed her down. I told him all that had happened. I was so angry and wanted them to have to sit in prison for the rest of their lives. I knew Kevin would help me find them. He was older than me, much more streetwise than me, and I was certain he could physically take down any man regardless of size. Lil Kevin and I left to find the car. I thought we needed to walk the road back to the Eagles, maybe they went back there afterward to drink some more. Talking as we walked, I knew Kevin felt really bad for Mama too. She had been good to him, and he obviously cared about her, sexual attraction aside.

As we walked through the "projects," government housing duplexes, I saw the car. My heart raced as I quickly told Kevin, "That's the one. That must be where they lived and that was probably where they took her." It was only two blocks from the Eagles so she would have just started her walk home. I needed to call the cops—but it was too late to knock on a door to ask someone to use their phone. I asked him to memorize the license plate for me—memorizing numbers and letters with dyslexia is a crapshoot—and then said, "Let's just run downtown to the police station and tell them where they are." As I took off, Kevin didn't follow. Instead, he gave me excuse after excuse as to why it was a bad idea to go to the cops. None of which I understood. My heart sank. *Was he afraid or maybe really didn't care?* Either way, in my eyes Lil Kevin fell from his pedestal that evening. He was now just another man who clearly didn't understand or care about the gravity or pain of sexual abuse. The disappointment was suffocating. I ran home, woke Mama, and gave her all the information I had. She told me she would talk to the police in the morning, but it was too late to wake someone up to use their phone. I loathed being so poor that we never had a phone or car. I hated that evil men fully expect to get away with such heinous acts.

The men were never caught.

Looking back, I wonder what all had happened to Lil Kevin to bring him to the situation he was in at the time. I'm not sure what he had been in prison for; I had heard it was multiple assault charges. Maybe he had been sexually abused and couldn't bring himself to face it. I'll never know, and I honestly never harbored ill feelings toward him over it. I still liked him plenty. But he was no longer invincible in my eyes. It was a lesson I needed to learn. I needed to stop falling for the myth of protection from men—papas, daddies, boy-friends—it simply didn't exist.

From the very beginning of our summer on Agnes Street, my dating scene really opened up. Weird to even say since I was only twelve. But that's how it was. The first guy I started "going with" was Greg. He had a cool car and tattooed my name on his arm right before I broke up with him for Steve. Steve was Dawn's boyfriend's brother, who used to give us rides to school. He also had a car, but he had a job as well. Steve was a lot of fun, bought me my first store-bought bathing suit, but he broke up with me because I was still a virgin and wasn't planning to change that until I was married. Again, I was in no way wanting to go to hell. Steve totally understood, as did I when he told me it just didn't work for him. I had plenty of other guys to flirt on and we all still hung out in the same crowd. Plus, that cheetah-print bikini he bought me for the swimming pool was an excellent parting gift.

We were all just a pack of misfits hanging out together. We all had a parent, a family member, or at least a grandparent, that we could call, or go home to, for emergencies. But most kids who prefer the streets prefer the streets because home, or needing an adult, comes with a price. All very different prices—getting a beating from a drunk, getting molested in the middle of the night—but everyone felt that Dawn and I pretty much won the lottery with Mama, so our front yard was the hangout spot.

After Mama's rape, I knew our time on Agnes Street was growing short. She quit her job, not able to face the place again that brought such pain, and Hippie wasn't fulfilling what she was looking for in a soul mate. She started showing signs of wanting to leave right about the time that I met Johnny. Johnny's brother PeeWee was one of the guys in our group. PeeWee was only fourteen years old, 5'2", and scrappy. Coal-black hair, brown Indian skin, and ice-blue eyes. His mom worked multiple jobs in the bars in the evenings. He had three older brothers; the oldest lived outside of town with his grandparents, and the second-oldest, Johnny, was eighteen years old and living in the county jail serving a year for receiving stolen merchandise. Bobby, two years older than PeeWee, lived at his girlfriend's house only a few blocks from us. So, that left PeeWee alone most of the time, hanging out with us.

PeeWee talked about Johnny all the time. How Johnny had basically raised him and Bobby because their mom worked all the time and their dad died in a car accident when they were young. Even Lil Kevin talked about Johnny. How tough he was and how no one messed with him. They would laugh and tell stories about Johnny's fighting reputation. It was just a sport for him. With three brothers and no money to do anything, if they weren't fighting other kids, they would just fight each other to have something to do.

Back to me meeting Johnny.

It was time for Johnny to get out of the county jail, which was sixteen miles away. No one knew what day, but PeeWee knew it was soon. PeeWee and I were hanging out on my front porch when Johnny and Bobby came walking down the street together. He had gotten out of jail that morning, walked to town, and first came to find his brothers.

Johnny was handsome. I mean *handsome*. Little girl's knight-in-shining-armor kind of handsome. He had everything I had ever thought a prince charming should have. Coal-black hair...check. Sapphire blue eyes...check. Dark tan skin and rock-hard muscles...check and check. We all sat on my front porch as he told stories about his time in the county jail. Lil Kevin showed up. Steve showed up. Dawn and her new friends from East Prairie showed up—who already knew who the infamous Johnny Griswell was. We laughed into the night. I was in love at first sight, and I told Dawn not to even think about it. She had her new guy from East Prairie and no way was I moving now. I needed to convince Mama to stay.

But Mama and I were already on edge by this time, and summer was about to end. I had asked repeatedly to spend time with my biological father, Steve. With Daddy John out of the picture, I thought it would be good to know the side of the family that I actually looked like, and certainly must act like. I just knew there had to be some commonsense, normal people I had gotten my no-drama and problem-solving skills from, and maybe, just maybe, I could find a better life with them. Daddy Steve was always up for seeing us when we called. However, it put Mama in a tailspin each time. It was worth the fight though. I had friends for the first time. Friends I didn't want to leave.

Living with Daddy Steve wouldn't actually solve my problem, because he lived in Portageville, an hour away. So, I still had some details to work through. I thought maybe I could stay with Aunt Cindy again, but she had too many living with her already. I checked in with Bobby's girlfriend, Cathy. Bobby had moved back to his mom's since Johnny was home. She and I had become friends and her mom was really cool. I hoped since Bobby wasn't there, she wouldn't mind me for a while. Cathy's mom was strict—a you-have-a-bedtime type of mama—but I loved her even more for that. She really worked hard and provided for her kids. I knew it would be a different life than what I was used to, but knowing the guys could come hang out was a huge plus.

Mama agreed. She was tired of the fight and wanted to head to her next location. Having two teenage daughters that wouldn't blindly drop everything and move when she wanted was beginning to be a problem for her, and for whatever man she was moving with. Cathy's mom and my daddy agreed to a plan. My dad paid her mom a little each week for my stay. I would go to my daddy's house Saturday morning, spend Saturday night with him and his new wife and sons, then come back home Sunday evening. Daddy also gave me an allowance so I could go to the skating rink with Cathy every Friday night. Bobby and Johnny would hang outside the skating rink in the parking lot with the other kids that couldn't afford to get in. We would skate for a while and then sneak out to join them in the parking lot. Right before it was closing time, Cathy and I would go back in and wait for our ride. It was a great setup, and we all knew Mama wouldn't stay gone long so it worked out perfectly. I honestly don't know where she moved this time.

It was really nice getting to know Daddy. I enjoyed visiting and getting to know my brothers too—Brandon, who was two when his mama married my daddy, was now five, and Boone, Daddy's new baby, was sweet as could be. Honestly, I couldn't help but be a little envious of them. Not in a bad way—I was happy for them. They had a mom that enjoyed cooking and keeping the house clean. They got to be kids. They lived out in the country and had three-wheelers and chickens that laid eggs and dogs that loved to hang out and play with you. We would run to the grocery store together and pay with cash, something I hadn't gotten to do in a really long time. The embarrassment of using food stamps was always overwhelming for me. There was a lot going on at Daddy's that was very special for me to watch and be a part of.

We would clean and set the table for supper together while music played on the radio; you could hear the music throughout the house. It was a modern-day *Waltons* to me. I remember in preparation for Halloween, we went to a farm store and bought pumpkins and hay bales. Then we came home and made a scarecrow and a nice yard display for decorations. They were the American family I had always wanted. Sadly, no matter how much they welcomed me, and they really did, I felt like I was outside a glass wall looking in. I was never fully able to immerse myself in the experience I had always wanted because it wasn't my life. It wasn't my family. Dawn, Lisa, and my not-so-perfect, over-the-top mama were my family. As messed up as our lives had always been, I missed them. I missed the crazy. The crazy was my normal.

A couple of months went by and Mama returned. She moved back in with Terry, who was living with his mom at the time, in an old house across the tracks and down the hill. His sisters and little brother, Lil Terry, all lived there too. I was missing my crazy life, but not exactly this form of it. Johnny and I had just started "going together." He would meet me at the Piggly Wiggly after school and walk me the three miles home. Riding the bus was certainly an option, but it just got me there faster and I had no reason to want to be home. Plus, I was in love for the first time. Spending time alone with Johnny, even walking across town, was perfect to me. I had just turned thirteen, and he was eighteen. He had quit school in the eighth grade because it was just too hard for him, and home wasn't steady. With no support system, he didn't know how to make it work and just assumed he wasn't someone who was cut out for book learning. Without a job or school, Johnny could meet me and we had the entire afternoon and evening to hang out.

After a few weeks, we found a trailer just for us on the outskirts of town in the same trailer park as Johnny's mom.

Two-birds, one stone. Aunt Jan moved into the same trailer park and was working at the Eagles. Even though this is the place where Mama had her Pepsi spiked and was later attacked and raped, she felt safe going there to hang out with Aunt Jan while she worked. She knew she had nothing to worry about as long as Aunt Jan was with her. As I've mentioned before, Mama never drank or used street drugs, but she was a groupie at heart. Going to the Eagles to listen to the bands and dance was a good night out for her. Falling for a boy in the band was absolutely her definition of the perfect night, so she was looking for her soul mate every time she went. And she found him. Or so she thought.

The band was setting up one evening and one of the guys got her attention. All night long, this young Southern-rock guy sang and played his guitar to her like she was the only one in the bar. Her perfect shy smile, long legs, and big brown eyes had ensured that she always got the one she set her eyes on. Mama definitely had a way about her that was hard for the men to walk away from. He was only twenty-four years old; she was thirty-four. They were both head-over-heels before the end of the night.

Winston Wellington, whom I called Lucifer—but not to his face, became a regular outing for Mama each night. Wherever he was playing, she was there. Mama didn't worry about me and Lisa being out in the country alone late at night because Johnny had moved in with us. He was nineteen and I was thirteen. Dawn was back home too, which was always nice for me and Lisa. She was as wild as could be and even though many of her actions really bothered me—the responsible one—she kept me and Lisa entertained with her many stories, friends, and sheer fearlessness.

We didn't know much about Winston. He was from Charleston, a town sixteen miles east of Sikeston, and he played music and sang in the local Sikeston clubs weekly. He had wild, coarse black hair. His eyes always seemed black as well. Winston had an issue with Johnny living with us so I just ignored him as much as I could. I knew he wouldn't be around long, and Mama liked to flirt with Johnny, so I didn't see her booting him out anytime soon. Basically, the plan was to stay out of the way and Winston would be history soon enough without my help.

As the last day of school for my eighth-grade year came, I could say without a doubt that it was the best year I had had in forever. We had moved several times but even with that, I attended the same school the entire year. The *entire year*. This had only happened twice in my life—my first-grade year at the special school for dyslexia in Dallas, and then my second-grade year in Garland, a suburb of Dallas. It was amazing. I had made friends, best friends even. I stayed the night with girlfriends and everything. Leaving school that final day, I had phone numbers of friends and plans to still hang out on the weekends together at Skate World. Life was feeling alright.

Until Lisa and I got off the school bus, that is.

Walking through the gravel trailer lot, I was sad that school had to come to an end. I didn't mind the schoolwork; it was well worth it to get to have long-term friends like I had now. Looking to the end of the row where our trailer sat, I noticed the front door was slung open with the chain dangling in the sun. My heart sank. The only time Mama let the door hang open and let the heat and flies in was when we were moving in or moving out. *Dang it*, I said to myself as I kicked some gravel as hard as I could across the lot. Lisa ran on ahead, anxious to see what was happening, but I knew.

Mama had the trailer packed and told us to help load up; we were moving to Charleston with Winston. He was standing there next to his old beat-up pickup truck smiling at me like the cat that ate the canary. I knew he had told her not to tell me until it was happening. He knew I would talk her out of it. What an ass. Chipper, he was loading up our boxes and started ordering me and Lisa around. I tried to petition Mama, but he kept interrupting like he was already in charge of us. Unreal.

Winston had bought Mama a microwave a few weeks earlier. Microwaves were new technology at the time—something we never had—so us girls had been trying to give him the benefit of the doubt. This little trick of his ended any hope of that. I was unhappy about the move for many reasons. Mostly, I'll admit, was because I didn't want to leave Johnny. Moving into Winston's place, instead of him staying at ours, meant he was the boss. I knew he wouldn't have Johnny around. I was also unhappy because I finally had friends. Long-term friends. For nine months, I had gone to school and sat at the lunch table with the same people and seen them on the weekends at Skate World. I didn't want to leave again. I didn't want to be the new girl again. I was thirteen years old and it's a little more difficult to make friends in the summer when you're thirteen than when you're ten or eleven. Thirteen-year-olds don't exactly play kickball in the front yards or ride bikes around the neighborhood to see who else is outside their age. Regardless, Winston came off as very controlling, and some-how, Mama thought he hung the moon swooning her with his music. We were moving, and I was going.

Winston loaded all the final items in the back of the pickup. He had to do it himself because he didn't want to make a second trip and all of our things really filled that truck bed up. He had to position everything just right to get it all in the one load. After it was all loaded, we squeezed into the cab—Winston driving, me on Dawn's lap, and Lisa on Mama's. I was upset beyond words, so I stayed silent. Dawn asked a lot of questions about why we had to move like right now... today. Questions to which Mama told her it was her decision to move so we needed to deal with it and shut up. Dawn was totally pissed, and her anger was pretty clear toward Winston. We knew whose fault this was. Winston was none too happy about a kid questioning her mama the way Dawn did, and his irritation was pretty clear to us too. I assumed Dawn wouldn't be in Charleston long.

We drove slowly and took the back roads from Sikeston to Charleston since the truck bed was piled pretty high. We were all silent, holding our anger inside as there was no room to let it out anyways. About ten miles into the trip, we heard a loud *clunk!* Winston swerved to the right to stop as I looked out the back window just in time to see that fancy microwave take a few bounces on the blacktop. I didn't dare laugh and that's a good thing for sure because Winston, already on the brink, snapped. Throwing the truck into park, he jumped out and started cussing and yelling and throwing a fit in the middle of the road. He picked that microwave up from the blacktop, raised it above his head, and then smashed it down on the pavement again—cussing it and kicking it the entire time shouting about how Mama put that microwave on the back of the truck. Dawn, Lisa, and I looked at each other. First of all, he put that dang microwave on the back of the truck, and we knew it. Secondly, who acts like this? Mama had tears rolling down her face as she apologized, standing right in the middle of the road with him while he was acting like an idiot. They finally got back in the truck, and he pulled out like a maniac. Microwave in a million pieces scattered across the pavement.

The beginning of a very long, and horrific, road.

Winston moved us into a concrete house in Charleston. The house was a bait shop in front and had living quarters in the back with one bedroom, one bathroom, living room, kitchen, and garage. Mama and us girls cleaned and cleaned until it wasn't a bad place to move into. Dawn and I slept in the garage, Lisa on the couch, and Mama and Winston in the only bedroom. He painted the concrete walls in the bathroom and bedroom black, and then spray painted the tub and sink blood red. I'll be honest, it felt like taking a shower in hell. You couldn't see because it was so dark, lit by only a pull-string light bulb hanging from the middle of the ceiling. The spray paint didn't stick to the tub or the sink so it kept peeling and clogging up the drains. Winston's hair seemed to be everywhere. Clogged drains from paint chips and hair in a bathroom that felt like the bowels of hell made me never want to bathe again. I hated this place, but Mama kept acting like it was all going to work out. Winston had already shown us his temper during the microwave incident, so I just tried to remain helpful and not complain. But every little thing that didn't go right, bacon overcooked, running out of milk, anything big or small, seemed to set him off.

The bait shop business Winston was starting conveniently doubled as a front for his drug sales. I'm not certain what all he dabbled in. I only had to help with the weed on the drugs side of the business. That bothered me a little, but not a lot. I felt it was his sin and not mine in this case. I was just a kid and surely God knew the trouble me saying no would cause. When we lived in Morehouse, I did most of the joint rolling for Dawn and her friends. Again, I wasn't the one selling it—but their own rolls ended up very wrinkly, so I just did it for them. My long, slender fingers and light touch made me pretty good at it. On the bait shop side, I made the weekly runs with Winston to Kentucky to pick up crickets and worms. I also greeted the minnow driver for our minnow deliveries. The shop had a concrete rectangular pool in the middle that we kept those cute little guys in. I assumed the building had to have been built as a bait shop—why else would there be a concrete minnow pool right there in the middle of the store? Anyway, I also took the morning shift in the bait shop. I enjoyed working so that wasn't a problem. It kept my mind off of Winston and Mama's relationship, which had turned very dark very fast.

It started right after we moved in. So quick, in fact, I was surprised he had been able to hold it in for all of those weeks of dating Mama and coming back and forth to Sikeston. He was disturbed all of the time. Mama once told me that Winston had been a devil worshiper and most of his torment came from that. He had also thrown himself down into the belly of a barge when he worked on the riverboat. She said he had done that to get disability checks, but he didn't realize how bad it would mess up his back and leg, so he was dealing with constant pain and taking painkillers. I really did feel bad for him until the abuse started.

Mama had a cardboard box that she kept all of our baby pictures in. This made it easy to tape it, tag it, and get it on the Greyhound when we made our moves. Some of the pictures included our daddies with us as well. Lisa and I were digging through the box one evening for a photo of Dawn sitting on Elvis Presley's horse, with him, when she was almost two years old. It was one of our favorites for sure. My mama was very pregnant with me in the photo, and she was standing next to Elvis as he sat on his horse. Oh yes, you read that right. My mama was standing next to good-looking, sideburn *Elvis Presley*, 1969, while he was sitting on his horse and holding my sister Dawn. Unbelievable! But Mama and Daddy Steve lived in Memphis at the time and my daddy was a drummer, so he had connections. My mama was striking, so standing at Elvis's gate with the rest of the groupies, even pregnant, she absolutely still turned heads. This picture was our "go-to" photo for classroom show-and-tell.

The fight broke out later that night after we went to bed. We heard Winston screaming at Mama asking why she had hidden that box from him. He said it was because she was holding onto past relationships. Crying, I heard Mama explain it was all of her pictures of us as babies and as little kids. She said she was saving them for us when we were older. We heard him start hitting her. She was screaming and crying like we had never heard before. Dawn and I ran into the bedroom to stop him. It was so dark. So black. I grabbed up Lisa who ran in behind us. We all saw Winston standing over Mama with one hand holding the back of her hair as she lay on the bed, and the other with a raised fist ready to punch her in the head again. He looked like Lucifer himself with those crazy black eyes. He dropped Mama's head and pushed Dawn back forcefully as he stormed past us out of the room. I climbed to Mama's side on the bed, where she lay with blood on her face, holding her head. It was obvious that he had also banged her head against that concrete wall. As I tried to calm her down to see if I needed to run and call the police, he came back with the box of pictures and set it on fire in front of us.

And that was Winston Wellington.

The beatings became too many to count. Mama spent most of her time laying in that black room on a waterbed that took up most of it. I only went in twice—once to stop the initial beating and then once to check on her when she didn't respond to me hollering for her. She stayed there, available to service Lucifer any time of the day he wanted. He kept most of the beatings on her body and the back of her head, not wanting to harm her beautiful face, I guess. He must not have cared about the dark circles under her eyes or the sadness of her smile. She no longer looked like Mama to me. He seemed to eliminate the wild gypsy light that had been inside her. No matter her depression, we had always been able to get a hug, a smile, or a small laugh when we tried. But he stole even that from her. He would beat her, bang her head on that concrete wall, then have very loud sex with her immediately after. Lisa and I would go into my room in the garage where we couldn't hear. I really can't explain the torment of listening to your mother being abused like this. There just really aren't words.

I talked Mama into going on a walk around the block with us once. Winston was gone for the day, and I wanted her to get some fresh air. To see the sun. But it was almost like the dark spiritual forces that Mama said he used to pray to alerted him of our movement. We were almost back to the house when Lucifer's truck came to a screeching halt at the curb right behind us. Startled, I turned around quickly only to see his wild hair and head jerk back as he threw the truck into park. He got out, all in one motion it seemed, and I knew there was hell to pay. We were only two blocks away from the house at that time. Looking around like a madman while screaming at Mama that she knew she shouldn't have left the house, Winston grabbed a tree limb from a nearby yard—not a switch, a tree limb—and whipped her with it all the way home. In the middle of the day. In the middle of town. Drivers passed by. Porch sitters sat. No one even tried to help us.

From that day, I knew without a doubt that Winston was either literally crazy or possessed by the very devil he previously worshipped. We knew he would kill us if we fought back. We lived in the small town he had grown up in of only six thousand people. His mother was a pillar of the town's Baptist church and his father a long-term dispatcher at the police station. I called the cops on him once, early on. They came and visited with him on the sidewalk out in front of the bait shop. I watched carefully from behind the bait shop counter as they seemed to be awfully familiar for a serious complaint of beating up a woman. I had called from the pay-phone at the gas station a block down and told them I was walking by and I heard a lady and kids screaming and a man cussing and hitting her. I ran back to the house to tend the bait shop and they came shortly after I got back. When they came in, they asked for Winston, so I yelled into the house that the cops wanted him. Despite his limp, he came fast—almost running actually, through the kitchen and into the bait store. My guess was he was probably worried that his drug sales had been found out. They asked him to step outside, and there they stood—chatting like old buddies. Once they left, Winston came back in, passed me without saying a word, went back into the house, and beat Mama until she looked like a wounded stray cat curled up in the corner trying to either hide from her attacker or just die and get it over with.

I never called the cops in Charleston again.

Winston hated Dawn, seemed to just not see Lisa, but for some reason he liked me just fine. Helping with our new "family" business, I had to make runs with him to Kentucky to get the crickets and worms. On these trips, he talked to me like we were friends, asking about my favorite things like music, cars, and places I'd like to see in the world. I figured it was only because I worked so hard. I wanted to be pleasing to him so he would let Mama come out and have a normal life. It's interesting now looking back and seeing how easy we all fell into that cycle. Just trying to "behave" to keep the horror at bay.

Dawn, however, never even tried to be pleasing. He hated her, and she was just fine with that because she loathed him. One night while we were eating supper, Dawn made a comment that set him off. He and Mama were sitting on the couch eating in the living room, Dawn, Lisa, and I were at the small table in the kitchen. I don't even remember what Dawn said, but he threw his ceramic plate at her face just like it was a frisbee. Lisa and I hit the ground, making sure the flying plate missed us, but Dawn barely moved, staring him straight in the face. Thankfully, it missed her face, but it still hit the side of her head. Mama started screaming and crying. Dawn was crying and yelling too. Lisa and I ran to my bedroom in the garage to hide and get out of the way. I knew, sitting on my bed with my arms around Lisa, listening to the fight, that it would be the final straw for Dawn. Dawn was fifteen years old and could take care of herself. I knew she had only stayed this long for me and Lisa. She left in the night as she had in the past without saying goodbye. As much as it helped to have the three of us together, I didn't blame her one bit.

After Dawn left, it felt like Winston's demons went to even a new level. One morning I woke up to him nailing all of the windows shut. I didn't ask. I just went to cooking his breakfast. Next, he tied a shotgun to the only door that didn't have an outside padlock. We were no longer allowed to leave the house when he wasn't home. The shotgun had the trigger rigged by a string taped around it and then taped around the doorknob tight, so that if we turned the doorknob it would pull the string around with it, trip the trigger, and blow off our hands—or so he said. I knew I could easily cut that string, but if I did, it better be to get us out for good. Meaning Mama had to come too. Because if not, we would all be dead once he got back. But she was too afraid. He had her on pain pills along with her normal sack of antidepressants. I couldn't talk her into anything at that point. If we were going to get out of this hell on earth alive, I knew I had to come up with another plan.

School had just started back, and Lisa and I liked being in a somewhat normal setting for most of the day. My mind, and I'm sure Lisa's too, couldn't help but be on Mama all day, not knowing what she was going through without us there. Mentally, however, we both needed the break it gave us. From my relationships with Johnny and Lil Kevin, I knew that crimes under seventeen got you juvenile court; seventeen and over most likely got you adult court. It made sense; a child shouldn't be put in a prison cell with an adult. At that point, I was pretty sure I could kill Winston, free Mama and Lisa, and only have to spend a few years at most away in a group home. I was about to turn fourteen and in my mind, I had no other options. Dawn was gone, Lisa was only eleven, and Mama was no longer in her right mind. He would end up killing her if I didn't stop him.

Winston had many guns loaded throughout the house. I had never used one, but it didn't seem like rocket science to me. The entrance to the bait store from the kitchen was a swinging door on hinges. From the kitchen, you just pushed through the swinging door, stepped into the bait shop, and you were standing right behind the long checkout counter. We had the cash register on top and a loaded shotgun underneath in case any trouble came in. The rest of the bait shop was pretty basic. On the other side of the counter, sitting near the middle of the store, was the concrete minnow tank. A couple of refrigerators for the worms were against the walls and a tank for the crickets. The crickets sang a song all night long that was seriously irritating when we first got them. But it didn't take me long to get used to it. It actually became a comforting melody after a while. The front of the store was nothing but windows so during the summer months, the sun coming up lit the store up every morning. I gladly took the opening shift every Saturday. Winston would wake up around 8 a.m. and relieve me while I cooked him breakfast. His morning routine was like clockwork. I played it over and over for weeks in my mind. Lying in bed thinking it through, I knew I could sit on the bait shop countertop, legs crossed, and hold that shotgun steady. I would push the safety off and just wait for the swinging door to open. *I can do this.*

To the person who has had a normal life growing up, this seems extreme, I know. But for months I had lain awake to the sounds of my mother slowly dying, being murdered right in front of me and my little sister. Kissing my broken Mama goodnight every evening, her beautiful smile gone, the constant tears in her eyes and the bruises on her neck and arms—sometimes even bite marks—was enough to break anyone's mind. And it did mine.

The fall had settled in and this particular Saturday morning seemed colder and darker than normal. When I flipped the sign on the door and unlocked it, I didn't anticipate many, if any, customers. Just as I had planned, I mounted up—sitting cross-legged on that countertop—and waited. I decided if a customer came in and saw me sitting there with the shotgun, I would brush it off as admiring a new birthday present. As the sun started showing through the windows, my mind played out the scene that was to unfold before me. My hands started sweating and I was getting more and more uncomfortable with it all. The negatives of my carefully laid out plan rang out in my mind like church bells. I couldn't stop visualizing all of the things that could go wrong.

What if I miss?

Or: *What if I don't kill him with my first shot? Will I have time to figure out how to load another shell and ready myself to fire?* It didn't matter. If I didn't try, he was going to end up killing her. We all knew it. This was our only chance of survival.

The brighter it became in the store, the more tired my arms were from holding that cold, heavy thing. I wondered what could be taking so long. Finally, I heard rustling in the kitchen. My heart banged like a marching band's drum in my chest. I pulled the gun up quickly and readied my aim. My heartbeat grew louder and faster, filling up my chest and my ears—*good Lord, come through the door already!*

"Ready for some breakfast?"

Lisa's sweet voice talking to the dog cut through my heartbeat banging in my ears. I dropped the gun to my lap. I thought I might throw up. *What was she doing up so early?* I slid quietly, quickly, off the countertop, and put the gun away before she walked through the doors looking for me. *What if I had gotten scared and just fired when the door swung open, never imagining it could be anyone but him?*

Lisa pushed that swinging door open just enough to peek her smiling, beautiful face through, "Want some Fruity Pebbles?" Mama had just been allowed to go to the grocery store the previous day. Lisa, rightfully so, made plans to wake up early and get a bowl while there was still some left. "Yep! I'll be right in there with you." Words I managed to choke out while smiling back at her as she giggled—so excited over cereal.

I took a deep breath, physically sick from the thought of what might have happened. Lucifer had to die, but I needed to find another way.

My sister Dawn, as I've said before, seemed to pop up when I needed her most. She was in the parking lot with some guy driving an El Camino as school was letting out only days after my failed plan. I think the guy's name was Chris. Dawn had moved in with him in Sikeston. No doubt this nerdy guy didn't know what hit him, but now he had a beautiful girl living with him. She had a ride, a bed, and food. To her, it was survival and a worthy trade-off. To him, well let's just say I'm sure he didn't realize it was actually transactional.

After she was settled in, she had him bring her to Charleston to check on us, and to let us know she was fine. She was fifteen years old, about to turn sixteen, and hadn't gone to school regularly for a while now. In the school parking lot, I told her everything. Mama barely came out of the bedroom anymore and with the nightly beatings and sex, or maybe rape—I couldn't tell—no way she could survive much longer. No one was allowed to leave now except for school and occasional grocery shopping. We needed out. Dawn promised me she would find someone to help. I told her she couldn't ask Papa. Even with me not wanting him in my life any longer, I didn't want him killed by Winston. So, it had to be help from someone else. And we had no one. But Dawn said she would find help, and she did.

The following weekend, a car pulled up, honking. The bait shop was on a corner off the main drag and this old four-door, honking car turned the corner and pulled right up on the side street—the one that the kitchen door opened up to. I was in the kitchen and looked out the door window just as Dawn hopped out of the car. They were parked directly across the street. Next came Terry, and his brother, Lil Terry, climbing out of the car. Winston was in the bait shop and didn't have a great view of the side street like me, but he sure heard the honking. I yelled for Mama, knowing crap was about to go down. The kitchen door was still rigged with the shotgun so we couldn't open it by turning the doorknob—unless we cut the string. I quickly made the executive decision that with Dawn, Terry, *and* Lil Terry here, someone was about to die so it really didn't matter. I cut the string, moved the gun, and ran out that side kitchen door just in time to see a crazed Winston, black eyes glaring, afro a flyin', coming around the front of the store and onto the side street with his sawed-off, double-barrel shotgun in hand. He snapped that shotgun together with one swinging motion of the barrels, locked it hard against his hip, and then...

Winston paused.

I stopped dead in my tracks, frozen, unsure how to evaluate the situation directly in front of me.

You see, Terry and Lil Terry looked just alike. Tall, slender builds, scroungy facial hair that only grew in weirdly placed patches, and black, curly big hair—Winston's pause was only because he didn't know which one to shoot.

I couldn't breathe. Winston's eyes darted back and forth then he readied that sawed-off double-barrel to his hip once again when suddenly, a police officer rounded the corner from the front of the bait shop directly behind Winston. With a gun drawn, the officer shouted, "Winston! Don't make me shoot you!"

My brilliant sister.

Dawn, knowing what happened the only time I called the cops on Lucifer, had Terry stop at the gas station on the corner a block away. She called the cops from the payphone and said something like "Winston shot somebody outside the bait shop!" Then slammed the phone down, jumped in the car and they drove down the block to our house. Pulling up honking, whether she thought about this or not, drew Winston out of the bait shop, which kept him from trapping us inside and just killing us once he saw Terry. God protected us, no doubt. With the cop now behind Winston, gun pointed to the back of his head, Winston lowered his gun. The cop handcuffed him and got him in the cop car. By this time, my mama was standing on the sidewalk crying in her see-through nightgown. The three of us girls scurried to pack up our most essential things, then we got our butts into Terry's car and out of town, with Mama, before they released him. Because we all knew they were going to release him.

The backstory, I soon found out, went like this: After checking on me at the school, Dawn went back to Sikeston and found Terry. While Mama had left him again some time back, her men were always willing and ready to come back. You just didn't come across her kind of beauty, intelligence, and sexual confidence every day hanging out at the Eagles Lounge. She was a diamond in the rough. Her siren song just wouldn't leave their heads. Dawn used this well-known fact about Mama's men as she went to Terry and told him that Mama wanted him back, but Winston had her trapped in the house abusing her and not allowing her to leave. Much of that was true of course, except for the part of Mama wanting Terry back. Dawn, hands down, was the best liar I've ever known, and I will always be thankful for this one. Even though it put us in a bit of a pickle when we got back to Sikeston.

After a lot of discussion, crying, and drama, Terry dropped us off at Aunt Jan's. One thing was for certain, Mama wasn't leaving Winston for Terry, no matter how wonderful he had been coming to save us. She also wasn't leaving the rest of her belongings, no matter how little it was. We called to find out if Winston was still in jail. He was not. They had released him, no charges, unless of course, Mama wanted to come in and press some. But battered women seldom do—it only causes more beatings.

Mama, still reeling from the morning, decided to call Uncle Ben for help. I begged her not to. Uncle Ben was a big man, at least 6'5" and weighed probably close to 300 pounds. He was Mama's older brother and he had retired from the Army special forces; he was a Green Beret. So basically, no one messed with Uncle Ben. He had a dominance about him. Incredibly intelligent, government contractor, and making excellent money in IT. My issue, however, was that Uncle Ben was a perverted sex abuser who took advantage of the women in our family. I knew this because my mama told me. So did my cousins, my sister, and my aunt. So why call him?

Mama refused to lose everything once again. She was physically battered and emotionally spent, and she was afraid that Winston would come find us at any given moment. She knew we had no help through the police in Charleston and wondered if Sikeston police would get to us in time once he found us. As kind as Terry was to come get us, his home was certainly the first place Winston would look. I knew Mama was in solid fear. We didn't have a phone and him finding us in the middle of the night would be horrifying and very possibly deadly. Mama called Uncle Ben and asked if he could pick us up and take us to get the rest of our things in Charleston, and then let us stay in St. Louis a few days while she figured out what to do next. All it took was one phone call and he was on the road to save us. Anytime his sisters or nieces called, Uncle Ben wasted no time to help. Being an IT guy in the big city, he could pretty much write his own schedule and pay. I certainly appreciated Uncle Ben removing us from Lucifer's grip, but it was no doubt just choosing a lessor horror. Mama always felt like she didn't have other choices; I always felt she reacted too quickly and didn't know what her choices may be. Regardless, Uncle Ben had helped us many times and although he never tried anything with me, Mama was easy prey. She always expected the best in people. I didn't. My eyes were open to the ways of this world, and I wasn't going to be groomed or preyed upon. I had a newfound clarity of our current situation, as well as the previous times he had helped us. I knew well that this type of kindness always comes with a price.

Uncle Ben arrived in a matter of hours after Mama's call. Sikeston sits just two hours south of St. Louis on Interstate 55. He had a truck with a camper shell, so plenty of room to get all of our remaining things. Mama called the Charleston Police Department to let them know we were coming and they needed to be there if they wanted to prevent trouble. Uncle Ben could squash Winston like a daddy long-legs underfoot, so it was their choice. We loaded up our belongings in Charleston, with no sign of Winston, and got on the road to St. Louis.

As I sat in the back seat of Uncle Ben's double cab truck, I watched how he looked at Mama. Smiling, touching, and patting her hand. Being overly supportive of all that she'd been through. Asking why she hadn't called sooner and assured her that no matter what, he's always just a phone call away. I sat there listening and watching and then decided to just stare out the window at the passing headlights on the interstate. Usually, the familiarity of being on the road at night was comforting, but not tonight, knowing what lay ahead. My mind struggled to find a way out for her. To change the inevitable. I hated that she was so weak. That she seemed to willingly walk into these situations and that it meant dragging the rest of us right along with her. Or did she think this time would be different? Maybe his compassion for all that she had been through would override his sick desire for payoff? Not likely. As Lisa slept peacefully across the seat next to me, I longed for the days that I didn't know or understand the things going on around me.

Arrival at Uncle Ben's was better than expected. His long-time girlfriend that we loved, Marie, was there to greet us and make sure we were settled in. I asked her to please stay the night and explained how much I thought it would help Mama to have a friend to talk to. Mama jumped on the idea and talked Marie into staying with us. I knew God had blessed us once again. I went to bed with Lisa, knowing all was okay for the night.

Morning came and Marie cooked us breakfast and then headed off to work. Uncle Ben took the day off to spend with us and had a list of pampering he had planned for us girls. Make no mistake, it may have seemed like gifts, but this is where the grooming for the payoff begins. He insisted on getting us all a few things, saying it wasn't right for his sister and nieces to live like we do when he has so much. "No, thank you" was not an acceptable answer. We went to the mall and to some high-priced department stores. He bought me makeup, a blouse, some new underclothes, and a pair of tennis shoes. All brand new. Lisa was treated with books, clothes, and shoes, and then Mama got to pick some items as well. Our next stop was lunch out at an actual restaurant and then we ended with popcorn and soda at the movies. It was only my second time in a theater, and it was pretty cool. *The Muppets* was showing and even though I thought it was a funny show, the pit in my stomach prevented me from enjoying any of it. Not even my new eye shadow. I found myself watching Uncle Ben and Mama all day, suspicious of when the moves would be made. Terrified of the fact that I had zero chance of stopping any of it.

We got back to Uncle Ben's house late that afternoon. Uncle Ben wasted no time in telling me that he needed to talk to Mama alone, so I needed to explore the neighborhood for a bit with Lisa.

"Take your sister for a walk," Uncle Ben instructed.

"In St. Louis?" I questioned. "Isn't this the biggest city in our state?" I continued with as much confusion and pushback as I could muster up, not wanting him to know that I fully understood what was truly happening. I glanced at Mama; her face was pale white, and she shook her head no to me before Uncle Ben could see her. I tried my best to fix it for her. "I'm not feeling so great. I'm just not used to having soda and candy and I don't feel safe wandering the streets here. Lisa and I will sit and watch TV quietly." Nope. He wasn't buying it and insisted we leave. I argued back and held my position. He started getting mad, really mad, actually holding the door open for us to leave. Mama spoke up and told me to take Lisa, that she would be alright. Which I knew wasn't true. Reluctantly, I took Lisa and walked out.

Down one block is all that I would allow us to walk. I just needed to be in my head and not worried about being two small-frame girls walking the streets in a big, dangerous city. I sat us down on the corner curb and we watched the cars and people quietly. I held Lisa's hand and pulled my knees up under my chin to rest my head. I didn't want to talk. I had learned to have a darn good poker face but at this moment, I felt it was failing me. Better for Lisa to think I was sick to my stomach from the popcorn and soda. I never wanted her to know the things I knew. I missed the days of those cold stairwells, concrete stairs, Lisa playing on the rails, and Dawn being with me while we waited for Mama to finish her latest shag, come back out, and then take us home. It seemed less lonely. Less evil. Knowing we were going home to our own home afterward might have had something to do with it, or maybe just the fact that I still had an ounce of naivety in me back then. Sitting with my chin on my knees on that street corner, I could hear the Eagles song, "Lyin' Eyes," playing in my head. In the song, there's a line about all forms of refuge having a price. *The Eagles were spot-on*, I thought. I had already learned this lesson on Handy Street, but now it was cemented in my brain. *Men that love you and promise to care for you will expect payment at some point.* It was a harsh and sad reality.

Once a couple of days passed, Uncle Ben drove us back to Sikeston and helped Mama secure a trailer there at one of the larger trailer parks in town. The larger park would provide some safety by having more people around us. It was actually a pretty fun place to live. A lot of activity was going on all of the time. Soon, Aunt Jan moved into a trailer a few doors down and Johnny moved back in with us. Lucifer seemed to be nothing more than a dirty speck on my rearview mirror of life.

Mama was happy again, as well. Sometimes we would wake up to her and some traveling musician coming home in the middle of the night, but I didn't care. She was happy. The eternal gypsy in her was in a better place when she had a music man around. Dawn, having just turned sixteen, was out of the house and about to marry some guy in his thirties. He was a drug dealer, mainly pills, but seemed to treat her well. I was dating Johnny and he stayed with us on and off, so Mama didn't have to worry a lot about us being in the trailer at night by ourselves. I made sure Lisa and I got to bed on time throughout the week and to school every day.

I was fourteen but looked a few years older. Mama's favorite beau at this time was a guy that had a Bob Seger cover band. He played at King Tut's often, a club in Cairo, Illinois, just over the Mississippi river from Charleston. Mama would borrow Papa's car on a Thursday evening to use it Friday for laundry and groceries, then we would drive over to King Tut's that evening to see "Bobby." I called him Bobby because I had no idea what his name was. Thursday night was Ladies Night and for only five bucks, girls eighteen and older could get in and drink and dance all night for free. Mama didn't like driving over by herself so Lisa would stay the night at Aunt Jan's, and Dawn and I would ride over with Mama. They never carded us and dancing all night was a seriously good time. Between the band's sets, and then after the close of the show, Mama would be in the back room making out with Bobby until all of the cleanup was done. Then we would drive home.

Weird as this sounds, my life felt back to normal.

As was typical, normal meant it was time for a change. Winston came for a visit while we were in school one day. A changed man, he begged for Mama's forgiveness. He told her how he had gotten saved and was now preaching part-time at a nondenominational Pentecostal church in Charleston. He was ready to marry her and spend the rest of his life writing her songs and being the man she deserved. He had found Jesus.

Honestly, I had always felt that I was the only one in our family, other than my grandparents, that cared about God or his opinion of us. Having a chance at a normal God-fearing family was an exciting thought for me. So was Mama finding religion, and she did. She went to church with Winston the next evening and came home literally glowing. Smiling from ear to ear, Mama had accepted Jesus into her heart. It meant the world to me seeing her so happy, seeing her reading the Bible instead of her romance novels. To me, this was actually worth Winston getting a second chance. I knew God was capable of changing anyone. I was still afraid, but it was worth trying. This was my opportunity to have a family that went to church together, a family that cared about what our Lord and Savior cared about. I needed this. I was all in.

Unfortunately, Winston was not.

CHAPTER V

Blowing This Popsicle Stand

Growing up in and out of trailer parks, and moving around the country on a whim, lends a few life lessons that you may not learn otherwise. Some lessons are very simple, like how putting tinfoil on your windows in the summer will cool your trailer down and lower the electric bill. Some lessons are not so simple. One would be the tremendous value in being controlled enough to keep your mouth shut. "Snitches get stitches" is for real in the places that I grew up. You must weigh the pros and cons of telling anything bad or illegal that you've witnessed, regardless of your age. That's why when there is a shooting, a beating, or a break-in, it's often hard for police officers to get information, even when it happened in front of others.

Even so, I realized early on that there's long-term damage in not telling. How many other girls will be molested? How many more times can your mother take those beatings and live? It's not as cut and dry as you may think—especially for a young mind. Either response weighs heavily on you, knowing that whatever you decide to do will most likely have long-term detrimental effects—on you and those that you love. Do you choose to tell and put someone in jail for harming your mama only to have her be the one to go bail him out? Then you are treated badly, most likely abused, for doing the right thing—all while living right back in the same situation that you were in before it all happened. Trust me, it can be a lot to consider in a really short amount of time. You have to move all of the chess pieces in your head at record speed to decide the most likely outcome of both decisions, then you pray you've made the right choice.

With decisions like this at a young age, it is my belief that you become a little older in your heart and mind. A little wiser to the world, and to your surroundings. Calloused as well, I guess. I also realized early on that people don't usually change much. If he beats you, apologizes, and then does it all over again, he's most likely not going to change. I watched others closely to help predict their next move. And just like in Kenny Rogers's song "The Gambler," I learned pretty quickly when it's okay to stay, and when you should just turn and walk away.

Because of our past experiences with Lucifer, the thought of moving back to Charleston with him was scary, even though he had found Jesus. As much as I wanted a Christian home and was so very thankful that Mama was saved too, I knew what he was capable of. So, in my heart, I proceeded with caution.

The church Winston attended was a small Pentecostal church located in a rundown concrete building in downtown Charleston. It had a small sanctuary with a stage, and we used folding chairs to sit on during services. It had a room off to the side that included a kitchen with an open area where we used fold-out tables for potluck dinners after service. The second floor was an actual apartment where the pastor and his family lived. One of their daughters was Lisa's age, so she played at their house often.

Everyone treated us like family and I really enjoyed that feeling. It was a sense of belonging that included all three of us, Mama, Lisa, and me, so it was incredibly welcoming. I didn't really notice Mama making friends; she mostly stayed next to Winston. He sang and played his guitar in the praise band and even started preaching at some of the night services. The church was basically a hell-fire-and-brimstone church, meaning that most of the preaching was focused on teaching you to stay out of hell—which I appreciated. We had services multiple times a week and no one ever seemed to miss any of them. We were there on Tuesday night, Thursday night, Sunday morning, and Sunday night, with praise band practices in between. So our entire week revolved around the church. The house we moved into in Charleston was a really decent one, just across town from the church. Lisa and I shared a bedroom, Mama and Winston had the other bedroom, but we kept that to ourselves since it was a sin to live together without being married. We had a small kitchen in the back of the house, and the back door from the kitchen led to the carport. The house also had a small, square, concrete front porch with steps, so it was a nice place for sitting and watching the neighbors tend to their yards. Not a common sight for me, but I really enjoyed pulling weeds and participating in the daily waves and "good mornin'" nods.

Within weeks of us moving back to Charleston, I started noticing the sheer evil in Winston once again. Changes started off small, like him grabbing Mama and screaming in her face. Then just like that, he was full-on Lucifer with all of the physical abuse once again. We were sworn to secrecy because awful things could happen if the pastor found out. Winston was trying hard to be a religious man and it was important to let God work the needed changes out in him. Honestly, I didn't have anyone to tell anyways. Dawn had just gotten married, and I had broken up with Johnny, mainly because I didn't want to go to hell, and our church didn't have many teens my age that lived in town. So most days, I was stuck sitting in my room listening to my Christian albums on the record player, cleaning the house, and praying the beatings would stop. When they happened in the early mornings, I would quietly sneak out to sit on the front porch and try to muster a smile and a wave to the nice neighbors in their yards. I needed their kindness so many of those days as I sat holding back my tears as best I could.

One scorching hot afternoon, I was lying under my metal-frame twin bed hiding as Winston beat Mama. He had already beat her once that day, then they had very loud sex, and now he was back to hitting and pushing her some more. I decided it was time to tell the pastor. I sneaked out of the house and ran all the way across town to our church. I found the pastor and spilled my guts about it all. He had the power to kick someone out of church, and I was pretty sure that meant damn someone to hell as well. So me telling the pastor was a pretty bad deal for Winston. But I didn't care. I couldn't take it anymore and I wasn't sure how much more Mama could endure and live. The risk of not doing something was far greater than the risk of trying and failing.

As I let it all out, the pastor listened carefully. It seemed like I was speaking a hundred miles an hour, but oddly enough, he didn't appear to be moved by any of it. He always seemed kinda pious to me. Once I finished with the major points—living together, sex all the time, beating her all the time, twice today and happening now, the pastor got up, took his anointing oil and his Bible, then headed out of his apartment. I followed, not sure what was going to happen next. The pastor quietly opened the door of his shiny, long, fancy car, and along with an elder of the church that was visiting the pastor at the time, got in and told me to get in the back seat. As we headed to our house, I knew how much trouble I had coming to me once they left. However, I also knew it may be our only hope.

As we took the turn into the alley next to our house and rolled up to the carport, Winston had Mama out the back door, half-naked, beating her with everything he had. No way he could lie his way out of this! The pastor and the elder jumped out of the car, finally with some of the emotion I knew this deserved, and started yelling his name. As all of that was happening, I slipped out of the back seat from the far side of the car so Lucifer never even saw me. He was too busy looking like the cat that ate the canary, but make no mistake, he was still enraged even with the pastor and elder jumping out of the car in front of him. With his coal-black eyes, red face, and crazy, black, uncombed afro standing straight up, he looked like a man taken over by the devil for sure. I didn't have to explain anything further. Smartly, I opted to sneak my way back into the house so that they would never know why the pastor dropped by.

They all made it into the kitchen, and after what seemed like forever, the scuttle and the praying and calling that devil out was over. The men were talking with Winston and Mama and I could tell the voices were sounding more joyous. Even a few soft laughs. I quietly came out of my room to peek around the kitchen corner. Winston was on his knees still from praying and he was hugging Mama. I stood in silence thanking God in my heart and in my head. These men had come to our aid, and I wouldn't forget that.

Looking up, I saw a movement on the other side of the screen door that caught my eye. Squinting, I saw Winston's mama standing on the carport steps looking in through the screen. Mrs. Wellington was a sweet woman, only stood about five feet tall, and was always put together perfectly, it seemed. She had come by that afternoon to pick us up for grocery shopping. I had no idea how long she had been standing there, but from the look on her face, she didn't seem too keen on Pentecostal prayer.

As the pastor and the elder left, Winston seemed lighter, more at peace. I let Mama know that Mrs. Wellington was here and waiting for us in the car. They both cleaned up quickly and we all climbed in the car as if nothing had happened. I was getting pretty good at this charade. Mama got in the front seat, me behind her, and Winston behind his mama. I didn't have much to say, I was just thankful for it all. Winston's mama, however, was not. Before even moving her gear shift down to the drive position, she lit into him telling him how embarrassed he made her, how stupid it all was, and that she wasn't going to have her son—

—and that's about the time Lucifer reached up and started choking his little mama right in front of us.

My natural instincts kicked in and grabbing his hands, I tried to pull them away from her neck. Mama also reacted quickly trying to smack him back while almost climbing over and into the back seat. As we screamed at him and tried to get his hands off his mother's neck, he finally released her and got out of the car and started trashing everything in the yard around him. We got out too. Mrs. Wellington? She just drove away.

Very deep exhale.

Instead of leaving Winston this time, Mama decided it was time to marry him. She just knew that it was all happening once again because of the pressures of them living in sin. She was thirty-five years old and he was twenty-five years old at the time. They married twenty miles away in Wickliffe, Kentucky, at the courthouse. I stayed in the car.

After a short move to Wickliffe, we moved back into the trailer park down Crooked Creek Road in Sikeston. It felt like I had made it back home. A few years had gone by since we last lived in this park, and I was much older now. The trailer was newer this time, but I wasn't planning on hanging out in it much anyway. With us being back in Sikeston, I was pretty sure I could get by with not being home as much.

Once we got all of our boxes moved into the new trailer, it was getting pretty late. I knew putting everything away would be my job, so I left the boxes sitting on the countertops and kitchen table for the night. I always liked to get my things put away first so that nothing would get stepped on or torn up. All of the trailers we rented were furnished, so it made it a bit easier than having to set up beds or dressers. Once I was finished in my room, I went to bed knowing I could get up early and start unpacking the kitchen items before Winston or Mama even came out of the bedroom. Lisa had been dropped at my aunt's house to spend the night along the way.

Getting up early, I ran across a pair of my old jeans while unpacking. Sliding them on *really* felt good. I threw on a T shirt, and then my tennis shoes and was ready to tackle the rest of the house. I was so comfortable wearing my jeans. I wasn't sure if I would get into trouble for it, but if I did, I planned to say I didn't want to get my dresses dirty. We had been converted to the Pentecost way of life for a few months now and women were not allowed to wear jeans or makeup. Now, let me say for certain that I wasn't turning my back on God—I wasn't being rebellious either, well maybe I was being a tad bit rebellious. I just needed to be me for a minute. The last few months had worn on me. I had converted to an incredibly controlled religion and was trying my best to be pleasing to God. I had broken up with Johnny, who was actually my only friend, because I didn't want to go to hell. Dawn had gotten married, which made me realize she wasn't moving back home—ever. All of these things on top of managing life with this lunatic that my mother loved. I needed to wear the damn jeans.

Unpacking the kitchen boxes, I washed up all of the dishes and put them away as quietly as possible. I could hear Mama and Winston stirring in their bedroom in the back, but I didn't want to draw any attention to myself. It wasn't long before they started having loud, animated sex, but there was nowhere for me to go. I knew I had to get my work finished. I turned my music up a little and stayed the course until everything in the kitchen was put away. Taking a break, I fixed a bowl of Cocoa Puffs about the time the beating started. Their room was small and at one end of the trailer; the kitchen was smack in the middle. From my seat at the table with my cereal, I had the sink, refrigerator, and countertop all to my left and a big, double sliding glass door to my right. As I said earlier, this was a much nicer trailer than we had lived in before.

Straight ahead and to my left was the hallway. It had a back door off of it before it ended at Mama's and Winston's bedroom door. I could see it all from where I was sitting at the kitchen table eating my Cocoa Puffs. They were banging around in there real good when Mama came flying out, half naked, see-through nightshirt, and no panties, pants, or shorts. She screamed, "Run, he's got a knife!" on her way out the back door.

The door slammed shut behind her just as Lucifer emerged from the bedroom. Black slacks with the slit pockets on the side, which were about the only kind of pants he wore, no shirt, frazzled hair reaching for the roof it seemed, and black devil eyes darting everywhere. With the knife raised high in his right hand, he came straight toward me, "I'll kill you!" he screamed.

I took another bite of cereal.

Watching it all unfold, and him coming toward me, I felt a peace that I honestly do not have words for. God had my back. Looking at him straight in his crazed face, I said, "You need to get her first; she's naked and probably calling the cops right now." My words were flat, and very matter of fact. Instantly, he turned and ran out the back door, barefooted, with that knife to go find Mama. Without hesitation, I took off in the opposite direction. Exiting from the sliding glass doors to my right, I ran with all I had to the next trailer park. I didn't stop at a trailer in our park; I didn't want him to be able to grab me as I stood helplessly knocking on a trailer door that no one came to answer. I didn't know where he and Mama were, but I wasn't planning to look for them. I got to the neighboring trailer park and ran onto the porch of the trailer that looked like it had the most working cars out front; I prayed someone would answer the door.

A grandma-looking lady answered and quickly helped me call the sheriff's office. After I told them everything, I handed her the phone and I ran back out the door. I had to help Mama if there was any way possible. Running back to our trailer park, I carefully lurked and hid, moving in and out between the trailers and parked cars. I could hear Mama screaming but I couldn't see where she was. Within minutes, it seems, I saw the county cops pull off the roadway and into the park. Two cars, but they didn't have their lights on. It was more like they were cruising the park. I ran toward one of the cars to show them where we were about the time that Mama, still naked from the waist down, came running from around the back of a trailer where Winston had searched her out. He was right on her heels with his knife drawn high in the air. I screamed so he would see the cops and within seconds, it seemed, they had him face-down in the dirt. I ran to our trailer and grabbed Mama's robe and got it on her as they cuffed him and pushed him into the back of one of the cars.

Good thing I wore the jeans.

As the two county cops pulled out of the trailer park with Winston, I looked over at Mama. She was shaking, crying, and standing there in her bathrobe being comforted by the onlookers, but I knew in my innermost being that she wouldn't press charges. I turned and walked silently back to our trailer, and not so different from "The Gambler," this is the moment life told me to not only fold 'em, but that it was time to walk away.

Much to my surprise, Winston didn't come around in the following weeks. I didn't ask a lot of questions because it no longer mattered to me; my mind was made up. I was getting out. Mama found us a trailer in town, and it was good to be in walking distance to everything once again. Johnny and I got back together, and I told Mama I needed her to sign the papers come September so that he and I could get married. I would be turning fifteen and by state law, you could have one parent consent to marriage once you were fifteen. Johnny was twenty-one so he didn't need anyone to sign for him. Mama wasn't fully on board with all of it, but I spent the rest of the month talking her into it. Right about the time of my birthday, she received a settlement of back child support from my daddy, so she was able to buy a car for the first time. Seems really simple and weird to be a big deal, but I even got my first blow-dryer. Having a car of our own was an incredible experience. We could grocery shop, go to the laundromat, go visit family—all without bumming a ride or walking. Amazing. Mama started looking for apartments to move into since she could afford an upgrade. She also agreed to sign the papers, mostly because I refused to let it go.

Mama found a condo apartment a few miles west of Sikeston to rent. It was super fancy with two bedrooms upstairs and a living room and kitchen downstairs. We even had two bathrooms! All of the walls were sheetrock, the carpet was not old, and the kitchen had tile floors—I mean, fancy! The little town it was nearest to was Salcedo.

Mama seemed happier in the new apartment. Maybe it was because she didn't have as many financial worries, maybe it was because Winston seemed to be keeping his distance—I'm not sure. I didn't ask questions; I had made my decision and I was working my plan. Mama signed the papers, Johnny and I were working on setting a date, and that was that. I was in love with Johnny, and I was getting out. The reality of it all was that I knew it didn't matter what today looked like. Today, everything seemed good. But tomorrow... tomorrow I very well could be standing on a gravel road out in the middle of nowhere, in a new trailer park, watching with my own eyes as my mama was being hunted by a crazy man with a knife. I was done.

Lisa and I caught the school bus each morning while Mama made her plans for taking more college classes. We liked our new change, but Mama was really missing her relationship she had had with the Lord. We all did. Salvation may not have been life changing for Winston, but it truly was for us. Finding Jesus was for real—we had never been more spiritually satisfied, even feeling God's peace in the worst of the Winston moments. I had been going to church and loving and trusting Jesus since I was four years old. He was my compass and the voice in my head beginning at a very young age. But the dedication and knowledge that we had gained with the Pentecostal church was different. It was deeper. I told Mama I had heard many good things about the Oneness Pentecost Church in Morehouse, less than ten miles from where we were now living, and on that Tuesday night we decided it was time to return to church.

Walking into the Morehouse Pentecostal Church was like coming home. We were welcomed and hugged up like we had always been a part of their church. We knew a few faces, so it didn't seem unfamiliar and we loved the way the worship service and the prayer just washed over us. Being in God's presence is unmistakable. We knew we were right where we belonged.

Before the end of the night, we had all made our way down to the altar where we gave our hearts back to the Lord. It was a special service all around. We climbed into Mama's little Toyota Corolla and got on the road home. I was in the front seat, Mama driving of course, and Lisa sat in the back. This car was far from new but it was new to us and very nice. It had bucket-style seats in the front and back, and was a stick shift so we got better gas mileage.

Church had gone late, and it was probably after 9 p.m. when we left. Our route home was easy—head east on Highway 114, the main road in Morehouse, about four miles, then take a left turn on BB Highway and head north about three miles. Our apartment building sat right off of BB Highway, so just two turns all together. As we drove the dark county road home, Mama told us how much better she felt about life and our future. Lisa and I agreed. I knew Mama being saved and focusing on a life of serving God, without Winston, would benefit her in so many ways. I had always wished she could see herself as the beautiful and intelligent woman that she was. I had already seen many changes in her since she had gotten saved. I knew salvation, without Winston, could be a turning point for her.

The road was so dark as we drove along talking. Old county highways lined with towering trees never seem to have enough light for night driving. Lit-up farmhouses or a bright moon is sometimes the best that you can hope for. This fall night was no different, so I was happy when we started coming out into a clearing where the county roads cross. Slowing down for our BB highway left turn, we came to a complete stop as oncoming headlights were passing us in the opposite lane. Mama sat patiently with her clutch in, hand on the gear shift, and left blinker clicking as we waited for the oncoming cars to pass us. Glancing back between the seats chatting with Lisa, who was sitting in the middle on the hump, I noticed headlights coming up behind us.

A few seconds later, I realized the headlights were coming up really fast. "Mama, I don't think that car is slowing down," I said as Mama waited for the final oncoming cars to pass us. Glancing back again, panic overtook me. "Mama, it's not—"

Silence. Cold, dark, eerie silence.

I struggled to hear what was maybe a muffled cry in the distance. *Is that Lisa?* I thought to myself. Jumbled thoughts seemed to crawl very slowly and deliberately across my consciousness, or maybe unconsciousness. Feeling cold hardness under me, I thought, *What has happened?* My thoughts were uneven and struggling to come together.

My arms were stiff by my sides and I seemed to be bracing myself in place as I sat. I felt my hands very sturdily planted, with my palms flat down and my fingers spread wide on the bumpy cold. *Am I sitting on gravel?*

Coming to a little more, I thought I heard Mama's voice like a whimper in the distance.

"Mama?" I called out softly, almost like a loud whisper, feeling engulfed in the horror of my current moment but not yet comprehending what the moment was.

I heard my little sister for sure this time, and I struggled to focus my eyes. My brain felt like it was responding to me at turtle speed.

"Lisa? Lisa, can you hear me?"

"Holly?" I heard her cry softly, "Holly, where are you?"

As my vision began clearing, looking down, I could see I was sitting on a black, cold something with my legs straight out in front of me. *What has happened? Where am I?*

I lifted my left hand to touch my face and shattered glass fell from my palm. Fear's dark grip surrounded me as I suddenly realized what had happened. "Mama!" I screamed, but there was no answer.

A movement came closing in on me quickly to my left as my eyes tried to focus—a woman appeared close and looking straight in my face, "Are you okay?"

Trying to think about how my body felt, if my body felt, was still confusing to me.

"I don't know," I finally said as I tried to force my thoughts and words together.

"Is my sister okay; do you see her?" I asked in desperation.

I could hear a man's voice, but it seemed distant. "I think she's okay." The lady looking closely at me said as she bent down and started picking the glass off of me. Looking at her, trying to get my thoughts to work, I asked, "Is my mama okay?"

Searching my eyes, she didn't seem to understand my question.

"There's someone else with you?" she asked.

"What?" I asked, I didn't understand why they didn't understand me. I was still so confused as I tried to force the alphabet soup that was in my brain to come out.

"Do you see my mama?!"

The sirens came next, and I tried to stand up, but my legs refused to cooperate. They were like jelly, and my vision and brain were still swimming. *Someone hit us. We were in a car accident.* I realized this but I wasn't sure who or how. I tried to think. *I told Mama the car behind us wasn't slowing down; I turned to see her. The flash of the lights. I'm sitting in the middle of the road. But where is Mama?*

I needed my brain to stop moving so I could look for her.

The sirens finally stopped, and a man was shining a little flashlight in my eyes. "Can you move your legs?"

"Please find my mama." My tears started rolling as I looked at him.

"You weren't driving?" he seemed confused.

"What?" I couldn't understand his questions. *Why isn't anyone answering me? Maybe my words aren't really coming out.* My ears felt clogged and muffled.

"A woman!" a man's voice shouted from the distance.

My flashlight man disappeared.

The following moments were loud. Hurried. And so utterly confusing. Voices and people seemed to be everywhere, so many shiny yellow coats, and the questions were overwhelming. The flashing lights hurt my eyes and the noise hurt my head.

They moved me onto a bed and put me into an ambulance. It was cold and bright with noisy gadgets everywhere. I closed my eyes. Them loading me into the ambulance felt like the starting gate for a ride on an old wooden roller coaster. The lights came down and a woman was talking. I opened my eyes to two paramedics in the ambulance with me. "My sister?" I asked, looking at the lady.

"She's in the other ambulance; she's going to be fine."

"Is Mama with her?"

Their faces told me plenty. I knew that body language well and it wasn't good. She touched my hand, "We are doing all that we can; your Mama has been taken by helicopter." I lay my head back again and prayed. Fighting back my tears, I knew I needed to pull it together so that I could ask the questions that were floating in my brain. *Taken by helicopter where? What's wrong with her?*

The nurses at the hospital put me and Lisa together in the emergency room. They promised to find out all they could about Mama as Lisa and I went through our evaluations. I had a bad concussion. I knew that. I had been ejected from the car, but by the grace of God I didn't have anything else wrong with me other than some cuts from the windshield and some body bruising. Lisa had been thrown forward between the seats and then slammed back down. She had hip issues and an arm injury but other than that, was good. God sure protected her because the back seat was completely smashed against the front. Her having the space to be thrown between the seats saved her life. She could have easily been crushed had she been sitting in one of the seats.

Mama had not fared as well. She was found in the ditch. Her feet were somehow hooked under a guard rail so that stopped her from being thrown down into the water. Her neck was broken, and she coded four times on the way to Barnes Jewish Hospital in St. Louis. Once, the helicopter actually turned around to come back but she started breathing again. Mama wasn't ready to die; she had fought the devil many times and won. This time would be no different.

They released me and Lisa into Aunt Jan's care. When we got to her house, Johnny was there waiting for us. I told him I had to find our car to get my things out, and I had to get to St. Louis to Mama. He borrowed a car from his cousin, I left Lisa with our aunt, and we headed out. I wasn't sure what I would do when we got there, but I knew I would figure it out on the two-hour drive.

Navigating a big hospital was certainly not on my list of experiences, but I managed it fine. As we got off the elevator on her floor, the world seemed to stop. The frenzy of the ER wasn't happening here. This floor was dead silent other than the beeping of machines and the quiet whispers of nurses working. I refused to look anyone in the eyes for fear that they would try to stop me. I knew nothing about how visiting hours were managed, or if there were exceptions, so I wasn't about to ask and be told to leave. I knew my best option was to just keep walking and act like I knew what I was doing.

Entering Mama's room, I could only see her feet. There was a pale pink curtain drawn down the middle of the room and she was tucked behind it. "Mama?" I said quietly, as I cautiously peeked around the curtain. Mama didn't answer. She was laying there unaware of life with a metal cage around her head and tubes coming from everywhere it seemed.

"Mama?" I said again as I got closer, trying to speak around the very large knot that had formed in my throat.

"Can I help you?" a voice came in from behind me. Not taking my eyes off of Mama's face, I said, "I'm her daughter" with as much authority as I could muster.

Over the next couple of hours, I stayed by her side. The doctors and nurses explained all that was going on with her, all of the progress she was making, and some of the progress that she wasn't. Mama was in critical condition, and they couldn't make any promises. She had a broken neck, amnesia, and a whole list of other things that were described with words that were too big for me to understand. They had an issue with me only being fifteen years old and being there alone, but I assured them that family would arrive anytime.

In reality, I had no idea what I was going to do.

I had the paperwork that Mama had signed, so I could marry Johnny at any time and I would be an adult. But they wanted an adult now.

Weighing my options, I knew if I called Papa, he would take two hours to get to us and he would make me go home with him. No way he would leave me in the big city and he and Johnny really disliked each other. Johnny didn't like him because of what he had done to me, and Papa didn't like Johnny because he was so much older than me. I didn't have the ability to deal with all of that when I needed to stay next to Mama. My second thought was to call Daddy. Maybe he would know what to do.

Calling collect, from Mama's hospital room, I got Daddy on the phone. He was still living in Portageville, but I hadn't seen much of him since Mama took us off with Winston. I told Daddy about the wreck, that me and Lisa were okay, but that I was in the hospital in St. Louis with Mama, and they didn't know if she was going to live.

The silence was deafening.

"Daddy?"

"I'm here, Holly. I don't know what you want me to say. I don't like your Mama. She treated me really bad. If she dies, she dies."

My heart ached in my chest and at that moment; I just wanted to curl up and cry. I wasn't sure how much more I could handle.

"Daddy," I choked out sternly, swallowing my tears.

"*You* picked her," I said. The words actually burned in my throat as they came out. "I didn't. You did. So, no matter what happens, she is my mama. You need to remember that!"

With that, I hung up the phone, walked into the bathroom, sat down, and cried my eyes out. I wasn't really sure what I had wanted or expected from Daddy. He hadn't raised me; we didn't have that kind of relationship. Now, all of these years later, I can look back and see his side of things. He didn't know me super well at that point in my life. He had no idea what I needed from him. Heck, I didn't know what I needed from him. Maybe I felt that talking it through with him would help me figure out what I needed to do. He had always been a steady hand that talked through things with me whenever I called, but I seldom called. I'm not really sure what I was thinking when I decided to call him in the middle of this tornado, but regardless, at that moment in the bathroom, my heart was on fire and my tears wouldn't stop coming. But just like I had done so many times before, I swallowed my tears, wiped my face, prayed for direction, then walked out of that bathroom and handled it.

Uncle Ben made it to the hospital within an hour of my call. He may have been a lot of bad things, but he was dependable. I'll give him that.

Mama recovered quickly, miraculously actually, and within days they had her ready to come home. She would need constant care for a bit while she got used to the metal halo sitting on her shoulders with the screws going into her head, and she still had short-term amnesia—she knew me, she knew Lisa, she could talk to us, laugh with us, and all the normal things—but she didn't remember from one day to the next.

I had decided my best option was to just lay it out to Uncle Ben. I couldn't imagine him wanting to take care of Mama in this condition; she obviously couldn't do anything for him in return. I gave him my plan for taking care of Mama. I just needed him to get us home. I explained to him that we couldn't live with Aunt Jan because of Lisa's asthma and the cigarette smoke, not to mention the extra care Mama now needed. They said she needed quiet and rest; I knew it would be impossible to make her comfortable at my Aunt Jan's. I told Uncle Ben that I was prepared to take care of her and Lisa, and that I had already checked with the school. I could do my schoolwork from home, and we could take it a couple weeks at a time. Which wasn't true, but I knew with Mama in that head thing and all her new medications, we needed to be in our own home alone.

Uncle Ben agreed, and then broke the news to Aunt Jan. She wasn't happy, but she understood. By the time he got us home, I had a plan. Johnny would move back in with us and take care of Mama during the day while I was at school. He didn't have a job and we were about to get married, so this would be perfect. All he had to do was give her medication and I had it all broken down meticulously on a schedule for him. We got married as soon as the preacher could do it, and I had Papa walk me down the aisle, or stairs, because I wasn't speaking to Daddy. All was done. I was officially an adult. All future decisions could be made by me without having to work carefully around others. Life would be on my own terms now.

As with all great plans mixed with real life, mine didn't last long. After only a week or so, Johnny's brothers came by to let us know they were moving to Mississippi. His mom had met a guy and said there was a lot of work to be had in Mississippi at the chicken houses. Good-paying jobs, she said, so Johnny wanted to go. I couldn't blame him; staying in our apartment taking care of my mama wasn't what he had signed up for. However, him leaving meant no one to take care of Mama for me and no car borrowing to get us to places like the grocery store. I could drive. But no one was going to loan me their car since I was only fifteen and didn't have a license. I needed to move us back into town.

Me, Johnny, and Mama at our wedding a few days
after we got Mama home from the hospital.

I really didn't want to quit school. I wanted to be an educated lady and get out someday. My dream was to take care
of myself and never look back. But my options were getting
fewer and fewer. I talked to the high school principal and

explained what all I had going on and that I needed a few days to manage it. I promised to do my studies from home, and he agreed without much fanfare or many questions. I found us a trailer in town right off Smith Street, and Johnny and I got us moved before he left for Mississippi. Mama still had some money from the back child support, so she was able to make the deposit and get the electricity turned on. I tried attending school, doing some work from home, and going to school some days. Sadly, it was just a constant struggle that I couldn't keep going. I think it was harder mentally than physically. Some of Mama's old boyfriends and their friends had started coming by when I wasn't there. I assumed they were either after her pain medications or trying to move back into her heart, which also meant our small trailer. Even though she was managing herself decently while I was at school only a few blocks away, I knew her track record of needing a man around. I honestly couldn't handle dealing with a live-in boyfriend of hers at this moment in time. I decided to quit school and just focus on taking care of her and Lisa.

Johnny came to visit a couple of times over the next few months and told me how much he liked Mississippi. He was working in a local chicken house getting paid cash, so it was a good gig. He told me how it was the best-paying job he had ever had and the weather in Mississippi was great. I wanted so badly to just pack up and go. Walk out the door and never look back. But my plan to get married and get out had been completely derailed by a man that I didn't even know. A drunk driver who swore that he never even saw us changed our lives completely. I wanted my freedom. I wanted to go to school and work and only have me to take care of. But that wasn't how life was unfolding.

Instead, I stayed home with Mama. I cooked, cleaned, and ran off all the bums that seemed to find their way to our house. I wasn't nice about it, and she really had a problem with that. One thing you could never say about my mama was that she was rude. She was way too nice to others, in my opinion. Her smile was always welcoming, and she thought the best of people, even when they proved her wrong. She was certainly a woman of second chances for all. It became a daily battle between us because I saw people differently than she did. Mama's life had left her soft and pleasing. Mine had left me rigid and fiery. Many of the things that injured and weakened her jaded me. We were two very different women.

Mama's recovery progressed really quickly. Within four months of the accident, they removed her metal halo and the doctors were astounded. It was another miracle, no doubt. God had had his hand on us throughout this whole awful situation. Mama and I found an older station wagon to tide her over until the lawyer got done with the suing. Life was slowly getting pieced back together for her. She could stay by herself just fine, however, driving without us girls wasn't a great idea. Her brain was coming back but still not firing at 100 percent. But we were getting there.

One evening, after another heated argument with Mama after I ran some derelict off, she informed me that she could take care of herself. It was her house; she was paying the bills. Which was all true, regardless of what a bad idea I thought it was. Honestly, most of the issues I had with Mama were the same issues I had always had with her—her allowing men to run over her. I was too young to realize that some of the damage from the wreck was ever-present, and some of her actions were due to that and the medications she was on. However, what I did understand was that Lisa was now twelve years old and smart as could be. I knew she would be fine without me. My moment had finally come to walk away. Mentally, I think I needed Mama to blow up about it all. Otherwise, my deep sense of responsibility for everyone and everything would have never released me from playing the mama to her and Lisa. But, during a heated exchange, my temper can go from zero to one hundred in a New York minute. "Fine," I said, "I'm out!"

I gladly packed up my things and found Dawn, who was back out on the streets because her husband had been arrested for selling drugs.

"Wanna move to Mississippi with me?" I asked.

"Let's do it," she said. Dawn never turned down an adventure.

The freedom that I felt on that five-hour drive to Forest, Mississippi, is impossible to describe. I didn't know if it was because I was on my own for the first time, or because I was out from under the immense responsibilities of my life, but it felt like I could breathe again. The weight of the last few months had buried me—mind and soul.

Bobby, Johnny's brother, had been in town a few days and Dawn had been hanging with him. She let him know we wanted to ride back with him when he left. So that took care of that problem. As we climbed in the old jalopy that Bobby had borrowed for his trip, he warned me that he wasn't sure how Johnny was going to like me just showing up. I didn't care. I was married to Johnny and had dated him on and off for two years. I didn't need an invitation in my eyes; Dawn agreed, so we climbed in and headed for my first adventure as an adult.

Mississippi was a strange and beautiful place. As we drove south down Highway 55, I stared out the window, noticing the difference in the highway as we went from state to state. Once we were in Mississippi, much of the highway was divided between the northbound lanes and the southbound lanes and had different trees and vegetation growing in the middle section. Mississippi's pine trees were thick and towered as if trying to touch the sky. Their color of dark green was immensely lush and underneath their canopy lay blankets of their pine needles. I had lived in states from California to Florida, but felt I had never experienced such profound natural color with my own eyes. *I bet Mama would love to paint this!*

When we pulled into Forest, it didn't seem all that different from the many small towns that I had lived in. A grocery store in the middle of town, diner nearby, a pharmacy, a few closed up buildings, a couple of gas stations, and a Dollar General. Forest was pretty normal for rural America. It was obvious, though, that they had a large population of Indians. Indians were not a people that I had lived around before, so it certainly piqued my interests. Moving around so much, I was always intrigued and fascinated by the differences in people from one location to the next. It was the Choctaw tribes that had settled in this area, and I was excited to see the differences in our cultures.

Arriving in the government housing complex where Johnny and his brothers lived with their mother, butterflies hit my stomach. I had just assumed that Johnny's mom, Hazel, would be fine with me and Dawn staying with her a few days while I looked for work. I hadn't confirmed it, so I prayed that it would all be okay. My mama had let Johnny live with us several times, so I felt that I had some leeway if nothing else. In the past, Johnny's mom had always been gone working or wherever and never knew who all was crashing on the couch, but I realized it would have been smarter to find out before hopping a ride to a place I've never been. I needed to get better at being an adult—that was for sure.

When I walked into the apartment, Johnny was super excited to see me. He was surprised, no doubt, but very happy that I had come. The apartment was just like any other government housing. Cold feeling, white tile flooring throughout, with white walls and baseboards. Hazel had a thin throw rug under the coffee table but other than that, not much decoration. Johnny and his brothers had the place full of their friends just as I had imagined. My sights were now focused on making a new life that I was in charge of. Next up, I needed a job.

Being a fifteen-year-old without a license, and without a car, my job opportunities were bleak. Johnny's mom had a friend who ran bootleg and he had told her he was looking for help. Forest was in a dry county, meaning you couldn't buy alcohol anywhere in it. Mr. Jim would drive to Jackson, forty-five minutes west of Forest, twice a week, to stock up on the bestsellers and any special orders he had taken. His garage was the hottest place in town on the weekends, full of about any kind of alcohol you would want—at a marked-up price of course. The job sounded easy enough to me.

Mr. Jim came over the next day to meet me. He looked to be around sixty years old, salt and pepper hair—well mostly salt, and was about as tall as Papa, so maybe 6'2" or 6'3". He spoke with a thick Mississippi drawl—theirs was quite different from my Tennessee-Dallas-southeast Missouri hybrid. They seemed to speak in shorthand and a lot of words seemed to be, well, just different. "Pillow" was pronounced "piller" and "Daddy" was pronounced "Diddy." But my roots weren't so different, so it didn't take me long to catch on. Mr. Jim also had a bit of a limp and used a cane for most of his walking. I figured that was why he needed the help. It would be hard to load and unload boxes with a cane in one hand.

Mr. Jim took to me right off. "You strong 'nough for haulin' boxes, gurl?"

"Yes, sir. I've worked landscaping for the past two summers. I can carry a lot."

With that, he seemed surprised but pleased. His only other requirement was that I could keep my mouth shut. His business was "somewhat illegal," as he put it. Check and check! Wasn't a problem for me. He would pay me twenty dollars a day. Two days a week we would do the running, then two days a week we would stock and sell. *Eighty bucks a week! Hallelujah!* I wasn't too worried about the "somewhat."

I was savvy enough by now to know if we got busted, no cop would worry about the fifteen-year-old ride-along. I waited out front the next morning for my new employer to pick me up. Good things were happening for me already!

It didn't take me long to realize that being a grown-up for real had its perks and its disadvantages. Going to work with Mr. Jim and having the promise of my very own paycheck was pretty exciting. The way it all played out in real life, however, was not.

My first day of work was at Mr. Jim's house taking inventory and shuffling boxes around in the garage. Pulling into the driveway of his modest ranch home, I had a pit in my stomach realizing I was about to go into an older man's house without anyone else around. It didn't feel good. *Hazel was his friend*, I reasoned to myself. *Surely he knew that I would tell if he tried anything.* Sizing him up, I decided that I could knock him off center and out-run him with that bum leg of his. I pushed the thoughts aside and focused on the cash I was going to have in my pocket in just a few days' time. I had already spent the night before looking in the paper for efficiency apartments for rent and I knew with this job, if Johnny split the bills with me, I could get one.

My new job wasn't hard work—mentally or physically. I enjoyed being in the garage alone that first morning. I had a radio turned on in the corner and my morning seemed to fly by. My type-A personality kicked in and I had detailed lists of our whiskey, beer, and wine stock made in no time. I then arranged and cleaned everything in the garage so that it was easier to find, and tossed empty boxes that seemed to just be taking up space. Mr. Jim was impressed by my organization and self-motivation skills.

"Yous cook too?" Mr. Jim said, halfway joking.

"Of course!" I responded, proud of my many skills at such a young age.

"Great, how 'bout you make us up some grill' cheese then we'll move the hooch from the house to the garage."

"Yes, sir!" I got right on it, pretty excited that I was about to get a free lunch as well. The kitchen was pretty old-ladyish with crochet potholders, some that looked like watermelon slices, and knickknacks everywhere. It was incredibly clean also, so I knew he must be married. That calmed my uneasiness a bit.

Mr. Jim asked me questions about my family while we ate. I asked him questions about his too. His wife worked in town, but he had been out of a job since getting hurt at work several years back. That's when he decided he could make plenty bootleggin'. Made perfect sense to me. I cleaned up our dishes and got straight back to work.

He showed me where the overflow stash was in his bedroom closet. I started moving those boxes to the garage and carefully placing them on the proper shelves. When I went in for my last box, Mr. Jim was sitting on the end of the carefully made bed waiting for me.

"Sit down here a minute, gurl," he said as he patted the spot next to him.

Reluctantly, I sat down and stared at my feet, feeling my face get hot and my heart start beating at twice the speed.

"I really like yous, you know it?" he began.

"Yes, sir, I'm a hard worker," I responded, trying to keep the conversation brief and off of what I knew this was leading to.

"More'n that" he said. "You're an awful pretty one," he said as he laid his left hand on my right thigh. Turning to look at me, he just kept on talkin', "I wanna make love to you." It came across as a statement, as if he was gonna do me a favor!

I stood up and bolted out of the house, yelling "No!" as I ran away. I grabbed my purse in the garage and I kept on running. All the way into town. All the way to the projects. *Is this how life is? One dirty old man after another? Mama has probably been telling the truth all along. This is just how men are.* My brain would not slow down.

Getting to the house, I went inside and laid down on the couch. Johnny was still at the chicken house working, and the others were still passed out in the beds from the all-night poker game the night before. I buried my face in my folded arm and faced the back cushions so I could pretend to be asleep if anyone came through. I didn't feel like talking to anyone, but I couldn't wait to tell Johnny about this. *He's gonna be so mad. No telling what he might do to that old man.* I thought. Or maybe hoped.

Wrong again.

Johnny finally made it home and was exhausted from a long, physically tolling day in the chicken houses. He smelled like chicken poop and didn't look much better. He headed straight for the shower, so I followed him in and told him about my day with Mr. Jim.

Crickets.

"Johnny?"

He didn't seem to have much to say. Or at least, not what I wanted to hear. "So, he didn't come after you, hold you down, or anything like that?" Johnny asked as he showered.

"No, I ran! That old man couldn't have caught me if he wanted to," I responded with 100 percent disgust.

More crickets.

"So, are you going over there?" I asked, irritated by the lack of concern I was starting to feel.

"What do you want me to do, Holly? He didn't touch you, you told him no, end of story," he snapped, equally irritated with me.

"I ran and yelled 'No!' in the process, Johnny," I replied with great annoyance. "Doesn't this bother you? I'm your wife, an old man just asked me to have sex with him?!" I was all but yelling.

"Holly, I'm tired. Me whippin' an old man's ass won't change any of this. You said no so it's over."

Johnny clearly didn't see this the way that I did. With that, I slammed the bathroom door and went back to the couch. For two years now, Johnny had scared and beat the snot out of any guy that he thought was even flirting on me. *Now an old man tries to put moves on me, says he wants to have sex with me, and nothing? I get nothing?* I was heartbroken and mad. *Men don't defend you. Ever.* I guess I didn't need that explained to me, but I knew this would be the last time I fell for the false sense of security of having a man who loves me around. That means nothing on the protection side of things. *A big, fat nothing.*

The next morning, I was up and about reading through the newspaper's help-wanted ads when I heard a horn honking. Searching the ads, I thought maybe I could find a job cleaning people's houses or babysitting. The horn kept honking. Walking from the kitchen to look out the big window of the apartment, I saw Mr. Jim's car, pulled up and waiting for me. I stood there staring at it for a minute. Finally, I took a deep breath, grabbed my purse, and headed down—*I guess we'll see how day two goes.*

Climbing in the car, I gave Mr. Jim a stern look straight in his face. Before I could open my mouth, he said, "I'm sorry, I thought yous a different kinda gurl, that's all." At that, I nodded, put my seat-belt on, and moved on. Maybe Mr. Jim was used to girls who were happy to do those things. Maybe Johnny was too tired with his own struggles in his new job to understand the gravity of what I had been through the previous day. I figured I'd never know, but if I was going to truly be out on my own, I needed to make some money and get on with it. So that's what I focused on.

Mr. Jim and I drove to Jackson listening to the radio and going over the day's plans. Four liquor store stops. Mr. Jim would park, go in, and make the purchases. I would stay in the car watching the store parking lot, and all parking lots around us, to make sure no police cars had pulled in and started watching us. When Mr. Jim came back out, he would open the trunk, and I would go in and start hauling the boxes out while he took over the watch. Usually, with me being a skinny girl and all, I would naturally have help from the store owners or workers. This also helped in cutting back Mr. Jim's normal time spent in the wide-open parking lots loading up. I was a good hire for him all around.

With my first week's pay, I got Johnny and me into a little efficiency apartment. It was fifty dollars a week and Johnny paid half. We decided that splitting all of the bills was the fairest way. He made more than me at the time, but he smoked cigarettes, drank alcohol, and played poker so his expenses were way more than mine. I knew once I turned sixteen in September, I could find a better-paying job, so I wasn't too worried about it at the time. After splitting the first week of rent, we had enough money to get us a ten-dollar set of pots and pans from the Dollar General, food for the week, and enough change to wash our clothes at the laundromat. We loaded up on bread from the local Bread Store, where we could buy "day-old" bread. I'm pretty sure it was older than a day, regardless of what those orange stickers said, but it was perfectly fine. Mama always got our bread and any treats from the Bread Store. I knew how to stretch a dollar.

With cheap bread and potted meat, we had plenty for our lunches. On the days that I worked at Mr. Jim's house, I got to eat whatever he had me cooking for lunch. That was a life-saver because I was never crazy about potted meat. Our dinners consisted mostly of things like Ramen noodles, mac and cheese, frozen pizzas, and bacon and eggs—budget foods. On the weekends, we would cook at Hazel's and all hang out together. She wasn't home much but she usually had all the ingredients we needed to make a pot of beans, fry up some potatoes and onions, and make cornbread. What I didn't already know how to cook, Johnny taught me.

We seemed to have a good system going in Mississippi. We were figuring it out. It wasn't long before we realized I was pregnant. This really didn't worry me too much; I knew several girls my age with babies. If they could figure it out, I knew I could too. My little sister was only three years younger than me, so I had never really been around babies. But that still didn't scare us. Johnny and I knew we could figure it out.

I wrote to Mama to let her know she was going to be a grandma. At thirty-five years old, you can imagine she wasn't really happy about it. When Mama wrote me back, she said I had to start seeing a doctor, and that she needed me to come back and sign some papers. The settlement from the wreck was about ready. Johnny and I decided planning a trip home would be good, so we started working on borrowing a car to make it happen. That very same week, however, Johnny fell off a truss at the chicken house while working on an overhead light. He had climbed to the top to get it going, lost his balance, and plummeted to the concrete floor. He hit the water fountain with his back on his way down. They sent him to the emergency room to get looked at and then sent him home to rest. Nothing broken, thank the good Lord, but he had pulled some muscles and had bad spasms happening in his back. After being off work for a couple of weeks with the doctor's permission, they decided to fill his position at the chicken plant and would let us know if they had an opening again. With him getting paid cash, there really wasn't much we could do. He would just have to start looking for another job once his back was better.

With a back that wasn't quite right, no job, and a pregnant wife, Johnny and I loaded up our very few belongings, borrowed Hazel's boyfriend's car, and Bobby drove us back to Missouri to my mama's house. Mama was happy to see us for about a minute. She had moved to the outskirts of town to a different trailer park. She and Lisa were the only ones living there, and everything was going good. They had been going to church in Morehouse religiously and Mama was actually happy. She was smiling more again and all deficits from the wreck seemed to be gone. Mama said she didn't mind me and Johnny staying there while we found jobs. It was only a two-bedroom trailer, but Lisa usually slept with Mama anyhow. Life was really starting to feel weird with me being pregnant, so it was incredibly nice being home again. I was far from my skinny, tree-climbing self and had been gaining weight like crazy. I desperately needed to find some clothes that fit. Mama explained that once we signed the papers at the lawyer's office, she would be able to get me a few things. Music to my ears.

Signing the papers at the lawyer's office didn't take long. Mama drove us to Joe Fenton's office in downtown Sikeston. The office wasn't impressive like I expected a lawyer's office to be. Nothing like the one in New Madrid when Dawn got in that fight on the school bus. Mr. Fenton's office had ugly brown paneling on all the walls, chocolate-milk-colored carpet, and a musty smell. I thought he should probably spend some of that money he made to make it more appealing, but what did I know anyways. Mr. Fenton popped out from around a corner right after we walked in and said he had the papers ready to go. It was all a little too fast and confusing to me. He explained very little, and sped through quite a bit, before he got to the end where I was supposed to sign. I felt like he and Mama stared at me too much, and at each other too much, while I tried to read those confusing papers. You know how you feel when you're being told something, but it doesn't feel like it's the full story? Well, that's how I felt. I didn't feel like I could ask questions. Or maybe I just wasn't sure what questions to ask. I was married, pregnant, and only fifteen years old. It was all kinda embarrassing standing in this reputable man's office, even though it was incredibly smelly. I didn't want to seem like I was questioning him when it was clear that he was highly educated and intelligent, and I was not. But it sure didn't feel right.

Mr. Fenton explained that I had to sign for myself because I was now married. All of the documents had my married name, so we just needed to get them all signed to release the money. One of the documents was a check for $3,333 dollars, made out to me, "Holly Griswell." I asked if it was mine and the answer was as convoluted as the rest of the conversation had been. Basically, Mama got all of the money from the settlement; she was my guardian when it happened. All the medical bills had been paid, and all of us were now released from the doctors, even Mama. So, this is the remaining insurance money, and it all goes to Mama. But they still needed me to sign the papers, as well as the back of the check, because they had my married name on them. Hindsight is 20/20 and it didn't take me long to figure out what I was truly signing away in that office. But it was well after that day when I realized it.

We went straight to the bank. Mama's other check was close to $30,000, and I was happy for her. I knew she wouldn't have to struggle for a while, and it might even get her through the rest of her college. We went to the Dollar General next, where Mama made good on her promise. Well, kinda. She bought me two five-dollar shirts and two five-dollar sundresses to go over the shirts. This allowed my belly to grow but didn't give me much as far as clothing. I was pretty disappointed that was all she was willing to spend, but I should have known not to expect more. Mama was always worried whatever she had wasn't going to be enough to get by. She said she had spoken to Aunt Lisa, her little sister whom she named my little sister after, and that Aunt Lisa was coming to town soon and was bringing all her old maternity clothes for me. So, Mama felt I'd have some really nice things soon enough. Mama then took my little sister to the mall in Cape Girardeau and spent over $400 on her new clothes. Mama said that was because Lisa was still in school, and with them being Pentecostal, it was hard on Lisa not having nice things. I actually understood that; it just didn't make my moment any easier.

Within days, Mama started fussing about Johnny being around the house without a shirt on. I hated that he wouldn't respect her rules, but I was trying to find a job and just couldn't get him to understand how much it mattered to her. Johnny didn't care about her rules, and for some reason, didn't seem to care if we got booted. I, on the other hand, realized that you do what you have to do to not be homeless. Dealing with Mama's rules until we had some money coming in didn't seem like a lot to ask. Johnny and I didn't see eye to eye on a lot of things though. Mama was a religious woman now and she was also concerned that us being there was using more electricity. With that, she said we had to go. Johnny had just gotten a job at a wood truss company on the outskirts of town, and I had been cleaning some houses for people. Things were looking up; we just didn't have a place to live.

For the next couple of weeks, we stayed at different friends' houses waiting on Johnny's first check. I was cautious to never stay more than a couple nights at a time; I wanted to be sure we didn't wear our welcome out. I also always helped cook, clean, or whatever was needed, but even with that, it was hard not to feel like a lowlife moocher. The cash coming in from me cleaning houses held us over for food, so we were able to help pay for whatever dinner we ate. Once we had Johnny's first check, we were able to rent a room at the old Dunn Hotel in downtown Sikeston.

The Dunn Hotel had been a big deal in its day. It once had an upscale restaurant, swanky bar, ornate decor, velvet curtains, and all the fancy things you can imagine. Now it was just an old hotel turned into weekly room rentals. It was a little over a mile walk to Aldi's grocery store, so it worked out well for me. The folks I cleaned for usually picked me up and gave me a ride home, so the grocery store and laundromat were the only places I had to walk to. By the time we moved into the Dunn, it was late summer, and I was pretty large. My one-hundred-pound frame had turned into 125 overnight it seemed, and with a few months to go, walking the mile there and back was needed exercise. Walking through the Goodyear parking lot to get to the Aldi's grocery, however, was the tough part.

The Goodyear parking lot was the place to be back when I was skinny, not pregnant, still in school, and not a responsible adult. Night after night, we had parked there with friends, music blaring and just living life. Now I was fifteen, a high school dropout, married, fat, pregnant, and wearing awful clothes—not to mention I had gone back to my Oneness Pentecost faith, so I was a no-makeup girl also. The walks across that parking lot for my groceries were beyond humiliating. It was still the place the cool kids went to park, squeal tires, and hang out. I just didn't seem to know anyone there any longer. A couple of times, I had guys drive through and pass me walking and yell some pretty ugly things at me. I often wondered how I had gotten from there to here. And not just how, but how so incredibly fast? From being the girl who bloomed so early that the older guys always flirted on me, to dating the older, tough guy that everyone was afraid of. Not so long before this, I had a level of respect among those in our "class" who knew me, and those who didn't. Not class in a high school sense—class in a social pecking order type sense. Even though we were total trailer park, I had landed as the cream of that crop, and not so long ago. But now, walking through the Goodyear parking lot with my sack of groceries wearing flip-flops and a faded sun dress, I was just a plain-faced, pregnant, high school dropout.

I hated my life.

My marriage wasn't so great either. Johnny didn't always come home after work; his life really hadn't changed. He was twenty-two years old, still able to work, run around, and act like he always had. I don't mean to come down on him. He had grown up in a family that drank and played poker most nights, and where the men weren't expected home at any certain time. That was what a family looked like to him. We didn't have a phone, so him calling to tell me he wasn't coming home wasn't possible, even if he wanted to. He was incredibly handsome, and I was incredibly pear-shaped. I understood what was happening and why. I didn't like it, but I sure couldn't say that I didn't get it.

I, on the other hand, had a completely different-looking life in less than a year's time. I tried not to be mad at Mama but felt she could have helped a bit more with all the money she had gotten. Being pregnant and only fifteen, my options were slim. There wasn't a way for me to make enough money to fully support myself right now, so I needed Johnny. I knew full well this was all on me, and Mama would even tell me: "You made your bed. Now you have to lay in it." I understood that too. I took full responsibility for the place I was in. And right at that moment in my life, I knew I had to just play the cards in my hand.

But come hell or high water, I was going to be a better mama. I knew that. I also knew this would be the last time I allowed myself to be dependent, even if just partially, on someone else.

CHAPTER VI

Carpe Diem

Vowing to not be dependent on anyone ever again when you're uneducated, unemployed, and about to be a teenage mama is pretty pie in the sky. But I meant it. I didn't know when or how, but that was my goal in life. I was hell-bent on working my way out of the hole I had dug for myself.

Carpe diem, seize the day, gather ye rosebuds while ye may...

Long before I had ever heard that phrase, my life began shaping up based on that simple principle. Over thirty-five years later, I can look back and say that whether you're raised poor or with many advantages, taking chances, watching for opportunities, and owning your mistakes and responsibilities are the things that will set you apart from others. I knew from watching those around me that whining about your life won't change things. Be thankful. Put your head down, close your mouth, and outwork everyone in the job you have. The Bible says in Proverbs 18:21 that "life and death are in the power of the tongue." If you go about your day moaning and groaning, you're basically cursing yourself and your situation. Saying things like "This is just a dead-end job," or "My boss is such a jerk," can speak that right into existence. I've never been that kind of girl. Regardless of my emotions, regardless of my today, I'm moving forward for tomorrow. I trust God to do the rest.

As a new mama, I had to recognize and "seize" whatever opportunities came my way. *Seize* actually means to take possession by force, so we are talking about aggressive action. Nothing had ever been handed to me. I knew that wasn't going to change. Playing by the proverbial "wait your turn" rules wasn't an option for me. Not if I wanted out—out of the trailer park, out of poverty, out of the bad statistic column that people seemed to love to quote. I had to just go for it at every turn. A person's gut sense of right and wrong are not always black and white when you have a helpless, seven-pound and twelve-ounce human counting on you to get it right. You can wade into the ocean of survival very innocently only to find those waves suddenly overtaking you. Then all you can do is keep fighting for the surface or drown.

The waves seemed never ending during this time in my life.

On and off throughout my pregnancy, we were homeless and just staying here and there between family and friends. Every week was different, but I'm thankful it was always somewhere safe. One evening, when I was about six months pregnant, Johnny and I were staying at our friend Jeannie's house because we didn't have rent money for that week. Jeannie was a single mom and several years older than Johnny. Very attractive, with dark eyes, and short, dark, curly hair. She reminded me a lot of Betty Boop. Her eyes always had a pretty sparkle to them. She flirted on Johnny often, but it never bothered me. I had too much other stuff to worry about.

Jeannie's mama stopped by this particular evening. We had never met her, but the three of us had been friends since we all lived out in the trailer park on Highway 61. Jeannie's mom was a sweet little ole Pentecost lady, I'd say around sixty-five years old. Her name was Mrs. Nan, which kinda screams "little sweet grandma." Mrs. Nan seemed to know a lot about a lot; she took care of several people's houses on the north end of town—also known as "the rich people." She asked me plenty of questions, which only seemed natural since she was the grandma type. Mrs. Nan had to be wondering who this young, pregnant couple was that's at her daughter's so much. I explained that we had just moved back from Mississippi, and we were getting on our feet. With me being pregnant, it was difficult to find work. With that tidbit of information, I could tell Mrs. Nan's wheels started turning. She mentioned that she knew a family that needed a full-time nanny. Someone to come every day, take care of their two-year-old daughter, help with light cleaning and cooking, and then care for a new infant once he was born. The family's incoming baby was due in just a few weeks. Mrs. Nan explained that they were looking for someone that had experience with children and was eighteen or older. She said she would be happy to pass my name along if I wanted her to.

Freeze frame—*I'm not eighteen, and not exactly experienced with kids. Other than the very active one growing inside of me.*

"Yes, please!" I said, without missing a beat. Those words came forth like a bull bursting through a gate. "Sounds like the perfect job for me!" Wow, I seemed to have no shame.

The truth was, I never said that I was eighteen or that I had experience with children. My guess is that Mrs. Nan just assumed I fit those qualifications. I was pregnant, looked older, and we were friends with her daughter who was a lot older than me. So, it makes sense. I'm certain Mrs. Nan never even thought two things about confirming my age. I knew I was in the wrong, but I didn't even think at that very moment. I just reacted. Deep in my soul, it bothered me. But those words just flew right out of me and then seemed too late, or maybe too important, to take back. I had a baby coming. The consequences of my husband missing work, something I had no control over, were us getting kicked out of our apartment. A baby couldn't be in that kind of situation. It was time for me to make my own hay while the sun was shining.

I seized the day. I was back in survival mode, but it wasn't just for me this time.

After an impressive interview, I landed the nanny job. I made certain I was shined up, arrived early, and had my best manners. I wasn't about to walk out of there without that job. Pay would be sixty-five dollars a week. I needed to be there at 7 a.m. every morning, Monday through Friday. I was to cook, clean, and take care of her little two-year-old girl. Give baths, keep her fed, play, and do her laundry. How hard could this be? Mrs. Black would be home by 6 p.m. every evening. Once Mrs. Black's new baby arrived, I'd get seventy-five dollars a week to take care of them both. This meant a free meal every day for me, sixty-five bucks a week for the first few weeks, then seventy-five dollars a week after that. *Wow!* Plus, I asked if I could do a load of my laundry each week and she was fine with that. Most importantly, to be sure, I would stay working after my baby was born; Mrs. Black said I could bring her to work with me! This had to be a job from God, I thought.

If only I hadn't lied to get it.

Little Katie wasn't a hard kid to take care of. It was all new to me for sure, but it came pretty naturally. I was exhausted most of the time from literally growing a human, so I was excited about nap time each day. I gave her a bath in the morning after breakfast, then play time, then lunch, nap, and then we played a little more. If it was nice out, I'd put Katie in her stroller and we would go around the block a few times before I put supper on. Mrs. Black would leave me a list of chores to do, which was pretty common for me. I work well with lists and Mrs. Black was a serious schedule maker. The job and Mrs. Black were a perfect fit for me and my situation.

Perfect, that is, except for the nagging big black cloud of untruth that hung over my head and around my neck, suffocating me with any ounce of joy that I had found in my gainful employment.

My grieved and convicted soul wouldn't allow me to continue.

I had only been working for Mrs. Black a few weeks before my sixteenth birthday rolled around. I slipped up and mentioned my birthday and she asked how old I would be. "Nineteen," I choked out as the cold, sharp knife of dishonesty twisted in my gut.

"Katie and I will bake you some cupcakes this week to take home!" Mrs. Black said with her warm, motherly smile on her way out the door.

No longer was my age something I was just avoiding. I had now bald-faced lied to someone. And not just any someone, but someone who was teaching me to be a mama. Someone who had trusted me with her babies and her house. I was pond scum.

After wallowing in my disgrace for a couple of hours, which is about all that I could handle of that kind of guilt, I picked up the phone and called Mrs. Black's office. I asked for her; the sweat beaded on my face as my heart raced. I had no idea how I was going to tell her, but I knew I was going to tell her. She would accept me or not, but I couldn't continue another moment engulfed in this shame.

"Everything okay?" she said with a breathless gasp. They had told her it was me on the line.

"Yeah, well, I guess so..."

I may have started out clumsily, but then my truth came on like a rocket ship.

"Mrs. Black, I have to be honest with you. I lied to you about my age because I needed a job. I'm only fifteen. I'll be sixteen this week. I don't want you to hate me, but I couldn't hold it in any longer. I understand if you fire me. I'm just so sorry I've lied to—"

"You're fifteen?" she interrupted quietly and slowly, piercing me with every syllable.

"Yes, ma'am," I responded, in total and utter shame.

Her silence was deafening. Letting her down cut through me, heart and soul.

"I need to hang up now. We will talk about this when I get home."

"Yes, ma'am," I said, and then hung up the phone.

Lower than pond scum.

My day drug on as you can imagine, and I carried a heavy and aching heart through every hour of it. Fully prepared to be yelled at, cussed at, and then fired once she got home, I did my best to do my job the rest of the day as perfectly as possible. Well, honestly, I had hoped she would yell and cuss. I knew I dealt with anger much better than with disappointment. When I heard her car pull in the carport, my heart banged hard on my chest walls. I was so very ready to just get this over with. I had a clean conscience now, and that I felt better about. But our actions most certainly have consequences, and I was about to learn mine.

Walking in the carport door, Mrs. Black sat her things down slowly on the kitchen counter. She wasn't struggling for her words—but certainly seemed to be measured with them. She started out by telling me how disappointed she was in me. Had we been playing Battleship; she would have sunk me with that one sentence. Tears welled up in my eyes. Nothing hurt worse than that. Beat the hell out of me. Yell, scream, throw me out, just please, please, don't say I've been a disappointment to you.

Lower than whatever it is that grows underneath the underneath of pond scum.

To my relief, once she was finished giving me a lecture like I'd never experienced before, she told me she wanted me to keep working for her. Mrs. Black was pleased with my work, and as long as I promised to always be honest and ask for help when I didn't know what I was doing, she wanted to be helpful to me as well. Even in my disobedience, or my breaking of the Ten Commandments, whichever way you want to look at it, God still blessed me. There's a lot to be learned in this. Maybe she would have given me the job in the first place had I been honest from the beginning. I'm not sure. But what I do know is that God really took control of the situation. I got to keep my job and my conscience was clear. Downside from not doing it right from the beginning was that I had definitely sown some distrust with Mrs. Black. I'm certain that getting to keep my job was God honoring my honesty. Even if it was a bit late.

Once Mrs. Black's baby arrived, my job was quite a bit harder. I had the good fortune of Mrs. Black wanting me at the house working and taking care of Katie immediately upon her return home from the hospital. Watching her with a newborn helped me tremendously because I had no idea how to care for an infant. I read books and pamphlets at the health department and found *Dr. Spock's Baby and Child Care* at the Book Bug where Mama traded in her novels. I traded three of Mama's novels for that one book and kept it in my backpack for quick reference. Mrs. Black was type A, like me, so that was helpful. She taught me how to boil the bottles, mix the formula, feed on a schedule, and how to bathe a baby. I never said I didn't know how, I just watched her like my life depended on it. Mine didn't, but I knew my baby's sure did.

With the steady income, Johnny and I were able to find a two-bedroom trailer on the edge of town for $150 a month rent. We were also able to purchase an old Ford Pinto from a friend for seventy-five dollars. We paid for it in installments of twenty-five dollars a week. Not bad. I put a nursery together with all of the items Aunt Lisa had given me that she was no longer using. We had a cradle, sheets, blankets, bottles, baby gowns, socks, and cloth diapers all from Aunt Lisa, and then several ladies from church gave me their used items as well. I bought some material and made a comforter for Raychel's crib, and with that, we were ready to go. As always, God greatly provided for us.

I've always felt bad about lying to Mrs. Black to get that job. I'm thankful for the Holy Spirit's constant nagging on my heart so that I never felt comfortable living in my lie. I was homeless, I was pregnant, I was desperate. That changes things. I'm not saying it was the right way to handle it, but I'm thankful God never leaves us, even when we don't get it right at first.

On my actual due date, December 2, 1985, I decided we needed to go to the hospital. I honestly felt like I couldn't handle being pregnant a day longer. I had gained forty-seven pounds and I thought my skin would pop if I gained another ounce. I had been going to the health department each month for a check-up with their nurse, and then more frequently the last couple of weeks, so medically I knew everything was fine. Mentally, I just couldn't take it any longer. I told Johnny, "Let's go; maybe they will keep me."

I was no longer on the medical card because I was married, so the health department was my only option for prenatal care. They did a wonderful job. My thankfulness to those ladies runs as deep as it can get. The nurses and health department workers explained everything in detail to me, sent me home with pamphlets, and made sure I got signed up for WIC—the Special Supplemental Nutrition Program for Women, Infants, and Children—a government program that provides milk to low-income mamas and babies. It was a godsend. With the health department as my prenatal care, I was supposed to just show up at the emergency room when I went into labor. The doctor on call would deliver my baby.

When I arrived at the ER, my water had not broken, and I wasn't having labor pains. So, I didn't think I was technically in labor. However, like with other things in my life once they become unbearable, my personal breaking point had come. It was time for me to change my situation. After I checked in, they moved me straight to the baby floor to be checked to see how far along my labor was. I explained I wasn't having any sharp, constant pains, but my lower back had been aching for some time now—days at least, maybe even a week. They went ahead and gave me a full check over and thank the good Lord, I was dilated over halfway already. I was, in fact, in full labor.

They admitted me quickly, broke my water themselves, and that's when the torture began. Not just labor pains, although that was certainly awful—but Mama...

Being a woman who could never deal with watching her babies in pain, Mama was a mess. Add that drama to me being someone who prefers to hurt alone, not wanting an audience, my hospital room was nothing short of a three-ring circus. Johnny was so good being in my room every minute. I knew he only wanted to help. But even though he wanted to help, he had trouble dealing with Mama. Because of this, I didn't want either of them in there. Johnny was nervous for sure, and when he's nervous, he's giddy. He talks too much and constantly cracks jokes. If Mama wasn't crying, asking how I felt, she was rubbing my hair and forehead and telling me she just didn't want me to die like this. Not something a sixteen-year-old needs to hear when she is trying to figure out how to get something the size of a watermelon out of her body. The sideshow seemed never ending. On top of Barnum & Bailey's, it was 1985 so there weren't medications to help with the pain. They kept giving me something they called "dream away" in the IV. It wasn't anything like dreaming or going away. I dealt with it the best that I could—I threw Mama out of my hospital room and told the nurses not to let her back in. Johnny... was going next.

Daddy called my room to check on me not long after I tossed Mama. I filled him in on all of the crazy and he said he was on his way. Once he got to the hospital, he told me he'd go find Mama and make sure she stayed out. Okay, *no*. Last thing I needed was Mama and Daddy having a face-to-face confrontation, one where Mama was already over the top in all of her feelings. I asked him to steer clear of her and just pray this doesn't last long. After almost six hours of pain, our seven-pound, twelve-and-a-half-ounce baby girl was born. Full head of coal-black hair and olive skin, she looked just like her daddy. Johnny was proud, Daddy was proud, Mama was calmed down and happy. Me? I was about to starve to death.

The nurses quickly got me moved into a joint hospital room while they took my baby to get cleaned up. My joint hospital room consisted of six beds, four of which were already filled by other new mothers. I didn't mind, I just wanted to eat and sleep. I quickly found out that sleep really wasn't in the cards. If they weren't bringing her to me to feed and diaper, they were waking me up to push on my stomach, check my vitals, and tell me all the things I needed to do next. I used my time in the hospital wisely, asking as many questions as possible. I wanted to make sure I didn't break her once we left. My weeks of taking care of Mrs. Black's little guy had sure come in handy. I knew how to change her diaper already, and how to make sure I burped her after a couple ounces of milk. I was exhausted, but ready.

Holding Raychel for the first time, without others staring at me, changed things in me. The fear that had been growing in me over the last few weeks of having a baby that was my full responsibility didn't worry me so much at that moment. I felt confident and strong. From the first moments of me staring at her in my arms, I knew I was her sole protector and provider. Johnny was there for us, but I couldn't control how much he would be. I felt like a lioness ready to protect her cub at all costs. A lioness doesn't wait for a male to show up with food, or to fight her battles. She just does it all. She's ever watchful, smart, and shrewd. From day one, that's how I felt.

In my group hospital room that first morning, I quickly found out how aggressive I had become literally overnight. One of the other new moms in my room lit a cigarette while our babies were in the room with us. I was only sixteen, and this woman was a grown-up. Even with that, it only took me about two seconds to holler across the room and tell her to put that thing out because my baby wasn't going to be around her cigarette smoke. That was the first of many moments to come of me turning into a full-on, hell-bent lioness when it comes to my babies before my brain could check my mouth. God made each of us individually. He put those protective instincts inside me. I was wise to what kind of world I had brought Raychel into—wise to the good, and to the bad. From that moment forward, I knew with every fiber in my being that she fully relied on me to survive. I felt it in my soul every time I looked at her tiny face. To her, I was her life source. To the world around us, I was a bit colder. I had to make certain that we would survive.

Me at sixteen years old, and Raychel at one week.

Raychel was just a few months old when Johnny decided he had better work opportunities in Mississippi, so he thought we needed to move back. It had been a long, hard winter on us in that cold trailer; that was for sure. But I wasn't going to move my baby into some situation I didn't know anything about. Johnny went down and found work and then started asking me to come with Raychel. She was spoiled by him, so the separation had been hard on them both. Johnny had more of an ease with Raychel. He could just sit and love on her, snuggle her up, and spend time with her just playing. I couldn't be so carefree. To me, raising Raychel was the ultimate job and it actually held life-or-death outcomes. I knew the stakes if I screwed this up. She was a live human literally depending on me for everything but breathing.

Life was intense. I...was intense.

Managing everything all by myself once Johnny left was incredibly hard. I had thought it was hard before he left, but then found out how difficult it was doing 100 percent of it on my own. Work, baby, managing bills, cleaning the house, making sure we were fed and bathed—it was exhausting. I was sixteen and still in survival mode all the time. I let Dawn stay whenever she wanted; she could be a pretty big help. Even with all the work, the worst part after Johnny left was the loneliness. Realizing that my friends were hanging out together, cruising town, and working part-time fun jobs was just a lot to accept. I knew I had done this to myself. There was no one to blame but me. But immense sadness over it all did come more often than I like to admit. It was just me and Raychel—staying on our rigorous schedule so none of the balls dropped, and me clinging to God to help me not screw it up.

As fall set in, Johnny needed the car in Mississippi. This meant I had to manage my own rides to work after that. But not just to work; to Raychel's doctor's appointments, to get groceries, to do laundry—you get the picture. With living on the outskirts of town, I couldn't walk to work. It was a good four miles away. I found a few friends to pay a couple of dollars for a ride each way, but they were never reliable. I ended up giving my notice because I couldn't stand being late again, and begging for rides just wasn't working. Life seemed to just keep getting a little harder every day. I took a job cleaning rooms at a hotel less than a mile away. I could walk to work and pay my sister Dawn to watch Raychel at our trailer. It was just from 7 a.m. to noon, so I figured it wouldn't cut into anything she had going in the evenings. This worked out great for the first week or so, but Dawn didn't really like being tied down and I knew this setup was asking a lot of her. She wasn't the one that went off and got pregnant. I gave in, packed us up, and told Johnny to come get us. *Maybe I can get us out of this hole in Mississippi*, I thought.

Always up for change, Dawn once again came to Mississippi with me. I had just turned seventeen, and Dawn nineteen. I knew if it ended up being a bad situation when we got there, two heads would be better than one. I had a baby to protect now. Having my sister beside me if we needed to get back home was an important part of my moving equation.

If she hadn't wanted to go, I'm not sure I would have gone. I had learned long before this day that you can't always trust others when it comes to describing living conditions, and if you can't confirm things for yourself, you need to be prepared for the worst.

Moving back to Forest was very different this time around. It was early November, so the days were getting shorter and cooler. We had a bedroom in a house that Hazel had rented. Johnny's brothers lived there also, but Hazel was staying with a boyfriend across town. When we arrived, it was pretty dark out and the yard was scattered with cars. I couldn't tell which actually belonged to someone and which were broken down and now a part of the yard decor. Hearing us pull in, Johnny came running out the front door, jumped off the porch, and grabbed up his little girl right out of my arms. They were so excited to see each other, and I was happy to have a minute to stretch my legs without holding a moving kid. I grabbed our bags and went straight to where Johnny told me our bedroom was. It was just down a short hall from the living room, in the back of the house.

When I walked in, the house smelled musty, with a strong mix of feet and cigarettes. Welcome to the boys' pad. Not surprised, I just held my breath and kept walking. The only person with a better nose than me was my mama. With Lisa's asthma, Mama had to be extra sensitive, so I grew up with a zero tolerance for negative smells. Besides the aroma, the living room seemed really cold. I quickly ignored that and walked on through with our bags. When Johnny came in with Raychel, I asked him to turn the heat up and give me a few more minutes to change the sheets and get the bedroom moved around. I was on a cleaning mission to make room for her pop-up playpen and find and remove all smells coming from dirty socks, sneakers, trash, ash trays, and so on.

"Heat?" Johnny questioned, half ignoring me while laying Raychel on the bed for a full-on tickle tackle.

Irritated and tired, I said, "Yes, Johnny, the heat? I need to change her and clean her up. I ain't letting her freeze while I do it," I snapped.

With an apologetic look and a quick shrug, Johnny tossed out nonchalantly, "We don't have heat right now, but we will get it back on in a couple of days."

"What?" I said, holding back as much frustration as I possibly could, but you better believe my eyebrows were raised just like the hair on the back of my neck.

"Well," he started slowly, seeing this was clearly a bigger deal to me than he had realized, "the gas got shut off because we didn't pay the bill. I'll pay it, Holly, damn," Johnny tried to brush it off as a nonissue. "I get paid on Friday and it's not even winter yet; we are fine."

Little things like *no heat* never bothered Johnny the way that they did me. We both grew up poor, no doubt. But my mama grew up in a middle-class home, with balanced meals every night, hot water, and indoor plumbing, and most certainly heat. She may have moved us every other full moon, but we were accustomed to some luxuries in life that Johnny and his brothers just weren't always guaranteed. At my young age, I really didn't understand the reasons why. All I understood was that now I was subjecting my daughter to living conditions that were unacceptable, and that was on me.

With my hand on my hip and my body language in full trailer-park mode, I pushed forward, unable to let this drop. "Why didn't you bother telling me there's no heat before I brought Raychel here?!"

With that, Johnny started cussing on his way out of the bedroom. To him, I was overreacting, so he slammed the door shut behind him. Unfortunately, this was how we communicated most of the time.

An hour or so later, I could hear people coming in and the living room getting louder and louder. I was trying to get Raychel to sleep, but a new place, loud noises, and having Daddy in the house was just a little too much stimulation for an eleven-month-old to settle in. I lay next to her singing her favorite ni-night songs—"Rock-a-Bye Baby," "Twinkle, Twinkle Little Star," "Hush Little Baby"—nothing was working. The living room was getting louder with music and strange voices. My patience was wearing thin, and I was getting madder by the minute that Johnny was out there playing poker and not running everyone off so his daughter could sleep. It wasn't long before things started getting knocked over.

I loathe drunks.

I knew the sounds well and I wasn't about to let my daughter be subjected to the same life I had been. We had only been there a couple of hours, but I was regretting every ounce of my decision to come. I hated the thought of going out there to lay down rules on my first night, and possibly getting into it with Johnny at the same time, but the louder it got, the madder I got. I knew this wasn't going to work for us. I placed Raychel in her small playpen and walked to the living room to ask everyone to keep it down. Before I could get anything out of my mouth, I was greeted by a belligerent, drunk teenage girl wanting to fight me because she thought I was Bobby's girlfriend from Sikeston.

That was all the motivation this little girl from the trailer park needed.

My temper skyrocketed, and I had a full-on Southern-mama meltdown. *This...was not going to be my child's life.* After my come-apart on the girl, my glare turned to Johnny, who was sitting at the kitchen table, just to dare him to have a different opinion. Seeing his half smile and head nod toward me may have actually made me madder. I quickly turned and went back to my baby in the cold bedroom. Johnny not weighing in was probably because he had gotten into his card game and totally zoned out of everything going on around him. He was always quick to put Raychel's needs first when it came to others around us. His slight show of approval of my meltdown most likely was because he just hadn't realized that things had gotten out of control. Back in the bedroom, still mad as a wet cat, I put a small chair in the middle of the bed and piled the covers on top to make a warm tent for me and Raychel to hang out in. With my blood still boiling, there was no way either of us was falling asleep anytime soon.

What had I gotten us into?

The next morning, I bundled us up and walked to a nearby gas station and small grocery store. We lived just outside of town, but we were super lucky this little gem was in walking distance. It wasn't freezing cold, but it was an uncomfortable cold for sure. I never seemed to have a warm enough coat in the winter. I had twenty dollars in food stamps and about the same in cash stashed away that no one knew about, not even Johnny. After Johnny moved to Mississippi, I signed up for welfare to supplement my jobs. They wouldn't help us when Johnny lived with us since we were married. But once he didn't, I qualified for food stamps, a medical card, and a welfare check. I didn't want to be on it long, but I most certainly didn't want us to get behind on our bills while I looked for a full-time job. It actually turned out to be a little more combined than what we had previously lived on, so anything extra I hid away for future tough times. Walking to the store and thinking about what a mess I let us land in, I was super thankful for the extra that I had tucked away. Stepping into the little country store, I must have looked pretty lost in my thoughts.

"Cana-hep yous?" the kind, older man said from behind the counter with the thickest Mississippi drawl I'd heard in a while.

"Yes, sir. I'm looking for some cans of Vienna sausage, or maybe potted meat?" I said with my normal big smile.

"Rat down that aisle, babe," he said, nodding and pointing in the direction I needed to go. "Yous sittin' today?" he continued.

"Oh no, sir, she's mine!" I had gotten used to the question by now. My oversized smile seemed to give my age away at times.

"Well, she's a dandy!" he said. "Lemme come hep you gals get all y'all's need'n."

I love Mississippi people. They have always treated me so nice and never an ounce of judgement. That sweet man spent his time helping me find the Vienna sausages and a small carton of milk for Raychel. I knew if I bought a full gallon of milk, I would have to put it in the fridge, and it would be gone as soon as I took my eyes off it. So, I opted for a small carton and bought a small box of powdered milk as well. I knew the powdered milk could carry Raychel over until I figured out how to sign up for Mississippi's WIC program. I also knew that not many would know what to do with powdered milk so if someone was in our room snooping, it might not get taken. My new store clerk friend helped me add it all up to make sure I had enough before he rang it in the cash register.

When I sneaked back into the house, the sun was full up, so it was easy to see the mess and people passed out on the furniture. The smell of feet lingered in the air. Beer cans and trash lay on the floor and on the end tables. To the left was the kitchen where they had played poker all night. Dishes were piled up in the sink and on the kitchen countertops. Cigarette ashes seemed to be everywhere. *What a mess.* I just walked through quickly back to our room carrying Raychel and my small sack. No way would I have my daughter in a bachelor pad for long. I knew where the bus station was and I let Johnny know we'd be on one if things didn't change fast. That evening, we went to the local drug store, and I purchased a small plug-in space heater for our room for ten dollars. This was a good start to making things better. The nights were cold, and the days were not much better. That little heater did wonders for our room.

I set up a house schedule for warming people up. I had to hide our food because I knew with as many people in and out of the house, someone might steal it if they knew it was there. I bought ten cans of Vienna sausages, knowing if I rationed those just right between me and Raychel during the day, they would last the full week until Johnny's check. I would let everyone come in to warm for thirty minutes at a time, but not when Raychel was napping. Everyone but Dawn, of course. She could come in when she wanted to.

While Johnny worked, I got busy fixing things. I secured a two-bedroom trailer out in the country for $175 a month. It was a little higher than we were paying in Sikeston, but it was really nice. With me just turning seventeen, I figured I'd have more job opportunities than I had had in the past. Our trailer was not too far outside the city limits, and easy to get to. Once you passed the city-limits sign on the north side of town, you took the first dirt road on the right, next to a yellow house. About half a mile down, way back in a field on the right, sat our brown and tan trailer. It was beautifully hidden behind towering pines. The only neighbor nearby was the little yellow house at the corner. Once I had our living conditions fixed, it was time to find a job.

First day out on the hunt, I was disappointed to find out I wasn't old enough to work in the factories. Factories were where you could make really good money, but with that off the table, I decided to check out all of the restaurants. My first stop was the diner in the middle of town. Excited to see a "Help Wanted" sign on the door, I went in and got the job on the spot. I had never been a waitress before, but how hard could it be? I had watched Flo on the TV show *Alice* say, "Kiss my grits" a thousand times! I had this. Problem was, I really didn't. Dyslexia spans many areas of learning and living, not just how you write and see numbers and letters. Your brain is wired differently; I know that now. I sure didn't know it then. Something so simple as taking an order had several issues and wasn't simple at all. Spelling, for starters. Memorizing and sounding words out has always been incredibly difficult for me. My second problem was focusing and writing down verbatim what the customer wanted. With so many others talking in the café, I was easily confused. To read and to write, I have to do so with purpose. That's just a part of it. Unfortunately, the two things I struggled with were the main parts of my new job. The cooks who had to read my tickets sure didn't like me, but the customers and the boss did because I worked really hard, and I was dependable. With those things on my side, I kept my job, but I sure wasn't good at it.

Every day on my break, I would walk across the street to the Dollar General to spend my tips on what we needed for the house. Shampoo, dish detergent, broom, mop—it could all be found at the Dollar General. Once I was off work, I'd pick up Raychel and then pick Johnny up from work. I still didn't have my driver's license, but I had been driving long enough that I never really thought about it anymore. We had a good system down, but even as determined and scheduled as I was, I still made some pretty big mistakes.

One of those mistakes, I'll remember forever. Raychel and I were home alone, and I was feeding her breakfast in her highchair. Now, growing up in trailers, there are some things that you know. The windows are gonna pinch your fingers, every wind gust sounds like a tornado, and the doors will lock on you. I know these things. But on that day, I wasn't thinking.

Mama and I always wrote letters back and forth. Getting a letter from her would be the highlight of my day. Being terrible at my job and having those cooks getting onto me constantly was pretty hard to handle day after day. I'm a perfectionist, so I certainly wanted to be the best. It just wasn't working out that way. Any letters from Mama, my main cheerleader in life despite her shortcomings, were needed blessings. While I had Raychel busy in her highchair, I decided to run down our long drive to our mailbox to see if I had a letter. I moved fast out the door and it slammed behind me. I darted like the wind to the mailbox, grabbed the mail, and ran all the way back to the door.

The locked door.

Looking through the narrow, vertical window in the door, I could see Raychel smiling at me, eating her Cocoa Puffs. She thought we were playing peekaboo and I was trying with everything I had not to freak out. I worked to pry the door open with anything I could find in the yard. No luck. I ran to the back, praying for it to be easier to get into; it was not.

Knowing I was the worst mother that God had ever placed on the earth, I ran back to the front door and started talking to her through the window. She was still calm, eating, smiling, and waving at me. I knew my only option was to run for help. No one would be out to us until nightfall. I was so afraid she would try to climb out; she was very mobile and already starting to climb. I knew I had no other option. I told Raychel I would be right back. I always spoke to her like she understood everything I was saying—she had been my only friend most days for the past year. Running as fast as I could, I got to the dirt road and didn't stop until I was banging on the door of the yellow house. I frantically explained what was happening. She told me to run back and she would get someone there to help me. God sure had my back because she knew the owner of my trailer!

Back on my doorstep, I peeked through the glass pane in the door once again. There was my girl, still smiling at me. She was out of Cocoa Puffs and had snot rubbed all over her face, but she was still sitting in her chair. My heart hurt with what an awful mama I was, certainly not deserving of her smiles and waves. We sang fun songs through the door—"Deep and Wide," "This Little Light of Mine," "Jesus Loves Me," and anything else I could think of. I needed her to be busy and I was frantic inside knowing I had zero control over this situation. I remained calm, however, on the outside, knowing it was my only hope to keep her safe.

After what seemed like forever, a dirty old pickup came racing and bouncing down the pothole-filled dirt road before coming to a fast stop in my front yard. Our landlord got out, unlocked the door, and started giving me the good tongue lashing that I deserved. I didn't stick around on the steps to hear it. All I cared about was holding Raychel tight and thanking God for her protection.

Not long after that day, we had Raychel's first birthday party. Next came Christmas. Both were good, but lonely. It was starting to wear on Johnny and me that we didn't have our big families around. We had both missed Christmas dinner with our cousins, aunts, and uncles. I missed my mama and my sisters. Dawn had left just before Christmas and a couple of Johnny's brothers had moved back to Missouri also. After our lonely Christmas, we decided it was time to go home. We loaded up that old Ford Pinto and moved back to Missouri.

Mama and Lisa were living in Cape Girardeau, where Mama was back in college. Moving back, we went straight to Mama's. She said we could stay a few days while we found work and a place to live. That worked just fine for me. We both had our checks for the week, so I found an efficiency apartment to keep us from needing deposit money for utilities. Cape Girardeau had several to choose from with it being a college town. Even more awesome and straight from God was that our next-door neighbor ran a daycare in her home! I was hired at Taco Bell right off, and Johnny was hired by Service Master. We had zero cash once we paid for our rent and Raychel's daycare, but I was able to call around to churches and got a couple of food baskets given to us. With brown beans, canned goods, and a sack of rice, I knew we could make it until we got our first paychecks. It was a mile and a half to my work, and with the babysitter next door, walking to work wasn't a problem.

I started GED classes after work a couple days a week. As crazy as it sounds, I felt foolish in those classes. We were all there for the same program, but most of the others were teens that had gotten into trouble at the high school. They were just in the classes to finish up and get done. I, on the other hand, was their age, but I was married and had a child, a job, and bills to pay. I wanted to get it over with and move on with my life. I didn't seem to fit in no matter what group I was around. Too old in experience for those my age, too young in age for those with my experience. Johnny and I were not doing so well either. Things always seemed to be on and off with us and I didn't want to find myself in the same situation as before—no car and not making enough money to keep a roof over our heads. I needed to get my GED so that I could qualify for more jobs and maybe even take college classes like Mama.

As soon as I turned eighteen, I applied at Thorngate, the sewing factory in town, and got hired really fast. One thing I knew how to do well was run a sewing machine. My pay was $6.25 an hour and then "piece-work" on top of that. Piece-work meant that the faster I worked, the more I would get paid. I could work fast when it came to sewing, so I was set. I made good money at my job, had steady hours, and was still able to pull some shifts at Taco Bell on the weekends. Plus, there was a location to take my GED nearby once I was ready. Unfortunately, before my master plan materialized, Johnny and I split again, leaving me with no car and no one to watch Raychel while I worked those extra shifts. Mama had her own life going and wasn't the babysitting kind, which I knew, so that took away any extra money that Raychel and I had. That, we could live with, but I absolutely could not lose my job at Thorngate. Walking to work wasn't an option because my shift was early, and I couldn't drop Raychel at the sitters early enough to get to work on time. I needed a car and a driver's license. I was once again in that ocean of survival and the waves just kept coming.

As I mulled over my options, Dawn reminded me that Uncle Ben had offered all us girls in the family who had quit high school a cheap car if we get our GED. My problem with this very kind offer was that every time he mentioned it, it came with some giggle-giggle crap about him getting to say how we pay for it if we don't come through with the GED. Deep, deep breaths.

I knew without a shadow of a doubt that I would be getting my GED. My concern, however, was that I had been out of school for three full years and there were a lot of subjects covered in the GED test that I had never learned in school, since I didn't attend the tenth, eleventh, or twelfth grades. Classes like government, geometry, and so on. I was worried I would fail, and then owe Uncle Ben, but I needed a car now. I feared that without one, I would lose my job. I swallowed my pride and called my uncle. He was excited to hear from me and he would bring me a car down at the end of the week. As I sat the phone down, my stomach felt sick. *It's going to be alright*, I kept telling myself. *It's going to be fine.*

Uncle Ben and a friend drove the car down from St. Louis. When they got to Mama's with the car, it had "As Is" and "$1,200" written on the windshield in white shoe polish. It wasn't awful looking at all. Nice even. It was an older model Buick Skylark, white in color with a blue interior. The defrost and air didn't work, but it was a car. My car! Uncle Ben was happy to help me. I never allowed him to, so it really gave him an ego boost to finally have me call and need him. I played along because I knew I needed to. He was wonderful, yada yada, and all the other nice things. I sure don't mean to sound unappreciative. Full truth was, Uncle Ben was saving me and Raychel. Telling him that just hurt for a myriad of reasons. Any type of voiced appreciation from me was immediately followed by his gross yukking it up about how if I didn't come through with the GED, he got to pick how he would get paid back. It was never spoken of more than that, but I knew, I mean *knew*, what he was saying. I was damn sure gonna pass that test.

I did my best to work, take care of Raychel, and take the GED classes in the evenings. It was so hard making it all work. Thorngate closed, and Johnny and I had been talking again, so Raychel and I moved to Sikeston with him. I got hired on pretty quickly at the sewing factory in Sikeston and I got into GED classes there to finish up. I needed to get that test out of the way, but I had to make sure I passed it. I was so nervous when my test day came. It was given at Southeast Missouri State University in the main academic hall under the gold dome. I walked across the tree-filled campus and then down those ginormous halls, and I could just see myself going to college there someday. I knew that passing this test was my first step. I took it, felt awful about it, then waited for weeks for my score to arrive in the mail. I passed with flying colors! You can betcha Uncle Ben was the first person I called.

I felt I had made a deal with the devil because I was backed into a corner. I wouldn't have given in to any of his demands had I not passed it, but I had been fearful of what that day may look like. I'm so thankful I didn't have to find out.

Seize the day, work like hell, and pray even harder.

Johnny and I found a little one-bedroom, white-board house on 5th Street in Sikeston. I bet it wasn't more than 350 square feet total, but it looked plenty big for the three of us. Even in its obvious run-down state, I could sure see promise in that little house. To others, I'm sure it looked like its best days were way past gone. But I saw a little white cottage sitting in a field, ready to be loved, painted, and filled with a little girl's laughter. The owner was an elderly man that owned other rental property in town. He explained to us that he was ready to sell off his places so he could retire, and offered to sell the house to us on monthly payments. After a few years it would be ours, and we didn't even have to have any money down! Unbelievable. Just like that, we were property owners!

Our new little dream cottage, on the other hand, had a few secrets of its own. It sat back between two pieces of property on 5th Street—way back. You had to turn onto a long dirt driveway, drive back between and behind the other houses on the street, and there it sat. Open fields on both sides. What I didn't know before moving in, that I found out really fast, is that open fields are where rats live. *Many* long-tailed, long-nosed, beady-eyed rats. Our house was pretty rickety and needed a lot of attention right away. The front living room wall was separated a bit from the floor because that side was sinking into the ground. It was only by a couple of inches, so we just tucked some old blankets all the way along the bottom of that wall to carefully plug the hole. It seemed to work great at keeping most of the heat in, and the rain and cold out, but apparently it was still like an open door for the rats. I spent most nights making sure they didn't get in the bed with Raychel. That weighed on me greatly but was doable. Regardless of the rats, walls not touching the floor, and all other issues, it was ours and that's all that mattered to us.

Living back in Sikeston had a few challenges of its own. I had not spoken to Papa in a while, and that was just the way I liked it. However, Papa saw me driving through town one evening after work and he followed me home. I had kept myself pretty well at a distance from him since he hurt me, mainly just seeing him at family gatherings. I loved him, I forgave him, but I was smart enough to know that if he did that to my mama, Aunt Cindy, and to me...it could happen again. Me having a daughter of my own now made me even more cautious. As I turned down my long dirt drive, Papa pulled in behind me.

Getting out of the car, I unbuckled Raychel and let her down into the yard to play. Papa was getting out of his car, so I walked to meet him.

"Hey Papa," I said with my usual side hug. "Everything okay?"

"I found you!" Papa said with a smile. His crystal-clear, baby blue eyes always seemed to have a twinkle. "I've been wondering where you lived. Now that I see it's behind the other houses; it makes sense why I couldn't find you!"

Picking Raychel up, I really didn't want to invite him inside. Our living conditions were not gross; I cleaned continually. I was trying so hard to be a good mama, and with the rats and the structural problems our house had, I just didn't want any judgment or worry on his part.

It was nice out and to my surprise, Papa never walked toward the door. It was obvious he was troubled by something, and I had always been the closest of us girls to him. I could tell this visit was more than just finding out where I lived. As Papa played with Raychel a little bit in the yard, we caught up on the family, my job, Raychel—obviously stalling a more needed conversation, I could tell. I've never been someone who could hang out talking about nothing when there was something that needed to be said. Elephants don't stay in the room with me long.

"Papa, tell me what's going on...something's wrong, isn't it?"

With a little bit of a sad half-smile, he looked at me and said, "Holly Bells, I have to go for some tests next week in Memphis. They think I have cancer and I don't want to go by myself."

He didn't have to say anything else. With a big hug, I told him I would make sure I could go with him. He gave me the details so I could ask off work and get Raychel taken care of. Regardless of our history, I wasn't going to let him go through this alone. He may have hurt me, but he was my papa and I loved him. I wasn't a child that couldn't protect herself anymore. Helping him was the right thing to do. Papa had always been a strong and proud man, but I saw fear in his eyes that day. The thought of this was weighing heavy on his heart and I knew the responsibility of helping him fell on me.

The next couple of weeks were quite a blur of driving back and forth to Memphis, tests and more tests, doctors using big words, and treatment plans being decided. Papa had pleural mesothelioma lung cancer from all his years working as a Navy Seabee. It's a rare form of mesothelioma, and this was in a time before all those trial attorney commercials, so both words were very foreign-sounding to me. Papa, however, was a seventy-three-year-old retired naval officer who had traveled the world. He decided quickly what treatment he was willing to undergo and then got started on that plan. My job doing alterations at a local dry cleaners allowed me to be flexible somewhat, so I visited Papa in the Memphis hospital a couple of times a week; Mama even went once, too.

Once home, Papa had to eat through a feeding tube that ran from his nose into his throat and down to his stomach, which totally grossed me out. It was a rubber tube that was kinda yellow from the stain of the food, which made it even harder for me to look at. The end of the tube had a little plug cap, and he would swing it over one ear to keep it from just dangling straight from his nose hole. *Ewww!* That was so hard for me to handle! Papa was pretty good at blending up his food, and we purchased cases of Ensure meal replacement drinks for him. Even with getting the proper nourishment, he was super frail from the cancer treatments, so I kept a good eye on him. Raychel and I would run by his house in the mornings on the way to work and I would make sure he was getting some breakfast in his belly. I would then come over on my lunch break and do the same, then after work I'd pick Raychel up from daycare and we would head back to Papa's where I would cook supper, blend his up for his feeding tube, and then feed and bathe Raychel. Getting Raychel's bath at

Papa's house was a lot easier than at our little house, so that was a help on my side of things.

I knew Papa realized and appreciated how much time I spent taking care of him. He loved sitting in his chair outside and watching Raychel play in the evenings, even though he was too frail at times to get up. He kept Dairy Queen Dilly Bars in his freezer so anytime we were outside in the evenings, he made sure she had one. Papa told me often how much he appreciated and loved me. I am thankful God gave us that time to work through the past pain, even though it wasn't worked through in spoken form. Actions mean more to me than words. They always have.

One night over dinner, Papa told me he had a CD at the bank that was maturing in the amount of $90,000. I didn't really understand what a CD was, but he explained it's where you put money in the bank, and you can't touch it for a period of time; it draws more interest that way. Okay, got it—but not really. I had no idea what he was talking about so I just listened.

Papa continued walking me through his intentions. He was going to value the house at $25,000, add the $90,000 to it, and split the total between Mama, me, and my sisters. He wanted to do the splitting before he died. As much as I hated us talking about his imminent death, I knew we needed to. I had helped with Grandma's services, and I knew Papa's would be solely mine to take care of. I wanted to be sure I made him proud. We discussed his thoughts and wishes for the service, and then he told me where he had money stashed around the house to pay for flowers, a love offering for the preacher, and the additional expenses that were certain to come up. It was a good conversation for sure, and just when I thought it was over, Papa looked at me straight in the face and said, "Holly, I want you to choose first."

"Choose what Papa?" I asked, no longer sure what we were talking about.

"Tell me what you want before I talk to your mother. You've been the one to care for me, you tell me what you want, then I'll split the rest between your mother and sisters," he explained.

I knew he meant the house. In my heart of hearts, I knew immediately he was asking if I wanted the house. *He meant the house!* It may have been only 1,300 square feet—and trust me, Papa kept telling me how old it was and all of the work it needed done—but that house had been my sanctuary the majority of my childhood. It looked like a castle to me.

"I want the house, Papa," I said without hesitation.

A home of my own, mine and Raychel's, that nobody can take from me.

"I want the house."

With that, Papa set up an appointment with his attorney and added me to all his accounts and the house. This change made it possible for me to pay for all funeral expenses and bills as they came in. The following weekend, Papa had Mama and the girls come over and he gave them each a cashier's check for $28,750, and me a check for $3,750. No one complained or asked Papa why I had first dibs on the house. But I'm pretty sure they would have chosen the cash even if given a choice.

It was a new day for me and Raychel for sure. We had turned a corner. My girl was never going to have to wonder where we would be sleeping. She was even going to have her own bedroom, with big windows, and without rats. My heart is so full right now just thinking back on this incredible day. Taking care of Papa was the right thing to do. It didn't seem like something that was going to be any kind of blessing for me in the long run. It was my responsibility and I take my responsibilities seriously. But God...God honors hard work and a kind heart. You can't always see a blessing coming, but trust me, it will come. He honors those who put their feelings aside and do what is right. What an unbelievable blessing he had bestowed on me. Words cannot describe.

Choosing the house, and not the cash, is one of the wisest decisions of my life. Papa passed in the summer of 1990, in the middle of the night, with me in the bedroom just across the hall from him.

Without Papa, and my work surrounding his care, I decided it was time to check into college classes. With my GED and enough cash left over from helping Papa, I was able to sign up for a full semester. I couldn't work full-time and take classes, so I found a part-time job in the mailroom at Galaxy Cablevision. I also picked up a house-cleaning gig every other week for Johnny's boss, so that helped make up some of my loss in wages. I was terrified, but I was determined to go for it.

I'll be honest, it was a struggle. A ton of reading and memorization is really hard for someone with dyslexia, and that sure is what college turned out to be. I didn't knock it out of the park, but I passed all my classes and that was all that mattered to me. Signing up for the next semester, I knew that if I worked hard, I could actually get my college degree. I had my own car, I had my own house, I had my GED certificate framed and hanging in the foyer—I was on my way.

Raychel was almost five at this time, and I had turned twenty-one. I was busier than ever, but Johnny and I wanted to have a second child before too many years would be between Raychel and a sibling. Regardless of the fact that we were still riding that roller-coaster relationship, I had come from a home of many divorces, and I wasn't about to let that be my children's lives. I was determined to make our family work come hell or high water. With that, Johnny and I tried for a second child and one month of trying was all it took. Johnny Ray Griswell, Jr., was born on June 4, 1991. My little JJ. He was a few weeks early but perfect in every way. My marriage, however, was not. We had hit some seriously rocky ground, and my intentions of never letting my children experience a broken home fell flat—that was exactly where we landed.

Johnny and I had started dating as kids—me thirteen, and him nineteen. We had made our marriage last seven years, but by the end of '91, it was clear to us that we weren't going to make it to eight. I filed for divorce, and with me as our only income, I decided the next semester of college would have to wait. I had moved from Galaxy Cablevision to Falcon Cable a few months before having JJ because they were able to give me more hours a week. But even with that, I knew I wasn't going to get the bills paid so I started my frantic search for a full-time job and a roommate. Lisa, my little sister, had recently finished her business college program in St. Louis and was excited when I asked if she wanted to move in with us. She needed an inexpensive place to live and I needed help with the kids and bills. It was a perfect solution. Lisa worked a couple of part-time jobs while she looked for something to match her business school training. I was open to do whatever; I just needed more hours than the twenty I was getting working evening dispatch at Falcon Cable.

When I answered the phone one morning, my former boss from the mailroom at Galaxy Cablevision was on the other end of the line. After chitchat and catching up, she explained she was actually calling for my sister. They had a daytime position open in the mailroom, part-time, but promised thirty-five hours a week. She said Lisa had put an application in some time ago, so she was calling to see if she was still interested.

Now let me pause right here to say, I love my sister with all my heart. But she was nineteen, no kids, and had a business school certificate. *Not today, Lisa, not today.*

"I need that job," I blurted out.

With a half-laugh, Donna said, "You know I'd love to have you back. Are you sure?"

"Just tell me when to be there," I said, and I never looked back.

This simple telephone call that wasn't even for me turned out to be one of the biggest milestones in my life. But at that moment, I had no idea of the path it was actually setting me on.

All of the milestones I've mentioned in this chapter catapulted me forward in life. Focusing on the long game, not simply on the needs of today, is key. Like me choosing the house, and not the pile of cash. That was a total *life* changer. We never know what tomorrow will bring, so making decisions based on long-term goals is vital. Soon after choosing the house, I went through a divorce—two small children to support on my own at just twenty-two years old. My "today" looked and felt bleak, but not so bleak as it would have if I had not chosen the house. My starting over position this time around had significantly improved. I had a car and a home that were both mine. If I had not chosen the house, my focus most likely would have been on trying to keep a roof over my babies' heads. It would have consumed most of my energy, time, and money during and after my divorce. I already knew how difficult it was being a mother of a small child, without a car, trying to get to daycare and work. But I was no longer on that starting block. Instead, with my own car and home, I was able to focus on being the hardest worker in that mailroom.

My job at Galaxy Cablevision may have started out at thirty-five hours a week and working in the mailroom, but it ended fourteen years later with me as director of government affairs, lobbying in Jefferson City, and Washington, DC, at times, on policy that affected our industry. I also handled all mergers and acquisitions of our cable systems across thirteen states. It was all on-the-job training, and before I had finished my college degree. Let that sink in a minute: simply unbelievable. Talk about a game changer.

Decisions that may seem inconsequential at the time can turn out to be a major fork in the road of life. Working in the mailroom, I didn't grumble. I kept my head down and I worked hard. I made sure the bosses knew I wanted to do more, learn more, and then I took chances by applying for job openings that came available. Some I got, some I didn't. God honors and blesses hard work. When I left Galaxy for my next adventure, I was one of the top five directors in the company, making an excellent salary. I also had industry connections and years of training that opened doors for me and my husband to start our own business.

Now that's the power of an almighty God.

I'm telling you my milestone stories for multiple reasons. First, I made it out of poverty. Many have asked me how; *this* is how. Second, having opportunity is not all that it's about. You can give people opportunity until you're blue in the face—they have to want it. They have to be hungry for it. They also have to work for it. When you have to struggle to get something, you take care of it. You remember the cost. You literally *feel* the cost. It's valuable to you. I was hungry.

CHAPTER VII

Mama

By this point in my story, I'm certain you have the wrong impression of my mother. Just as I did growing up. She was definitely a complex woman; aren't we all? Many layers are formed on top of each other by the seasons of our life. Some layers are more dramatic in color than others. Some, more dark and painful. I can look back now and see the many things that I have learned from being raised by her. I've learned you cannot judge a book by its cover. I've learned mental illness has many faces. And I have learned, most importantly, that the words she always spoke to us girls, "*until you've walked a mile in their moccasins...*" reveal a truth about humanity that few people are ever lucky enough to embrace.

What I haven't told you yet is about her journey. The things my mother saw, the life she endured, and the lessons she learned—whether right or wrong—at a very young age. The journey that made her into the woman that she became. Because that truly matters as well. I don't say that to excuse anyone's behavior. I firmly believe the person we become is based on the many choices, turns, and curves we take throughout our lives. But I also believe that what gets ingrained underneath those layers of life most certainly comes back to haunt us if not dealt with appropriately. I'm not a psychiatrist and in no way know if these canyon-size impressions left in my mother's life's layers contributed to the struggles she had with manic depression. But once you know her story, I think you will wonder just as I have.

When you live with manic depression, you have erratic behaviors that can wreak havoc on yourself and your family. I have also learned that another trait of manic depression is promiscuity. It is my belief that Mama never felt unconditionally loved; add this to her manic depression and it was a powder keg always waiting to blow. I also believe that her constant attention-seeking behavior was a byproduct of it all. She couldn't seem to help herself from always being the victim. She allowed man after man to abuse her mentally and physically. She allowed family and neighbors to run over her. She would then get upset as if she had no choice in the matter whatsoever. As her daughter, I stood up for her often, but I desperately wanted her to stand up for herself. I hated all who abused and took advantage of her, and I tried one by one to remove them from our lives. I couldn't understand why she allowed it, but growing up, I also never understood the complexity of her mental illness. I perceived her nonaction and playing the victim as weakness, and I loathed it in her. I vowed to never be like her.

Looking back, it seems like I started assuming some of the role of the parent in our house at about the age of eleven. Mama's decisions were emotion-based and impulsive, and mostly dictated by whatever boyfriend she had succumbed to at the time. Because of this, we seemed to clash often. My fights with her, however, are actually how I knew about many of the demons she struggled with. Her frequent meltdowns sometimes included her yelling about the things she went through as a child and how lucky we were to be so protected by her, which I did appreciate. Many of the kids living around us didn't have a clean house, groceries, clean clothes, or a mama that cared for them. We did. But during her meltdowns, Mama would tell us incredibly graphic and painful stories. Stories of how her teenage uncle, who was mentally retarded, started sexually abusing her when she was only four years old. She said her grandmother would look the other way because it was my mama's mother who originally dropped him on his head when he was a baby. They blamed his mental retardation on that accident. So essentially, she was told to deal with it because it was her mom's fault to begin with. I was probably ten years old when she first told me about this. No words can convey what that must have been like for her; it's unconscionable. It was also a pile of horrific information for a child to hear about and try to process. But my mother had no boundaries when upset. In those years, her life was driven by raw emotion.

I can look back now and see clearly how something so evil as being sexually abused at only four years of age would shape your opinion of yourself. Of course, I had no way of understanding it then. My breadth of knowledge and understanding was far too limited at my young age. However, the many stories of abuse that she told us did allow me to see that our family, and the world, had some scary tall dark shadows in it. Now, looking back, I can understand some of what it must have been like for her. She was never cared for or protected by the adults in her life. They allowed her to be abused by a teenage uncle because of the supposed sin of her mother. On top of that, she was also sexually abused by her older brother. She said the family didn't believe her, but felt that if it was true, he was only doing what he learned from his young uncle. This twisted mentality formed her very first opinions of herself. Of her self-worth.

My mother was a victim of this abuse on and off for several years until her mother, at only twenty-seven, passed away from cancer. Not long after, Mama was sent to an orphanage. She was only eight years old at the time. Her father tried but wasn't able to manage the kids alone. He had consistent problems with making sure they were all in school while he was working. After so many days absent, the school started inquiring and found the children's home life not acceptable. Her grandmother's home was seen as unfit as well, so they were removed. All to different locations. My mother's youngest sister, who was four years old at the time, was adopted immediately. My mother's older sister was sent across town to live with extended family. Her brother was sent to a boy's orphanage, and was later adopted, and Mama was sent to an orphanage in St. Louis.

At about ten years old, Mama was adopted by her maternal grandmother's brother and his wife. They weren't able to have children of their own, so they chose to adopt Mama. That was my Grandma and Papa. As you already know from previous chapters, Papa sexually abused her too. As I have mentioned, Mama told me often that she told Grandma about the sexual abuse, but Grandma refused to believe her. As much as I am certain my Grandma walked on water, I believe Mama. Other things in my childhood have somewhat confirmed that Grandma had suspicions about Papa, or was at least worried it could be true. For example, when I would go to mow Papa's vacant lots with him, Grandma would always ask me if he did anything that made me uncomfortable in any way. I always honestly answered "no." I guess she didn't want to believe what Mama told her, but those questions make me believe that she knew in her heart it could be true. I wish so much she would have stood up for my mother. I wish so much that someone, anyone, in her childhood would have stood up for her and said that her safety, her life, was most important to them. But they didn't. No one ever did.

So, you have a child who has lost her mother at a young age and has been continually used for the sexual pleasure of the men in her life. A child who reached out for help and was either told it's okay for her to be treated like that, or not believed altogether. I can absolutely see how that would change your psychological understanding of the entire world around you, as well as your understanding of yourself. She was beautiful and smart, and she knew that, but Mama had zero self-esteem. She was never taught that she could have boundaries. I fear that her years of sexual abuse as a child, and then as a teen, made her think that *was* her self-worth—her sexuality.

Does any of this excuse the fact that she let a fifteen-year-old sleep with her and become her boyfriend when she was in her mid-twenties? Absolutely not. I don't understand why an intelligent woman, regardless of her past, would think that was acceptable. At the very least, it had to be against the law. Her sleeping with underage guys wasn't necessarily a pattern, but there was at least one other that I know of that was under eighteen. I wished my whole life growing up that she wasn't such a sexual being. All of it bothered me. All of it. It still does forty years later. But Mama danced to the beat of her own emotional drum. She was a free spirit, eccentric and beautiful. A child of the sixties, free love and all. We always knew that if Mama hadn't been strapped with us girls back then, she would have been touring with some band as a groupie, somewhere exotic and fantastic, I'm certain.

What might surprise you from reading this memoir so far is that Mama spent a lot of time with us girls one on one in our younger years. She was an avid reader, and many evenings she would read to us. She sang us to sleep often, and Mama never missed an opportunity to tell us she loved us. She also told us often how important school was and that she had been in the top 10 percent of her class. I wasn't exactly sure what that meant at the time, however, I knew it meant she was really smart. But just as some days Mama was so laid-back and nurturing, other days she could be totally over the top. When we were little, we rolled with whatever the day would bring. It was just Mama: artistic, loving, and emotional. Some days, she saw such beauty in the clouds while other days, she could only see a storm coming.

There are several moments in my life that really stick out to give you a better understanding of the beautiful mess that was my mother. As just a child living with a mama with manic depression, I really didn't realize that any of her issues had an actual diagnosis. Again, it was just Mama. Her high drama and frequent outbursts didn't change how affectionate she was toward us, showering us with hugs and kisses often. I have heard of many adults that spent their childhoods with all their physical needs met but they never felt loved by their parents. I never, ever, doubted her love for us.

During her times of depression, Mama would sleep a lot, so we managed ourselves often. With that being said, if Mama realized we needed her, come hell or high water she would get to us. Immediately. Without regard to anything. An example of this would be when I was about four years old and I started catching the church bus in front of our house each Sunday. My friend, Sheila, who lived next door, was a few years older than me and invited me to go with her. She had been catching the church bus for some time, so to her the process was a well-oiled machine. I fell in love with Jesus and I adored church. Since Mama and Daddy John didn't go, I always had permission to go with Sheila.

Every Sunday morning, I would wake up, get myself dressed, make myself cereal or toast, brush my hair and teeth, and then meet Sheila in front of our house. Most of the time, my mama was still asleep. Sometimes Daddy was up, but then later he would be out on the road with his truck-driving job. It didn't matter because I didn't need help. Mama wasn't worried; she knew where I was on Sunday mornings when she woke up. Sometimes my sisters would be up so they both knew where I was as well. Like I said, a well-oiled machine.

One Sunday morning, Sheila didn't show up for the church bus. I still remember wondering to myself if this was a problem, but then I quickly decided it wasn't. I knew what I was doing. The church bus came down the street as always. Stopped in front of me and opened the door. Nice bus driver man said, "good morning." Me, too shy to speak to adults, smiled and dropped my head as I walked up the stairs. What could go wrong?

Without Sheila as my mouthpiece, it honestly was a little scary. The ceiling of the church seemed incredibly far away as I sat in the pew looking around. I remember looking at the rafters across the A-frame sanctuary wondering why I had never noticed them before. And the doormen—they sure seemed really, really tall that day. I was usually holding Sheila's hand, so it's possible that I had never looked up at them. I'm not completely sure, but gosh they were tall and quite creepy looking.

Once Sunday school was over and all the kids were shuffled into the main sanctuary, I realized I had to pee. I sat there holding it through the song service. Once the offering plate began to be passed, I knew I couldn't hold it a minute longer.

I whispered to the old papa with the offering plate when he got to our pew, "May I go to the bathroom, sir?"

"Of course!" he said, motioning to the door on the side of the sanctuary.

I knew exactly where it was, so I jetted out of there like my feet were on fire.

The doorman stopped me, "Slow down, no running," he sternly said.

Shocked, I felt the tears form in my eyes and a lump in my throat. He may as well have spanked me. I quietly said "Yes, sir" and went straight into the bathroom. Once finished, I wiped the tears from my eyes, washed my hands, and headed back to the sanctuary. I kept my head down, walked slowly, and prayed that the doorman wouldn't speak to me again. I found my spot back on the pew with the other bus kids and waited patiently for service to be over. Without Sheila, it felt like an eternity.

Once service was over, bus riders were shuffled out to the church buses. I climbed in and took the first empty seat, just a few seats behind the driver. As we dropped kids off, I kept watching out the bus window knowing we would be at my house soon. The driver turned down Wasina Drive as always. There was my house, just up ahead and on the right. I continued watching as we got closer, and...as we drove right on past. *We passed my house!* I thought to myself. *We didn't stop!* My insides were growing frantic, and the tears were welling up in my eyes. My face was so hot; I honestly could not find my voice. I was terrified. I said nothing. Not a peep. My throat burned with words, but none would come out. We continued to drive. Only two more stops, which we made, as I sat there in silence. I never uttered a sound.

The seconds felt like hours as I tried to ponder my next move. Or any move, actually. In my mind, I begged myself to speak. My voice just wasn't there. My heart was in my throat, and it was throbbing so loud I couldn't think. I could see myself locked up in the church bus parking lot until next week when Sheila got back on. *I'll be wearing this same dress...Mama will think I'm dead.* My mind reeled with all that a week alone on a church bus could do to me. But just as I realized all hope was lost, I heard a loud car horn honking. Frantically, over and over honking. Next came my mama's voice. *My mama's voice!* She was honking and yelling at the driver to "STOP!" I stood straight up, scared the driver—who clearly didn't realize I was still on the bus—looked out the back, and there she was. Right behind us, driving all over the road. Honking the horn of our station wagon. Her and my sisters, all with their heads out the windows, screaming for the driver to "Stop the bus!" My mama was looking just like the crazy woman that she could be when we needed her. And I loved every minute of it.

The driver pulled the bus over. By the time he opened those doors, my mama was already standing in them, silky nightgown, no undergarments, and barefooted, of course. She grabbed me up and held me tight. I don't think I've ever been so happy to see her! Mama had seen the bus drive by. She immediately grabbed her keys, told the girls to get in the car, then she darted out the door to save me. She didn't care what she looked like or what she was wearing. Come hell or high water, she would snap out of whatever depression or aloofness she was in at the time, and she would get to us.

My mother also struggled with being quite jealous of my and Grandma's relationship. Feeling as though one of us girls preferred anyone over her seemed to throw her into depression or cause her to be incredibly defensive with her words. I truly believe this had a lot to do with us being "hers." We were really all she had that no one could take away. My relationship with Grandma was hard for her because I clung to my grandma wanting the normal life that she could give me. She loved me and protected me. Grandma's home was my safe place. I could sleep and not worry about the things going on around me. My grandma had it all together. She was awake in the mornings before I was. She cooked me breakfast and made sure I had a bath at night with good-smelling shampoo. I got to be a kid when I was with her. She was nothing less than a saint and was like a mother to me. I think Mama realized I felt that way and that's what she hated the most. It was a constant tightrope between Mama and Grandma, but I walked it gladly for fear of her not letting me go visit if I didn't.

My grandma hated the way my mama dragged us around the country. She hated that men were in and out of our lives constantly and she felt like my mother was too loose, selfish, and dressed inappropriately. One Friday evening, when I was in the fifth grade and we lived in Cape Girardeau, Grandma and Papa came to pick me up for the weekend. My sisters and I were cleaning up after supper and Mama was sitting cross-legged in her cutoff short shorts on the living room floor, working on her college homework. She was thirty years old at the time. Mama didn't bother getting up when Grandma and Papa came in. I think that may have been what set Grandma off—that we were doing the housework and Mama didn't even bother to get up to help me gather my things.

Standing in the living room, Grandma looked down at my mama and said, "Lynn, get up and get some damn clothes on; you're sitting there with your twat hanging out!" *Lawd!* It sends chills up my spine even thinking about it! I froze. Never in my life had this saint of a woman ever even said a cuss word in front of me. Not even a common cuss word! *Twat?* Oh, my goodness.

They had a not-so-great relationship, to say the least.

Along those same lines, Mama was very jealous of our daddies. An example of this would be when I cried because I was tired of the life we had, the moving and the boyfriend merry-go-round, and wanted to live with my biological father at about twelve years of age. She promptly started screaming at me, which was expected. She then, however, proceeded to tell me that *first*, when I was dying in the hospital as an infant with scarlatina, my daddy wouldn't come to the hospital. Even when she called to tell him that I may die. She said his response was "If it's her time to go, it's her time to go." *Second*, he may not even be my father.

Long, deep, sigh. What the hell.

When she was about forty, other things started changing. It was no longer just Mama's impulsiveness, mood swings, or high drama that were over the top. For a woman who had always been academically brilliant, she started having some trouble connecting simple cause-and-effect situations. Between the car wreck and her many years of domestic violence, I assumed that this new trouble was just brain changes that we would need to get used to. My mama, however, was afraid of something more serious: Huntington's chorea.

Huntington's chorea is a disease that is passed down from generation to generation. If you have a parent with it, you have a fifty-fifty chance of having the mutated gene as well. If your grandparent has it, but your parent does not, you cannot get it. It stops the generational transfer. Mama's biological father had this disease. He passed away when he was only fifty-one years old. We knew little about his family, but fortunately, my aunt knew everything. When the younger children were removed from the home after their mother passed, she was sent to live with family who also lived in Sikeston. This allowed her to stay in contact with her father. She knew how horrific this disease was.

My mother had researched Huntington's and knew the basics. That's what led her to believe she had it. Huntington's is said to be a cross among Parkinson's, ALS, and Alzheimer's. It results in the death of brain cells, you lose coordination, and your mental abilities decline quickly. Typically, it starts at around age forty. There are about 30,000 symptomatic Americans, and more than 200,000 at risk of inheriting the disease. Most in our family line make it about ten years after the symptoms begin.

My mother went to see a neurologist and then asked us girls to come with her to her next appointment. I was twenty-one years old and pregnant with my second child. The neurologist explained to us that Mama did, in fact, have Huntington's chorea. He tried to answer all our questions based on what limited medical knowledge was available at that time. Mama would need constant care in the coming years. Life would not be great, there wasn't a cure, but he would give her medication to help her with the uncontrolled movements and other symptoms. He would tweak her psychotropic medications to help with some of the "extra" we were all noticing. And, he explained, we each now had a fifty-fifty chance of having it, so it also should be considered when "family planning." At that time there wasn't an early detection test available—so our waiting began. Me at twenty-one, my little sister at eighteen, and my older sister at twenty-three. Riding home in the back seat of the car, I stared out the window. Would I have gotten pregnant again had I known this could possibly be my baby's future as well? It was all so surreal.

The following days and weeks, I went to the library and checked out books and learned as much as I could on the subject. Things quickly started adding up. Mama's impulsiveness was getting worse and that absolutely was a symptom. Her most recent issues with not connecting cause and effect were symptoms as well. I didn't have any of those symptoms yet. I remember thinking positively that I'm the one of us three girls that is the farthest from being like her. Maybe I didn't get this gene from her either. I don't show emotion. I am very much a planner and pragmatic. I can think clearly under pressure. Those thoughts gave me some peace in the short term. I would love to tell you that I researched the subject to try to provide answers and a better quality of life for my mother. To be honest, I must say that is not the case. I desperately needed a sign to show me that this wouldn't be me. I was in mental anguish not knowing if I had done this to my children. I was consumed by the reality that there very well may come a day when I have to rely on others to be taken care of. The very thought of that tormented my days and my nights. That I might lay in a bed someday at the mercy of other people for things like food and water, in addition to cleanliness. Unimaginably horrific. My life's greatest fear.

Mama's "crazy" at least had a reason now. That alone gave me some form of sanity after years of trying my best to manage her public episodes as discreetly as possible. I now had something tangible to blame it on. I couldn't control it, but at least this was something clinical. When problems came up after her diagnosis, I was able to handle them differently. Even laugh about them later with her and my sisters. One of the loudest displays of her loss of cause and effect almost landed her in jail. It's still so bizarre to think about.

She and I were out getting groceries. Mama asked me to swing by the veterinarian so she could have a quick visit with her cat that had been sick and in the vet's care for a few days. She was totally "the cat lady." She always had six, or ten, cats. I pulled up, told her to go ahead and visit as long as she needed; Raychel and I would stay in the car. Raychel was about five years old, so I thought sitting in the car singing was better than hanging out in the waiting area. It was in the fall, so temperatures were good for windows down and minding our own business in the parking lot. The vet's office doors were even open because of the nice weather.

Sitting in the car, Raychel and I suddenly heard my mama scream. We darted out of the car to the inside of the office foyer. From there, I could see down the hall and out the open back door into the field behind the vet's office. The field where my mama now stood holding that cat after she had decided to grab him and run. Another instance of What. The. Hell.

The veterinarian explained that he had asked her for payment when she came in. Toby, her cat, could be released and was doing well but they needed to be paid first. My mama didn't have enough money. So, she grabbed the cat and ran. Seriously. Out the open back door into the field before she realized she really didn't have a workable getaway plan. Wow. I sprang into action as I always did with her. I ran out the back and calmed her down. Got the cat back inside and in the arms of someone who worked there.

"Go to the car with Raychel please and I'll make plans to get Toby home," I said.

She didn't budge.

"No," she said curtly, "I'm not leaving without *my* cat!"

She had an emphasis on "my" like you would expect from a mad child, not someone that was forty-one years old. I could see the cops pulling in the front parking lot from the corner of my eye. I looked at Mama and demanded, "*Mama, get* to the car with Raychel so I can keep them from taking you to jail." That must have sunk in because she grabbed Raychel's hand and half walked, half ran to the car.

My time was ticking at this point, and I knew it. Raychel may have only been five, but she was one savvy little lady who could spin up a case of righteous indignation pretty fast. She and her Nanny, which is what she called Mama, were a tag team when it came to Mama's animals. I was certain she would pepper Mama with enough questions to keep her busy long enough for me to get us out of this. However, I also knew that by the time Mama answered all her questions, my little hot-headed, sass-mouth girl would be laying new plans for her and Mama to steal the cat back while I was busy with the cops. So basically, time was ticking.

I explained to the officers, while keeping one eye on the car, that Mama wasn't well. I also expressed how sorry I was and that I would fix it with the vet. I quickly worked a deal so that I could pay Toby's medical bills and get Mama, and Toby, home without charges. I remember looking at my little girl's face in the car as the cops were asking me what felt like a gazillion questions. Since I was her age, I felt like I had been managing my mama. All I could think at that moment was: *Your life will not be like this; I will promise you that.*

Within a few years, Huntington's disease took Mama down the path that the neurologist told us it would. Throughout her forties, she became more dependent on me to manage her bills and banking, and on my little sister to manage her doctor's appointments, medication, and eventually her care. Before Mama moved in with Lisa, she had me take her to an attorney where she had a living will drawn up. She wanted me to be the executor of everything and she wanted me to make all medical decisions, such as administering or withholding life support. At the time, I really didn't think that part was necessary for a woman in her mid-forties but again, I didn't understand Huntington's. I believe she did. Mama told me that out of us three girls, I was the only one she could trust to not let her live without a life. My mother was a passionate and vain woman. I didn't get a lot passed on from my mother, but she knew I could identify with her: The thought of being hooked up to machines to live terrified her. She knew she could trust me to handle it if we came to that point.

We were out of town for the weekend about an hour away from home at my in-laws' when I got a call from my little sister, Lisa. She was taking Mama to the hospital because she had gotten a tickle in her throat that just wouldn't clear up. It was nothing serious, there was no need to come home, and she would call me once they were done. A few hours later, Lisa called me back pretty frustrated and said they were keeping Mama overnight in the ICU. They told her they were not familiar with Huntington's and just wanted to be cautious. Mama was only fifty-one years old but I could see them wanting to keep her under observation through the night. Still, Lisa said they told her no need to worry. The next morning, I got the family up early and drove home. I felt it wasn't fair for Lisa to be at the hospital all night and then have to deal with the discharge too. I went to the hospital to handle whatever was remaining and take Mama home. I got there and sent my little sister home. I hung out with Mama and soon realized the hospital staff wasn't moving too fast, so I called Dawn, who decided to come hang out with us as well.

Sometime about midday, the doctor arrived and went through Mama's tests with me. She had pneumonia, probably from getting a little choked on some food. With Huntington's, it can become difficult to move the food back and to swallow. Choking is something you have to be watchful of. I assumed they'd get her an antibiotic for the pneumonia, and we would head home. However, the doctor didn't feel that was where we were headed. He explained that they had been treating the pneumonia all night and she was getting worse. He said her body wasn't strong enough for the fight. To this day, I honestly don't understand what all was happening. It was so very fast. I stayed with her and called my aunt and cousins, and they all came to visit. I called Lisa and gave her the update—basically that the doctor seemed to think this wasn't going in a good direction and he would be back to talk to us in a few hours.

Lisa got back up to the hospital fast and was there by the time the doctor came back to talk to us. Mama was resting so I was standing outside her room talking to my aunt and both of my sisters when he arrived. The doctor spoke to me directly and said things were progressing quickly, she was not doing well, and he needed to know if I wanted her on life support. He said she may be able to live for a few months at home with an oxygen life machine and tube. I stared straight into his eyes as both of my sisters and my aunt started talking all at once. As with the other most difficult moments in my life, I couldn't find my words. As they argued back and forth and asked the doctor what the hell was going on, my heart pounded harder and harder.

Lisa was mad, saying, "She's only fifty-one, what are we talking about here?"

Dawn, our free spirit, responds with, "Lisa, who wants to live like this?"

My aunt was mad and asking, "Why wasn't I called sooner?" My head felt faint taking in all the conversations at once.

The doctor broke the chaos with a loud "Ladies!" I can hear his words now and see it so clearly in my mind's eye, "I understand you all have thoughts on this, but I need an answer very soon, and I have to hear the words from Mrs. Rehder's mouth." So, MY mouth only. I thought I would pass out.

They had her advance directive. I had given them a copy when I got to the hospital, just as Mama had instructed me several years before. In that moment, both of my sisters turned to look at me, dumbfounded. Mama had not told them. She had not told anyone. I looked him in the face with both of my sisters' eyes burning holes in me, as well as my aunts, and I said, "She does not want to live life on life support." The doctor wrote it down, closed his file, and left us in the hall. I explained to them once he left that Mama asked me to take her to the attorney some years before because she wanted to make these decisions while she still had all of her mind. I told them I was sorry, but this was not how she wanted to live.

I left to clear my head and let my family cool off a bit while they sat with Mama. I went to the funeral home and started the paperwork. After the funeral home, I went home and changed into some comfortable clothes to stay the night with her. I had seen God's miracles before. I prayed we would get another one this night. I made it back to her room and my little sister went home for a while with the promise that we would call her if anything turned either way. The ICU was quiet with only the sound of the machines in each room and the soft glow of the evening night lamps. Dawn and I sat there talking and giggling, telling stories of our crazy childhood while Mama slept. I was so glad it was just me and Dawn. I knew Lisa wasn't angry with me, but I knew Dawn agreed with my decision. My mama had just turned fifty-one and I alone had to make the call to decide her fate. The magnitude and finality of that decision was suffocating, but I was resolute as always. Just as Mama knew I would be.

As Dawn and I quietly visited at Mama's bedside, we heard her start choking a little. We both stood up and went to her bed, Dawn on one side and me the other, both of us holding her hands. As we stood there softly speaking to her as her cough calmed, she laid her head back peacefully once again. Suddenly, a loud buzzer went off.

Nurses started running in and screaming: "No code!"

In that split second, Dawn and I looked at each other, my eyes quickly filled with tears and my chest burned deep inside. Dawn bent down and whispered in Mama's ear, "Fly away, Mama, just fly away. You're finally free."

But I had no words. Once again. I just stood there squeezing her hand as the tears silently streamed down my face.

My life of managing Mama was suddenly over.

As I have stated many times now, I'm not a doctor or mental health professional, but looking back, I can clearly see that Mama's actions told a story that her words never could. Maybe I had initially heard the stories of her childhood abuses at too young of an age. Maybe I heard them too often and was just calloused by the time I was old enough to understand what she had actually been through. I believe the constant moving around the country with us was because she kept believing she would find a better life for us. She would hit a high and think that this time, this guy, will work out for us. Or, in Winston's case, that maybe he's really changed and won't end up trying to kill her again.

I truly believe we have come a long way in our society in our quest to successfully detect and treat mental illness. Only fifty years ago, we were locking people up regularly in mental institutions. But even as far as we have come, reports still show that about 50 percent of individuals with severe psychiatric disorders are receiving no treatment at all. That is inexcusable, not to mention detrimental to our entire society. The mind is such a beautiful and complex organ. It can be in complete and utter agony and hide it all from the entire world.

Much can be said about the way my mother raised us. For someone who suffered from such a serious mental illness and such a painful and abusive childhood, I think she did the best she could. We always had food, and we always had shelter. She loved us and we knew that without a doubt. A friend made a comment once about Mama that really struck me. He said it was actually pretty astounding that even with the life that we grew up in, my mother somehow raised three of the most nonjudgmental women he's ever met. And that she never passed judgement as well. Until that moment, I had never thought about it, but it is very true. We were each other's biggest fans and we never concerned ourselves with what others were doing—

"...until you've walked a mile in their moccasins..."

CHAPTER VIII

DELTA DAWN

She died way too soon, but man, did she live. —My daughter Raychel at her Aunt DD's funeral.

I'm going to start off by saying you're not going to believe this. A person with a normal upbringing will have a hard time getting their head around my sister Dawn. If I hadn't witnessed her throughout my first forty-nine years of life, with my own eyes, I might not believe it either. It's interesting how two girls, same mother and father—so, DNA not too far off—both raised together, could be so very different. Both of us had to be pretty fearless throughout our lives. Both of us were thick skinned and we bounced back regardless of what life threw at us. The only difference, I believe, is that I've always clung to God. Careful, responsible, focused, and planned, always looking forward to God's promises of a better life. But my beautiful sister...well, she had a different take on life. Dawn was born set on "go." She was daring, carefree, chill, and always up for adventure. Dawn lived life.

Me and Dawn in our twenties.

Up until this point in this memoir, you've gotten a pretty good picture of my older sister. From her experimenting with boys and drugs at such a young age, rebelling against Mama at every turn, to moving on when life as we knew it held too much unhappiness for her. With this chapter, I'd like to peel back a few of those layers to give you more insight, and touch a bit more on my mama's favorite saying, "Until you've walked a mile in their moccasins..."

I started noticing Dawn had a lot more options when it came to boyfriends when we lived down Crooked Creek Road and Grandma was sick. She was so shapely, even at only thirteen. Dawn had a small waist, a killer booty, and big boobs. Her figure alone would have made her popular, but she was beautiful on top of that. Her feminine, yet chiseled jawline, seemed just the perfect shape to go with her small nose, blonde hair, and blue eyes. She seemed to have it all. I was eleven years old and certainly had the boobs coming along, but with my way-too-slender build, no butt, long nose, and red hair—well, let's just say I had plenty of reasons to be envious of my seriously cool sister. Every morning she would lay back on the bed with her bell-bottom, low-rise blue jeans pulled on, and I would straddle her and pull the zipper up while she held the zipper sides together. I would then stand in front of her, stick out my hand for her to grab, and hoist her up off the bed because the jeans were too tight for her to bend. Man, did she look great in those jeans. I was happy to assist.

The guy she was in love with, Rusty, was back in jail, but his little brother, Steve, would still give us a ride to school sometimes. I always knew he liked my sister too. When Steve wasn't picking us up, we would ride the school bus where all the boys flirted on her, it seemed. Even high school boys from nice neighborhoods! Now that was impressive to all of us girls in the trailer parks, to have wealthy boys interested in you. We knew that was a way out. Marry someone you can have that dream family with. It seemed way more important than love. Love was a wonderful dream, too. But what was really our understanding of love? Men who forget to come home at night because they're out drinking? Daddies who leave and don't come back? No thanks. When you're raised without much heat, when you have to run to the neighbors to beg for a phone in an emergency, and when your winter coats are always too thin to keep you warm, your priorities are just set a little differently. And it has nothing to do with being materialistic; it's wanting to have the necessities that others take for granted.

Dawn seemed to have all the tools to get out. Lisa and I were super excited when one of those wealthy boys asked her on a date, and not just any ole Joe Schmo. It was the handsomest and coolest of the guys, Mike Lambert. He already had an afternoon and weekend job that he talked about. He wasn't just a catch; he was a major catch. Dawn agreed to go out with him and, reluctantly, explained where we lived. There was no way around this since he was going to pick her up in his sweet Cutlass Supreme. Up until this point, we had been lucky and only a few kids knew where we lived since we were at the end of the bus route. Dawn was worried this might change his mind, but as Dawn often did, she tossed caution to the wind. She sure acted cool about it all, but we knew she had to be over the moon.

Friday came and after school Dawn spent time getting ready, curling her hair, and reapplying her makeup. I got her zipped up in her best jeans and she was ready to go. All three of us girls piled on the couch watching our black-and-white television, with the volume turned down low, as we waited to hear his car pull up. With the plastic stapled up over the windows to help keep the cold out, it was impossible to see his car coming down the gravel road, but we could hear engine noises and see headlights pulling in easy enough. So we watched, listened, and waited.

At some point that evening, we realized he wasn't coming. Dawn shrugged it off, acting like it wasn't a big thing, but I knew it had to really hurt. My heart broke watching it all. Us thinking that one of us could be someone that a wealthy boy would find interesting or attractive, well, I'll just say this was a hard double kick in the heart and the gut. Embarrassing to the max. I wondered to myself if maybe it was all just a cruel joke on her that those rich kids were playing. I didn't know and she didn't talk about it. She went back to our room and shut the bedroom door. At that moment, I wouldn't have spit on Mike if he was on fire and I really didn't even know him. We didn't have a phone, so I guess something could've come up and he had no way of telling her. But we all pretty much knew in our guts what happened.

After the Friday night Channel 12 shows went off, I went down the hall to our room and climbed in bed. Dawn was talking out of her head and was slurring her words and just being weird all the way around. I got up and turned the lights on. I wasn't sure if she was just dreaming or what. With the lights on, I saw Mama's pill bottle by Dawn's pillow. I grabbed it up, but it was empty. By this time, Dawn was sitting up and thrashing about, pulling the covers and pillows back and forth like she was drunk. I started yelling for Mama while I was yelling at Dawn.

"Did you take all those pills?"

"Dawn! Did you take Mama's pills?!"

"Dawn! Dawn!" I kept yelling and shaking her.

"Stick your finger down your throat before you die!"

I was eleven; I didn't know what to do. Mama ran through the trailer to see what was happening. I handed her the pill bottle, and in a flash, Mama was gone. The trailer door slammed and I knew she was going for help. I kept trying to get Dawn to throw up, but she just wanted to sleep. Mama ran back in, screaming and crying, and I knew an ambulance was on its way. Dawn had taken Mama's bottle of Librium, her "nerve medication," as we called it. When the ambulance got there, the people pushed me out of the way, got her in the ambulance, and rushed off to the hospital, where they said they would pump her stomach. Imagining all that was involved with a stomach pump was just too much. Mama went with the ambulance while Lisa and I sat on the couch and waited. Honestly, I was more worried about her heart than her dying from an overdose. *How would she face the kids at school Monday? Would Mike and his friends laugh at her knowing she waited and thought she really had a date? Would they ever realize how mean-spirited they are, or would they always be so cruel?*

My sister had tried to kill herself. Was my sister in love with Mike and just couldn't handle the rejection? No. Did she maybe in her young brain feel like dying would be much easier than facing the humiliation of the bus ride to school Monday morning? That would be my guess. Life wasn't so great anyways. Our grandma had just died. Mama was engulfed in depression. At just thirteen, Dawn honestly didn't have much hope for a better tomorrow.

One thing I knew for sure was that we had to figure out how to keep it all between us as much as possible. As ugly as those kids had been to my sister already, there's no telling how they would act knowing this.

Thankfully, our bus hop to Houston was right around the corner.

When we arrived in Houston in the middle of the night, Terry met us at the bus station. Mama had given in after the Sambo's incident and fight with Papa, so Terry was waiting and ready for her with open arms. The Houston bus station was bigger than the one in Memphis, but even with all of the people and busses everywhere, it didn't take us long to find him. I could spot his black afro, and thin, tall frame about anywhere by now. He seemed like the itch that just wouldn't go away.

Loading up, we drove south thirty miles to Pearland, where Terry's two-bedroom trailer sat back off the county road. Several trailers faced that busy roadway in a straight line with the landlord's house down just a bit, situated on a corner, with a car wash right across the street. Behind us sat a large trailer park with several streets and rows of trailers. We would have to walk about a football field back to get to it, but there were several kids who lived there, so it was worth the hike.

Pearland turned out to be quite the stomping grounds for my sister. Her beauty, coolness, and daring personality were a whole lot of fun to be around. She had moved on fast since her night spent waiting on the couch for that handsome rich kid that never showed. She had found her groove hanging with the kids that were like her. No more trying to hide from where we lived, or from what parents we had or didn't have. Within only a month or two after that awful night, she seemed to have the guys, and friends, lined up waiting for her.

One night just before dark, Dawn wanted to meet some friends down at the car wash. Knowing that Mama, or actually Terry, wouldn't let her go, she had me ask if we could go down there to do some roller skating. When we promised to stay off the roadway and just walk through the yards all the way to the well-lit car wash, and with me doing the asking, Terry agreed to let us go. To us kids, it never seemed like the men in Mama's life cared about what could happen to us as much as they cared about just having someone to be the boss of. Terry was at least the one that seemed to care more than he didn't.

Once we got to the car wash, I strapped the roller skates onto my tennis shoes. They were pretty neat, had an adjustable bottom for the length, and straps across the top to hold them on tight. I was really good at roller skating. Dawn had some friends show up in an old four-door car, so she stayed over by them talking and listening to music. I'm pretty sure they were smoking too, but I really didn't care. The music was playing, the air was warm, and the stars were out. It was a perfect time and place to work on my turns and skating backwards.

We hadn't been there long before Dawn called me over. "Get in," she said. "We're running down to pick a friend up and come right back."

"Nope! We ain't supposed to leave," I said, knowing her friends were shady to start with.

"I'm going, so you're going to be here by yourself, and you know what that cop told us."

The cop she was referring to was an officer who had stopped us a few evenings before when we were walking along the roadway in front of our house to go down to the little hamburger stand. He asked us where we were going, we told him, and he said we needed to be careful because, "Bad men love to pick up pretty little white girls around here" and "rape and kill them." Um, *wow*. He suggested we "get on home." He scared me to death, but Dawn pretty much thought he was full of it.

Regardless, remembering that conversation, I got into the car. Taking my skates off in the back seat, I watched closely where we were going and who all was in the car. Just in case I needed to tell the details to the police—because I absolutely would.

We didn't go far. Just down the road and then making a right to cross the ditch bridge, we were in another large trailer park. Once we came over the bridge, we pulled into a trailer just on the left. With it being pitch dark, it was harder to log all the details into my brain for later recall, but I felt like I was doing pretty well. Some guys in their early twenties came out of the trailer, leaving the door open so the blasting music could be heard. They were all laughing and smoking weed, so I got out and stood near the back of the car out of everyone's way—holding my skates, of course, just in case someone saw them in the back seat and decided to steal them.

Mad as could be, I stood there wondering why I always let Dawn talk me into these things. We were gonna be in trouble for leaving the car wash for sure. Before I had much time to brew on it, a couple of cop cars turned in and started across the ditch bridge toward us. Just as I looked up and saw them, I heard one of Dawn's friends yell, "Oh shit, *cops!*" and Dawn grabbed my arm and pulled me along with her yelling at me: "Run!"

I wasn't sure at that very moment what exactly *I* was running from. However, with the urgency of the moment, there was no time to ask. I followed her. Jumping into the ditch, Dawn waded through the water fast and climbed the concrete, slanted slab, under the bridge. She found a good place for us to curl up and be quiet as we listened to all of the commotion up above. Cops yelling, dogs barking, and what sounded like scuffles in the gravel. Scared, I didn't say a word. I may not have even been breathing, truth be told.

We weren't in our secret hideout long before we saw a flashlight scanning that ditch bank. My heart was pounding so loud in my ears I was certain that drug-sniffing dogs could find us from my heart noise alone. As we stayed focused on that flashlight moving closer and closer, another officer startled us from the opposite side of the bridge. Sliding his feet down the side in the mud, and ducking his head under the beams, he seemed to come out of nowhere.

"Let's go!" he shouted at us. "I've got two hiding under the bridge," he yelled to the flashlight cop.

Scared to death, I complied quickly. I was wet, muddy, and sure not looking forward to seeing my mama. The cop marched us like criminals toward the flashing lights of the two cop cars parked in the main entrance of the trailer park.

"Put your hands on the hood!" one shouted at us. Shaking, I put my hands up on the top of the car, just above the car door window.

"I said *the hood*," the cop yelled at me then pushed me down a little toward the front tire area.

"If you weren't on drugs, you'd understand what I'm saying," he continued, being as mean to me as possible.

With tears rolling down my face, I looked at Dawn who had her hands on the "hood" of the car and I realized what I had done wrong. I placed my hands in the right spot and scooted close enough to Dawn that I could say something to her, and you better bet I did.

"Mama's gonna beat you to death for this!" I whispered under my breath to her.

"Shut up and be cool," she said, with a little bit of a head shake. "We've done nothin' wrong." She sure had the "don't worry about it" face down pat.

"Be cool?" I questioned sarcastically, staring straight in her face, my eyes wide with disbelief at her calmness. "Are you kidding me?!" I continued, peering around at the shit show we were standing in the middle of.

Quietly studying me with her blue eyes, then glancing around still calm as can be, Dawn continued to school me in the ways of this world, "Holly...we are kids, it's gonna be fine."

Before I could say anymore, a car pulled up and out came Mama. Oh yes, most definitely in her nightgown. She talked to the cops, like only my mama could, then they quickly released us to her with a few stern warnings of hanging with the wrong people. Once we got home, I went straight to our room. Mama knew this had nothing to do with me, and after what I had been through, Dawn was 100 percent on her own.

Dawn didn't slow down after the car wash night. It certainly scared the fire out of me. But Dawn? Not so much. Her new friends may as well have been cemented in stone now. They were older, had all been in some form of trouble, and didn't seem to be living with rules in their houses. By the time we moved to Pearland, Dawn had already been a handful for Mama for a few years. Once we got there, it was like warp speed ahead. She was fearless, daring, and loved to have fun. You mix all that with a teenager's brain and a lax home life and you get some pretty wild moments. Mama actually grounded Dawn a lot. Dawn just wasn't too concerned about her groundings. If she had somewhere to go, and she couldn't wear Mama down enough to get her permission, she would just figure out a way and go anyways.

One of Dawn's groundings is a story that is so fantastic, so brazen, that it deserves to be told for generations to come. It went pretty much like this:

Grounded again, Dawn decided she was "going to bed" early. I use quotations there because I knew exactly what that meant when she announced it. Mama and Terry were already in bed, having sex, and making noises no one wanted to hear, but we had cable television for the first time, and it was a free-movie weekend, so Lisa and I were not leaving the living room. We didn't care how loud Mama and Terry got; *Xanadu* was on, and we were not going to miss it. We just turned the volume up to drown some of it out. Once our movie was over, we went to bed. As I entered our dark bedroom, I knew Dawn wasn't in her bed. A big lump of something was, but it wasn't Dawn. Not wanting to get her blown out of the water, I climbed in my bed and told Lisa to sleep with me, and I'd tell her a bedtime story. At eight years old, Lisa still loved hearing bedtime stories, and I knew if she climbed in bed with Dawn as she always did, Dawn's jig would be up.

After Lisa's bedtime story, we fell fast asleep. Sometime later, *boom, boom, boom!* came a hard, loud knock on the front door. Startled from a good sleep, I sprung from the bed while still waking up. I wasn't 100 percent just yet, but I was awake enough to realize that the knock sounded pretty aggressive, so we had a problem. With my heart racing, I ran to the front door with Lisa right behind me. Mama, waking from her sleeping meds, came out of her bedroom a little slower and headed to the door. *Boom, boom, boom!* Another knock that shook the trailer wall just as Mama was getting to the door. Unlocking the door, Mama pulled that door open fast, scared to death someone had died or been in a car accident. Lisa and I scurried up behind her to peek around and see who it was while Terry was just emerging from the bedroom, blue jeans pulled on, no shirt, afro standing tall in all directions.

A cop was standing on our rickety steps with his face set on unhappy. I guess since we didn't have a phone, he was mad about having to drive out to our place to wake and tell my mama that her thirteen-year-old daughter was in custody. Scrambling back to the bedroom, Lisa and I hurried to put some clothes on. We were so excited to go downtown to get Dawn out of jail. This was going to be fantastic!

"Y'all ain't goin,'" Mama said as we came flying out of the bedroom dressed. Mama was already mad and yelling, "Your sister stole our landlord's truck!"

Our mouths all but hit the floor. "What?!"

"Get back in bed. I'm not sure what all I'm going to have to do or how long this will take," Mama said. She had dealt with juvie before for Dawn, but this time, *Dawn stole a truck!*

Oh my gosh...Lisa and I were giddy with excitement. Dawn was always a good story just waitin' to be told. We couldn't wait for her to get home to give us all the details.

When Dawn and Mama walked in the door, the sun was coming up. They had been there for hours, and Mama was still yelling as they came in. Dawn came straight back to the bedroom the three of us shared and slammed the door—midstream of Mama's yelling.

"Tell us *everything*," I said, sitting up on the bed. "Don't leave anything out!"

This was gonna be good.

Sweet little Lisa piped in with a whisper, "How could you see over the steering wheel to drive?"

Giggling, we knew we had to keep it down so Mama didn't come in on us. This was a serious matter, and we knew it, but *Dawn stole a truck!*

Dawn undressed and climbed into her bed, just parallel with mine. Laying on her side facing us, head propped up on her hand, she gave us all the details we had been waiting on.

Just like I had thought, she sneaked out the back door while we were watching the movie. We had it up loud, and with Mama and Terry in the bedroom at the other end of the trailer, she had no trouble just waltzing right on out. We didn't have stairs up to that door, however, so after jumping down, she had to be a little more careful trying to get it closed without a slam. But she managed just fine.

Next, she told us, she walked down to the car wash to see if any of her friends were hanging out. She cut across the trailer yards instead of walking down the roadway to keep from gettin' another talkin' to by the cops if one drove by.

But on her way past our landlords' house on the corner, she noticed their pickup truck had the windows down. Looking inside to see if they left a pack of cigarettes on the seat, Dawn noticed the keys were just a-danglin' from the ignition.

It had to be fate, she decided.

Dawn had only been behind a wheel a time or two, pulling up in the driveway or moving someone's car for them. She figured it couldn't be too hard; she knew plenty of people who drive just fine, and they are far from right most of the time. With that, she climbed on in, started it up, and pulled out slowly onto the roadway.

Easy-peasy.

Once she had the hang of the foot pedals, Dawn decided to drive downtown to see if any of her friends were at the town lot since the car wash had been empty. She figured our landlords were old people, so she'd have the truck back *way* before they even notice it's gone. With such a great plan in place, Dawn said she turned the radio on and drove herself slowly right into town.

Pulling up to a stop sign, windows rolled down, arm out letting the warm air flow through her fingers, Joan Jett's hit song "I love Rock 'n' Roll" came on the radio. Well now, that just so happened to be Dawn's favorite song! So, with the night sky shining nothing down but twinkling stars, Dawn turned that baby up. She said she was way into that song, singing it out, and really feelin' it.

"I love Rock 'n' roll, so put another..."

As we listened to her tell the story, Lisa and I could see it all so vividly. Dawn movin' and groovin' in the driver's seat of that truck, blonde hair feathered back, singing into the night air, just livin' her best life—and then cop sirens cut through.

Looking in the rearview mirror, Dawn said that she saw that cop car behind her. Lights on, and sirens a-blarin'. She looked around to see if she could make a run for it, but she was downtown, stop signs at every corner, and people crossing the streets. No way to run. She pulled over.

The officer came to her window, "Do you realize we have a noise ordinance?"

"Oh! No, sir, I'm so sorry, I didn't know that," she said.

We could just see our sister, cool as a cucumber talking to that cop! Our hearts were beating fast as we hung on her every word. It was as if she was going to tell us he let her go, even though we knew the end of the story already!

"I thought he was gonna let me go, seemed like he just wanted me to know about the noise ordinance," she told us with a shrug.

Then she continued, "But then that cop says, 'I need to see your license and registration,' so I knew I was busted! But I didn't give up..."

She said she looked at him straight in the face, making sure she kept eye contact because it's obvious you're being shady when you don't, and she said, "I'm sorry, sir, when I ran out of the house, I forgot to grab my purse."

Dawn was an ice princess.

"Then what?" Lisa asked. We were both leaning in close listening intently.

"Well...he kinda looked at me like this..." she told us as she squinted her eyes and cocked her head to the side a little.

She continued, "Then he said, 'how old are you anyways?' so, I said, 'sixteen!'"

We squealed with laughter. Dawn would keep a lie going, way after being busted!

"Then," she said in a bit of a surrendering tone and shrug, "he told me to 'get out of the truck!'"

"Did he handcuff you?!" Lisa asked, wishing we could have watched this all unfold with our very own eyes.

"Heck yeah, he did!" Dawn said with pride, "*And* I rode in the back of the cop car!" We laughed so hard our bellies hurt.

She was fearless. We had no idea what all her punishment was going to be once she went to juvenile court, and that really worried me. But it just didn't seem to bother her.

Come Monday, Dawn's weekend escapades had already made it all over the school.

She was a legend—and she was only thirteen.

We weren't in Pearland long. I've already told you about our hot summer in the trailer in Morehouse, hanging at the park and getting some great lunches from the DAEOC program. What I didn't tell you about was exactly why Mama packed us up to leave this time.

Mama wasn't a party girl, but she sure enjoyed hanging out down at the Morehouse bar where Aunt Jan worked that summer. Who could blame her? Air conditioning, jukebox music, and kind men would buy her all the ice-cold Pepsis she could drink. She needed the attention this type of scene provided, and her beauty made it easy to get. Aunt Jan working there all afternoon made it extra nice because Mama could just hang out with her sister, something she enjoyed doing.

Mama always had a boyfriend, typically going from one to the next, and our time in Morehouse was no different. Dawn and I were usually glad to see the old one leave but never excited about the new one. Lisa seemed to be indifferent to most of Mama's boyfriends, but I think even she didn't care for the newest one. His name was Jesse.

One blistering hot afternoon, Mama was up at the bar with Aunt Jan and us girls were just hanging out in the trailer. I was eleven years old, Dawn was thirteen, and Lisa was about eight. Jesse showed up and came right on in. I remember thinking it was odd for him to come to the trailer with her up at the bar, but *whatever*, I thought. Jesse was a big guy. He seemed to tower over us and was just larger built than Mama's typical picks. He had dark brown hair and a thick beard, which was also weird for one of Mama's choices. Sitting on the floor with my word search book, I listened to his and Dawn's conversation. I never looked up to greet him; I didn't want him thinking I paid him any mind. I just kept listening and working my word search. I didn't trust him, or like him, so I hoped that he wasn't staying long.

Oddly enough, Jesse seemed to be most interested in talking to Dawn. He was telling her all about some new type of weed he had just picked up. Something different about the taste and the buzz it brought. I didn't smoke and didn't care to know about it, but I was nosey, so I kept listening. After only being there a few minutes, Jesse asked Dawn if she wanted to take a walk and try some out. Dawn was cool with that, and I was just glad he was leaving.

Dawn and Jesse hadn't been gone too terribly long when Mama got home. Maybe not even an hour. Mama asked where Dawn had run off to, so I let her know Jesse stopped by and they went for a walk. I thought about mentioning to her that he had some new weed and offered my sister some, just to get him kicked to the curb a little faster, but I didn't want to get Dawn into trouble like that. Mama was always suspicious about Dawn doing this or that, and I never gave her up. I knew better.

Mama stopped dead in her tracks when I told her they had gone for a walk. Next came the yelling and slamming things around in the kitchen. Lisa and I just sat there confused until she finally got it all out of her system. She and Jesse had broken up earlier. Mama had a new man, one of the Abernathy boys, on his way over to hang out at the house. She didn't want Jesse showing back up because he and the Abernathy guy had already gotten into it at the bar just a few hours before. Listening to Mama vent, I knew this could go on for a while, but I still had no idea where Dawn was, and we didn't know they had broken up. So, there was really nothing about this whole mess that was my fault or my problem.

I went back to my word search, and without an attentive audience, Mama left to go find them. Within minutes of her leaving, I heard the back trailer door open and slam shut and my sister sobbing. Dawn was alone and crying so hard she was having trouble catching her breath. Running down the hall to her, I could see she was very roughed up as if she'd been in a fight in the dirt and weeds. Her clothes were dirty, her arms and face had dirt and scratch marks all over them, and she had twigs and cockleburs stuck throughout her coarse hair.

"What happened?!" I said frantically, helping her into the bathroom that was near the back door.

Between her crying and catching her breath she managed to get out "Jesse" a couple of times.

In the bathroom, Dawn bent over the sink and turned on the water and started scrubbing her arms frantically with the soap. I did my best to hold her up, but she was crying so hard it was impossible. I got her to sit on the toilet and I grabbed a washcloth from the shelf and got it wet with cold water. She held that rag on her face crying into it as she told me what had happened. Jesse tackled her down and raped her. Horrified, I just didn't know what to say or do. I kept my arms around her while she cried, then I ran some bath water for her and helped her take her clothes off and get into the water.

As she sat in the tub, still crying uncontrollably, Lisa and I helped her scrub her whole body as clean as we possibly could. *Dang, my sister is so tough,* I thought over and over as we helped her get every bit of him off her. The scratches from the rocks were deep all over her back from having a cutoff shirt on. We tried to wash the small pieces of gravel out without hurting her too much—her body had been through so much already. Once we got her hair washed, I sat and picked the remaining cockleburs and weeds out the best that I could. She was still sobbing in the tub when Mama got back home.

Hearing Mama come in, Lisa ran to the living room to tell her what happened. Running back to the bathroom, Mama took one look at Dawn and started crying. Jesse had done this to Dawn to get back at my mama for breaking up with him. Mama went next door and called the police. I helped Dawn get some loose pajamas on because I knew her cuts and scratches didn't need clothing touching them. Her head hurt so bad. She said he really pulled her hair a lot. I could tell she had fought him with all that she had.

When the police got there, it made me sick to my stomach listening to her tell them everything that happened. It seemed so mean to make her go through it all again, tell such detail, to two men she didn't even know. I wondered if that was even right. *Were they supposed to be asking her such personal questions?*

I remember hearing the cops talking and pushing on their microphone walkie-talkies a lot. They decided she needed to go to the hospital in Sikeston to be checked, and they kept saying something about "sodomy" on top of them talking about her being raped. There were so many things happening that didn't make sense to me. Why weren't they leaving to go arrest him? We told them who did it. Mama knew where he lived. Heck, even they knew where he lived! We didn't need a doctor to say she had been raped; it was crystal clear what he did to her. My young brain simply could not understand the process for something like this.

I had so many questions. *What was "sodomy"? If she had not been high, would she have been able to run?* It didn't seem like a good time to ask questions or make comments. I looked "sodomy" up in Mama's dictionary. She said he raped her in other ways too, but I didn't know enough to know what that meant. Now I did. My heart ached for my sister once again. Dawn was so brave to tell the cops everything. She was so brave to allow the doctors to check her and to go through the details all over again with them. She was just so very brave.

Jesse was never arrested.

Life seemed to have a way of branding my sister. Another deep, smoldering sear on my sister's young soul.

And then there was that one time...when Dawn joined the carnival.

Oh yes, you read that right. After Dawn was hurt so badly in Morehouse, she kinda did her own thing for a while. Mostly staying with some of her friends in Sikeston, she waited out Mama's next move, knowing she wouldn't be gone too long. She was right; it wasn't very long at all before Mama and Lisa were back on a Greyhound bus headed back to Houston, where Dawn was happy to meet them. Soon thereafter, I was also on a Greyhound headed back to Mama from the Seventh-day Adventist boarding school.

All of us were back home together in Pearland once again. I was in the seventh grade and Dawn was back in the eighth. With all of the moving, and getting into trouble, Dawn was having a harder time keeping up in school than me. She was smart, very smart, in fact. She was street smart like it was nobody's business, but school was always another story. It's difficult to care or focus on schoolwork when your home life is a bit of a wreck. It just is. Dawn and Mama were like oil and water. The older Dawn got, the worse it got. She was fourteen years old and she pretty much felt like she could just take care of herself. One morning, we got on the school bus together, and both of us got off at Pearland Junior High. After that, she disappeared.

By the time the bus dropped me at home, all we knew was that she didn't come home from school, and school said she didn't go to classes that day either. We knew that she took my clothes before getting on the bus and left her books, so it was at least a few days that she had planned to be gone. We assumed she was out joyriding with friends, and that she would wander on home at some point in the next couple of days, at which time Mama would give her a good beating. But she never did. We just kept waiting and praying she would turn up.

Mama reported everything to the cops, and they had juvie out looking for her. When none of her friends seemed to know where she was, we had all our family in Sikeston looking for her too. Mama even called my daddy to see if she showed up at his place. Nothing. All we could do was pray and wait.

I don't remember how much time had gone by before we heard from her. But I remember well the day juvie came knocking on the door of the trailer. Opening the door, I fully expected to hear some audacious funny story about where and how they caught her, my fourteen-year-old sister who was "on the lam." But that's not exactly how it went.

The carnival had been in town the week Dawn left. No one realized that or put two and two together. She had made friends with some of the carnies and when they packed up to leave at the end of the week, Dawn met up with them and left too. She had told them she was eighteen years old and that her name was Tracy, not wanting anyone to know she was just running away. A few weeks into working as a carnie, her and her new boyfriend got into it, and she was tired of this weird life anyways, so she gathered her backpack and hit the road. She was in Florida at that time.

Since Dawn had been working as a carnie, she had some cash in her pocket. Her plan was to get to a bus station, buy a ticket to Houston, hitchhike to Pearland, and then maybe Mama would be so happy to see her alive that it would all blow over fast. Catching the bus, she met a guy that was about eighteen years old headed to his sister's house in Baton Rouge, Louisiana. They really hit it off, so she decided to get off at his stop and stay with him a few days and see how she liked Louisiana. He assured her that his sister wouldn't mind. She was pregnant and her husband worked nights, so she liked having people in the house at night so she wasn't alone. Dawn had known this guy for about a day, but again, she was fearless and always up for adventure.

Meeting his sister made Dawn feel right at home. She was young, personable, and very pregnant. Hearing the story, it sounded to me like the family was glad to see this guy with a friend, even if it was some stranger he met on a bus. He and Dawn looked for jobs the first day. He found one, but Dawn didn't. She was only fourteen and didn't have any real identification. She even had to have some guy purchase her ticket for her at the bus station.

Day one of her new boyfriend going to work, Dawn stayed at the house cleaning and trying to earn her keep a bit. The pregnant sister was gone at work, but her husband was home and sleeping from his night shift. Or she thought he was sleeping. The husband came down into the basement room that Dawn was sharing with her new friend, and he did many bad things to her that I won't go into detail about because they were far worse than her previous rape. He then threatened to kill her and drop her body somewhere if she told. A few days went by before Dawn could run. But at the first chance, she did. That's when juvie came knockin' on our trailer door. The authorities didn't have her in Texas yet, but they were working on it.

Dawn didn't talk about this trip like she would her other adventures. She would tell us about working for the carnival, the guy who tattooed her name, well actually "Tracy" because he thought that was her name, on his arm—and we would all laugh about it until our bellies hurt. But she would stop short of talking about Baton Rouge.

Layers of pain.

Joining the carnival wasn't the last time Dawn ran away. It actually became just the first of many over the next couple of years. Some had some great stories tied to them, but many only held more demons for her nightmares. Years after our childhood, Dawn started telling me some of the things that she held back before—like being sold on an auction block alongside other girls in an empty warehouse just outside a truck stop. I honestly cannot imagine. We may have grown up in the same house, but our experiences were very different.

For those who want to cast their stones at my sister, keep in mind that before the tender age of sixteen, when the typical American girl is worried about getting her driver's license, Dawn had already been raped multiple times by multiple men, tried to kill herself, and had been in fear for her life many times. The "good" kids from normal families didn't accept her. Didn't accept kids like us. That left her street friends, who had similar home lives to us, to very naturally become her family. The people she could trust, and the arms that would wrap around her when she was hurting, were kids who also had many moments in their heads that they desperately needed to forget. So, as it often happens, when Dawn experimented with drugs like many kids from all walks of life do, what she found was something that actually allowed her to forget the memories that haunted her. They made her feel good about herself. They were a method to numb her pain. Dawn had stumbled on a way to hide from the demons that chased her. To breathe.

I realize it's hard for many to put themselves in someone's shoes like my sister's, if they've never seen how cruel life can be. I tell you these stories to hopefully give you a glimpse from the other side. A song that always brings tears to my eyes is "What It's Like," by Everlast. It's very symbolic to me, reminding me of so many kids that grew up around us. One of the lines in that song talks about how you can tell someone's ending by looking at where they start. That's often true. I'm so thankful God let my life turn out differently. The song's video ends with all of the outcast people in the video staring into a large window that has a family having dinner together on the other side of it. They are laughing together and talking as they eat. Way before that song was ever written, and way before that video was made, that was my aspiration. *And it still is for many kids.*

Dawn's path in life was filled with many barriers, but even so, she never lost her ability to make everyone around her laugh; she never lost her love of life or her flair for the wild side. So fearless, so brazen...such a free and beautiful soul.

She passed away at only fifty-one, the same age that our mama passed.

CHAPTER IX

Addiction

As I begin this chapter on addiction, I want to start with the obvious but maybe something that isn't truly considered enough; addiction knows no socioeconomic background. It happens to those raised in poverty, and to those raised in a two-parent home and in a church pew multiple times a week. It simply doesn't matter. As you have seen from this memoir, I grew up around it. My sister became addicted by the time she was sixteen years old, my cousin died from long-term opioid abuse at just thirty-nine years old, and many that I grew up around have now since passed because of their addictions.

What I haven't told you about yet is my sweet little Raychel. That sassy-mouth five-year-old who would take up for her Nanny in a New York minute turned out to be even more fearless as a teenager. I may be like a strong cup of coffee sometimes, but Raychel is a double espresso. Bold, beautiful, and intelligent since the day she came into this world. She also has the kindest and most empathetic heart that you will ever find, and can outwork any man in the room.

Those are personal characteristics that I would bet on all day long as someone who will be successful if given a solid foundation. And she was given a very solid foundation. I remarried a couple of years after Johnny and I divorced, so Raychel grew up in a two-parent home. She was also raised sitting in the church pew several times a week, she had a mama up in her business most of the time, and she never had a concern over food, clothing, or shelter. Raychel had the opposite childhood that I had, and that's exactly what I fought for her to have. However, addiction knows no prejudices.

When she was seventeen years old, I started noticing some different behaviors in Raychel. She had been the normal teenage girl, giving us trouble here and there. I won't pretend she was an angel because she was far from it. My children are all spirited. They come from a spirited mother, so I've never expected them to be anything but. Raychel's sass mouth was ever-present, but it didn't get her into serious trouble. She was very respectful and kept her manners and boundaries. Her grades were always good; she took her schoolwork and future seriously. On top of keeping a part-time job, Raychel had begun shadowing at a local center for kids with disabilities after school. She knew she wanted her future college degree to allow her a career in pediatric physical therapy, so while in high school, she put in the necessary time to figure out how to obtain her goals in the most efficient manner. Then things started changing—rapidly.

Raychel had gotten a job at a local café. It was somewhat known for being a place where drugs were rampant, but I wasn't overly concerned. I spoke to her about it often, and I knew Raychel was laser focused on her future. My understanding of "drug addicts" at that time was what I had seen growing up—people without hope turning to them to feel better about their lives. Raychel was far from a kid without hope, so drugs were not on my mama radar—boys, however, were. I knew how quickly a serious relationship could derail her plans to go off to college. Boys and relationships were Raychel's blind spot; she was a lot like my sister and my mama, so that's where my attention stayed focused.

At first, she started coming in a little glassy-eyed. I had been raised around alcoholics and drug addicts; I knew the signs to watch for. Groundings, extra chores, and lectures of being forced to change her friends all ensued. She only dug in deeper. I was a thirty-three-year-old mother of a seventeen-year-old daughter. I knew the signs, but I didn't possess the knowledge that is needed to help a teen dealing with these issues. I was absolutely present in her daily life, very loving and supportive, but I was also tough and rigid. I had always had to be in order to keep the trains on time. Working more than forty hours a week, taking night and weekend classes, and being the teacher for the youth at church meant that my kids and I had a lot of balls in the air. We were the classic middle-class American family—we were overscheduled but spending a lot of time together.

Raychel's troubles escalated one night on her way home from a party when she was stopped and arrested for drinking and driving. She had scholarships with zero-tolerance policies; now she had pending charges that would tank them. When I got her picked up from the police station, I lit into her like only a Southern mama can. Up one side and down the other all the way to her daddy's house. I insisted she wake him so that she could tell him exactly what she had done to "completely ruin her life." Yes, I was way over the top.

Today, this fifty-plus-year-old mama can tell you how unhelpful my actions were. Not just unhelpful, but damaging. However, the thirty-three-year-old mama could only see red. Once we made it back home, Raychel stormed off to her room crying, saying she was leaving. In Missouri, you are an adult at seventeen years old. I took her car keys and told her she was welcome to take whatever she could carry. I called the police, but they couldn't help. She was well within her legal rights, so I could only wait, pray, and hope she returned. I never really thought she would stay gone long without her car. I was wrong. She packed three big bags that night and started walking. Raychel finished high school, with many more struggles that year, but she never moved back home.

My girl was gone. She didn't leave with a big goodbye celebration as if going off to college to live her dreams, and my dreams for her. Instead, she had moved just outside of town, in the middle of the night, with her boyfriend and his parents. I was so utterly disappointed for her. *In* her too, but mostly for her. Raychel continued working at the café and attending high school, but it became quite infrequent. My little girl was spiraling and there was nothing that I could do to stop her. I could only watch. Heartbroken, I started finding more pieces to the puzzle that I had missed. Many months before this, she had cut her finger at work. It was such a deep cut that the café sent her to the emergency room for stitches. Once finished in the ER, she was given a prescription for opioids. It was 2003, so only a few years after these types of pills had started being prescribed. We now know that at that time, doctors were being told that they were excellent for pain and not addicting. That has turned out to be very, very wrong.

I knew that she had cut her thumb. I knew that she had gone to the ER and was given stitches and a prescription pain reliever. She was seventeen, so they didn't need my permission or attendance for her treatment. What I didn't realize was that once Raychel's prescription ran out, she started purchasing pain pills from others at work.

Let me explain a little more about how this all works...

I am not a medical professional or specialist of any kind. I want to be sure I repeat that disclaimer. I am a mama. The fifty-plus-year-old mama that I am now knows a lot more about addiction than the thirty-three-year-old mama knew. What I have learned through years of fighting it in my home, and then in the legislature as an elected official, is that genetics play the largest role in this. A person's environment and age are huge factors as well.

Genetics, from what I understand, make up about 50 percent of the key factors. That is why you will notice that things like drug and alcohol addiction oftentimes run in families. Our DNA is different—some of us are more susceptible to addiction from the start. I can tell you from personal experience that when I have to take pain medication for my migraines, *if* I have to take it for more than a couple of days, I will have to wean myself off. If I don't wean myself off slowly, I have flulike symptoms because my body goes through withdrawals. I know many people who can take pain medication for a couple of weeks, like after surgery, for example, and stop taking it when their prescription runs out and they are just fine. That's a significant difference, and a very clear example of how people's genetics play a large role in this nightmare.

Environment is a giant factor as well. Parental care, peer pressure, access to drugs, abuses of any kind, all matter. If you grow up around people misusing or abusing pain medication or alcohol, you're either calloused to its ability to harm you, or very aware and afraid of its ability to harm you. I was lucky because mine was the latter.

Lastly, the age that you are when you start taking pain pills is significant when it comes to getting hooked. I've had specialists explain to me in great detail how a teen brain, still in the developmental stage, will attach to these powerful narcotics much faster than a fully developed twenty-something brain. Teens who received a prescription for opiates were 33 percent more likely to develop an addiction before they were twenty-five. Think about how many teenagers getting their wisdom teeth cut out are given a prescription for pain pills. This has been a sleeping giant for years.

When you put all those factors together, you can imagine how that might play out with a teenager who has no idea what's happening to her body. A teen with genetics like mine has a sports injury and is given a perfectly legal prescription of pain medication. She immediately feels on top of the world. The prescription doesn't seem dangerous in any way; it was written by a doctor. However, once the medication runs out, some feel awful—tired, aching, no energy, headache, and edgy. Most fall quickly into a deep depression as well. But on the medication, they felt like they could lasso the moon. What do you think many of them do? Yes, the same as my daughter. They buy them at school, work, or wherever they can find them. They are not thinking, "I want to be a drug addict." No one sets out for that. They only know they feel sick without the medication, so they don't see the harm in taking more.

Even without the age portion, the other two factors combined are hard to get beyond. Not too many years ago, when people were injured at work and in pain, they were quickly prescribed a painkiller. Many, for an extended period of time. Our bodies adapt to the pain medication, making us need to take a higher dose to relieve the pain. The outcome often becomes that the need for narcotics surpasses the original injury. By that time, many need treatment to successfully get off the medication. With the stigma surrounding addiction and scarce affordable resources, people often go a long time in this cycle. Some even lose their jobs or families because their addiction becomes the driver of their day. Sadly, many move to illicit drugs because their tolerance threshold has continued to rise, and they can no longer get enough relief from the pain pills. I've been told that three out of four heroin users started with a prescription pain pill addiction.

It's fascinating to me how different one person to the next can be when it comes to taking pain pills. Working on legislation to help with the opioid epidemic, I had a neurologist share a set of brain-image slides with me. One set showed the brain of a person who *wasn't* susceptible to addiction while on opioids. The slide of that brain had a few lights lit up in different places. The second set of slides showed the brain of a person who *was* susceptible to addiction after taking opioids.

The slide of that brain didn't have a few lights; it was lit up like a Christmas tree. The difference was unbelievable. The fact that this wasn't common knowledge for so many years while these were being prescribed frequently is how we find ourselves in the tragic situation we are in today.

So back to my daughter...

Raychel continued to delve deeper and deeper into her addiction. When she couldn't afford to buy the number of pills that she needed in a day, she moved on to meth. From meth, she moved to shooting up, and then to bath salts. Anything she could get her hands on. Once the addiction is in the driver's seat, you are no longer afraid of things like shooting up, losing your family, your job, and so on. Getting that drug so you can take it and stop your body from hurting consumes you. Your brain pathways have changed. You have changed.

We went through thirteen years of rehabs, a stint in prison, me not knowing where she was for weeks on end—or even if she was alive—her son being born with opioids in his system, and him being pulled from a meth lab when only a toddler. It was terrifying. It was exhausting—emotionally and financially. After my grandson was born, I had even more to worry about. He wasn't mine; I couldn't just take him away because he was in a dangerous situation. I would sit for hours watching her front door from across the street, waiting for someone to pull up that she would open the door to. With him just a baby, I never knew if he was there alone, possibly for days, with his mother overdosed and dead on the couch. The fear, the pain, it was all too much to bear.

The cycle of recovery and addiction has many triggers. Raychel had Kayden when she was twenty-three years old. She had been in recovery for several months and was doing well. However, the pregnancy threw her back off track. Triggers are what makes a person in recovery strongly feel the need to use again. Basically, anything that puts you in mental or emotional distress. Getting Raychel the proper treatment to learn how to manage her triggers was not something I understood. When something bad enough happened to make her want help, we would end up in a thirty- or sixty-day "treatment" program that would essentially get her body clean of the narcotics, but not much beyond that. We were doing nothing to get her the mental health help that she desperately needed to be able to move beyond the triggers. So, we stayed on the merry-go-round of addiction, treatment, recovery, addiction, treatment, recovery, addiction...an endless cycle of pain.

When Kayden was about twenty months old, Raychel was down to ninety pounds and had needle marks up and down her arms. One day, I knocked and knocked and she wouldn't come to the door. I knew she was there so I did as I had so many times in the previous weeks—I pulled into the parking lot across the street where she wouldn't notice me, and waited. After a couple of hours, one of her ex-boyfriends, Mike, pulled in and I knew he had a warrant out for him. I waited until she let Mike in, then I pulled in behind his car so he couldn't get away and then I banged on the door. She wasn't about to open it.

I kept banging. Still, no response.

Finally, I yelled through the door that I knew there was a warrant out for him and she could open the door to me, or she could open it for the police, but the door was getting opened today.

He opened the door.

Once inside, her ex began to tell me he was trying to help Raychel. To get her into rehab. Both of them begged me not to call the police and turn him in. I told her to gather Kayden's things for me, and if she went to rehab, I wouldn't call the police. They agreed. Kayden came home with me, and we were able to get Raychel into another treatment program. This one was a four-hour drive away and it was a long-term program, so that was good, but a treatment program can only help if you are ready for help.

She walked out of there within the first two weeks. We didn't hear from her for over a month.

Kayden had many rough nights and sporadic anger problems for the first year or so. When the other kids at the daycare were picked up by their mommies, Kayden would push their mommies away from them or knock them down and say *no*. He had me, his uncles—Johnny who was twenty, and Christian who was fifteen, and a house full of family, but he didn't have his mommy. He had been taking care of her and he wasn't even two yet. Her leaving was traumatic for him even though he was now in a safe and happy place. I just couldn't understand how she could choose that life over us. I had accepted the fact that I didn't matter enough to her long before this. But I couldn't understand for the life of me how Kayden didn't matter enough to her.

But you don't know what you don't know.

Raychel did love us enough. She also missed her life, her moments belly laughing with her brothers, and she missed her little man more than anything in the world. However, after over ten years of this addiction merry-go-round, her brain pathways were very different. Getting her body free of the narcotics and sending her on her happy little way was never the right answer.

Soon after I took Kayden full-time, I was elected to the Missouri House of Representatives. During my campaign, and this struggle with Raychel, I found out that Missouri was the only state without a prescription-drug monitoring program (PDMP). A PDMP is a tool that allows doctors to look up their patient's narcotic history before prescribing. The reason this is important is that Raychel started out buying pills from people at work who had them in droves. They had more than one doctor prescribing pills at the same time— without the PDMP, doctors had no way of knowing. Raychel could also go to the doctor and say she injured her back and get a prescription. While at the same time, she could go to the emergency room and say she had a toothache. The beginning of her addiction was fueled by an excess of pills. Countless other families were telling me very similar stories about their struggles as well.

Through the fight for Missouri to establish a PDMP, I got to know many medical professionals, recovery and treatment specialists, and mental health therapists who had been in the trenches of this epidemic for years—like the neurologist who explained the brain science of addiction to me with the slides. I was flooded with resources and educated on how addiction is a disease, documented by science and the medical community for years. What addiction wasn't was a moral failing, as so many had always thought. Just as I had thought my entire life. My eyes were opened. I was starting to understand what was really going on. Raychel had not just walked away from us, not caring, not loving us. There were actual neurological changes driving this in her. I finally understood, but I still didn't know how to help. My girl was still out there.

I was invited to be on a panel focused on addiction for a television program out of St. Louis a couple of years into my fight for a statewide PDMP. I had been getting several invitations like this because I had been very vocal about addiction and the need to remove the stigma. Since being elected, I spoke often on the House floor about the way that I was raised, and about my sister being addicted to drugs by the time she was sixteen. I also talked about my daughter becoming addicted even though she wasn't raised around drugs like I was. As you can imagine, this was a little odd coming from a very Christian conservative legislator. But I knew God didn't give me a microphone to keep my mouth shut, so I happily accepted the invitations.

At the time of my being on the TV program, Raychel actually had Kayden back in her house most nights. She had been doing well, though I started noticing some of the signs returning. Her new boyfriend had many of the same demons, so that gave me heightened concern. I was worried about Kayden's safety night and day—especially when I was out of town working at the capitol, which was four hours away from our home. Kayden was four years old and I would call him nightly from the capitol to make sure he was okay. What I had not realized was that Kayden wouldn't rat his mommy out for nothing. When I called, he sounded sad, and he wouldn't want to get off the phone, but he kept telling me everything was good. He protected his mommy, just like he always had.

During the panel discussion that night, I was learning so much from the other participants. Joining me was someone from the National Council on Alcoholism and Drug Abuse, a person from Washington University that had been providing addiction-related services for over fifteen years, an addiction therapist, and a teenage girl who had moved from prescription pills to heroin. It was incredible. I left there with the contact information of the therapist. His name was Jim, and I wanted to know more about the importance of mental health treatment for those struggling. It was clear to me, through our panel discussion, that Raychel was lacking some very important tools needed for a solid recovery.

Within a couple of months, things had blown up with Raychel once more. Kayden answered my call one evening, crying, saying that Mommy wouldn't wake up. I'm so thankful I was in town that evening. I kept him on the phone as I drove to their house to get him. He had packed his backpack full of his stuffed animals and was ready to leave the minute I walked inside the door. Oh, my heart! I was so sick and angry with myself for allowing him back into an unsafe situation, but at the same time, I wanted so badly for her to truly be doing well. I gathered the rest of Kayden's things, made sure Raychel was breathing, and left her a note that he was coming home with me for good. The next morning, I called my new therapist friend and asked his opinion. I needed to know if there was anything else I could possibly do for her. I knew forcing her back into rehab was a waste of time. We had bet on that and lost many times now. He had one suggestion that we had not tried yet: an intervention.

Our family wasn't really sure about this. We had seen interventions on TV, and we weren't so certain that would work with Raychel. I could just picture her walking straight out of the place as soon as she realized what was going on. She was one tough little 4'11" girl when she wasn't on drugs. Trust me, on drugs no one, and I mean no one, told Raychel what to do. Even knowing our plan could go south fast, I wasn't about to leave any stone unturned. It was my daughter's life we were talking about, and now my grandbaby's heart as well. We had to try.

Jim worked first to find a place for Raychel to check into immediately if the intervention worked. He explained that we had to have a bag secretly packed for Raychel and in the car for her, as well as a facility awaiting her arrival. The reason for being this stringent is because if you wait, even just overnight, many times the person needing treatment will change their mind. An intervention is different from someone going into rehab that might not really want to be there. With an intervention, you have the entire core family saying the same thing about the consequences of not going, in writing, as a solid front, all mixed with love and promises as well. After the intervention, you drive straight to the facility. If you stop by their house before getting on the road, something can go wrong, like him or her throwing drugs in the overnight bag. With this, I knew we had a little bit of prework that had to be done before the intervention could be scheduled.

I took care of getting a bag prepared for Raychel and placed it in my trunk with all the necessities that she would need short-term. Once she was checked in, I could take her the rest of what she needed or send it by mail. Jim found a place for Raychel about three hours away that had an opening, and that we could afford. It was incredibly expensive, but we were ready to throw everything we had at this last opportunity to get her back. I really liked this facility above the others that she had been in because they did an interview with me first to find out more about Raychel. They had different houses set up for different types of core issues. For example, one house was set up for those who used drugs to self-medicate because they had past abuses or trauma, in their lives. The house Raychel was going to join was for those whose issues stem from bad relationships. As I've said before, I had always felt that was Raychel's blind spot—relationships.

Once we had the facility locked in and the date that a bed would be available, we set the date and time for the intervention. Jim came to town the evening before and met with us; he wanted immediate family only. That meant both of Raychel's brothers, Johnny and Christian; my sister Dawn, whom Raychel had always been incredibly close to; and Raychel's stepdad (my husband) and me. We didn't have Johnny, Raychel's daddy, join because we felt it would be too hard on him. Jim walked us through writing very personal letters to Raychel that evening. Letters explaining how her addiction had harmed us, and what precautions we were going to take moving forward if she didn't go to rehab and fully complete the program. He went around the room and asked each of us how her actions made us feel. As we explained, out loud, he would tweak our words so that we were clearly saying it was her addiction that had harmed us. He explained how telling her over and over how awful she was and how much she hurt us was only going to trigger more drug use. We needed to express our love for her, but at the same time, we needed to be honest and set boundaries for our own health and future. He had notepads for us all and asked that we really put time into it that evening, and then we were to meet at the hotel room he had set aside the next morning for a run-through before Raychel joined us.

I was so very nervous. I knew she would throw a fit about not getting to see Kayden before she left—*if* she even agreed to go. The next morning's run-through with Jim went well. I was impressed with all that everyone wrote. I knew Dawn's would be really good, but I also figured it would be too soft. She never got onto Raychel, ever. Her letter was close to what I thought—loving, gentle, and understanding. But she was honest about being harmed by Raychel's addiction. I knew that would be powerful for her to hear.

I expected mine to come off more rigid; I'm just not as touchy-feely as my free-spirited sister. Raychel's addiction had taken a toll on me, and from what Jim advised, I wasn't supposed to ignore that. Raychel needed to hear it. I loved her with my whole heart. But the harm and the pain that my precious Kayden had gone through with her addiction—that had made me harder inside. She was my baby. Having her at only 16, and it often being just the two of us, it felt as if we grew up together. I couldn't imagine life without Raychel in it, but I also knew that we had to follow through with what we had decided as a family: to no longer allow her addiction to be a part of our, or a part of Kayden's, lives.

As the boys read theirs, I was so proud of the obvious time and thought they'd put into it. They wanted this so badly for their sister. Christian's was a little hard, very straight-forward, but Raychel had left home when he was only five years old, and it really hurt him. She was like a second mama to him, and then she was just gone. Because of the explosiveness of dealing with someone under the influence of drugs, he had never gotten to express how it had affected him. So, I pretty much expected a more pointed letter from the now seventeen-year-old that had lived her addiction in almost every memory he had with her. He loved her so very much, but he had some anger built up that writing about his feelings certainly released. Christian is also a writer by nature, and now by trade, so you can bet he laid his feelings bare. Her stepdad's was good, very thought out, with some humor in it. But it was Johnny's that surprised me. He is a man of few words, but when it's needed, he will hit you with the wisest, most thoughtful comment. He had just turned twenty-three, and he spoke about their childhood memories together in his letter. He had grown up witnessing the cool, funny, and daring sister. He spoke of how much he missed that, and missed her, over the years. How she would take him riding around listening to music when she was sixteen and he was just eleven, and how cool that made him feel. They had a special relationship, always laughing so hard together, usually when no one else even understood what was funny. I knew Johnny taking this seriously and putting his heart into his letter would matter greatly to her.

It was time to get started, and even with all the emotional letters and thoughts put into this day, I honestly wasn't sure if it was going to change a thing. I was all in, but skeptical. I left the hotel and headed to Raychel's. I asked if she would hit a drive-through with me so we could talk. We had had an enormous blowup the week before and we both knew we needed to talk. She agreed to go with me, got dressed, and met me in the car. We ran through the McDonald's drive-through and then I pulled up to the hotel across the street and parked. I explained we needed to run in and pick some things up from a work event I had there earlier in the week. She followed me in, casually talking, until we got to the room and I opened the door. Seeing her brothers and Dawn, her Aunt DD, she stopped cold. I thought she was about to turn and go, but, in true Raychel fashion, she started peppering us with questions.

Jim explained in a very concise and matter-of-fact way what was going on and asked her to sit with us and allow us to speak to her as a family. We then started around the room, reading our letters out loud to her. They were to tell her how much we loved her, something special to start with, then we needed to address how her addiction had harmed us. Next, we could offer what we missed about our relationship with her, and then end with what the outcome would be for our relationship moving forward—if she didn't take this last offer for rehab.

Jim directed everything. It was seriously high emotion, which isn't my wheelhouse, so it's hard to remember some of the details. But it was fine-tuned. It surprised me how putting the therapist's spin on something as simple as a word, or phrase, could make such a big difference in how it was received. As a child, Mama had taken us to therapists, and I never gave them the credit they were definitely due. Jim further cemented for me the importance of Raychel getting mental health care. She needed it to help her heal, and also to allow her to jump off this merry-go-round for good.

She agreed to go to rehab.

The facility for women was a ranch in the beautiful rolling hills of Tennessee. Way out in the country, with multiple houses for the girls, common work areas, and a main house with a nurse, admissions, and so forth. They had treatment with horses, treatment through old Indian rituals, group therapy, and many other programs for the girls. It was nothing like what we had ever experienced. Johnny and I checked her in, loved her up, and said goodbye. We weren't allowed to communicate with her for a couple of weeks. She would be there for thirty days at least, then we would discuss her progress, needs, and next steps.

When I first spoke to Raychel, she wasn't happy. Medically, she was still sick. She had been abusing both alcohol and drugs, drinking a ton of vodka a day on top of the drugs. Her body had very painful and long-lasting withdrawals. She couldn't really start the mental health aspect of the treatment program until her body was free from the drugs, alcohol, and pain associated with the withdrawal process. I believe she was there for six weeks total before moving to Nashville for the next phase of her rehabilitation—a sober living house for women.

In the new facility, Raychel had group therapy, individual therapy, and attended local AA meetings each week in the community. Honesty and participation in all classes were key. I took Kayden to see her one weekend each month for her entire stay, which ended up lasting a little over four months. She looked so good when we went to see her. A little quieter than her normal self, but positive change was setting in. Raychel was speaking differently about her addiction, about herself, and she was speaking differently about having hope for her future. God had her exactly where he wanted her.

After four months in the sober living house in Nashville, Raychel moved home to southeast Missouri, but this time she didn't go back to Sikeston. She moved into a halfway house thirty miles away in Cape Girardeau. There, Raychel would search for employment, do her own grocery shopping and cooking, and take the city bus to get to meetings and to church. We had just built our family home about ten miles outside of Cape Girardeau, so this allowed her to be away from running into old friends every day, but close enough to us that she could see Kayden as much as she would like. She was sober, equipped with the tools that she needed to continue successfully in her sobriety, and she had hope. My girl was coming back, slow but steady. I couldn't have been prouder of her.

Keep in mind that this is just one type of treatment and is not the program needed by everyone. Addiction is different from one person to the next. My point is that I believe that the mental health component must not be overlooked by anyone with long-term drug abuse.

I'm not going to act like it was all sunshine and roses. It wasn't. By the time of the intervention, Raychel had spent thirteen long years in the bowels of addiction hell. Raychel coming from the life she had lived for so long, back into our daily routine of work, supper, church, school, and so on, was strange to her. She was lonely and sad often. Depression is very common for someone who is in recovery. Without the drugs to forget the pain you've caused, you have to face it head-on every single day. That's rough. Typically, it takes someone in recovery a lot longer to forgive themselves than it takes for others to forgive them.

Restoration of the brain pathways I talked about earlier? It's different for everyone. I realized that after thirteen years of damage to Raychel's brain and body, it wasn't going to repair itself overnight. However, I longed for Raychel to have happiness again so badly. She was going through the motions every day. Finding a job at a local grocery store, she busted her butt like always and outworked everyone else on the team. That was my Raychel, no doubt about it, but the light in her eyes still seemed dim, and that broke my heart for her. She worked hard at her job, she worked her AA "steps," she took excellent care of Kayden—both of them living at home with us after a month or so in the halfway house, and she made new friends here and there. Raychel was doing all the things she had been taught that she needed to do. I just don't think she found a lot of joy in it for quite some time.

That was the really, really good part—Raychel being sober and staying the course. God was so good to us, and I never could have thanked him enough, even if that was the end of her progress. But it didn't end there...

Now to the amazing, over-the-moon, "thank you, my Lord and Savior" part!

Sitting in the living room of our house with Kayden on my lap giving him tickles one morning, I couldn't have been more thankful for the noises of all three of my kids coming from the kitchen. Christian was home from college for Christmas break, Raychel was off from work that day, and Johnny had come up to spend the night with all of us. All three of them were in the kitchen making coffee and picking at each other. Raychel had been home for exactly two years at this point. Most likely, it was movie lines they were all three going back and forth with, but out of nowhere it seemed, I heard Raychel's laugh. I paused Kayden's tickles. *Her laugh!*

My brain screamed at me as tears filled my eyes. Yes, Raychel had certainly laughed since being home. But it had not been *her* laugh. Her laugh is a gut laugh that will make you giggle just hearing it. I had not heard it since she was a teenager, and right then, standing in the kitchen, she was gut laughing once again with her brothers! My heart was overflowing.

Now, my girl is back.

I think it's important to note how long the recovery road can be because you need to know that restoration happens, but it takes time. We cannot live by believing in only what we can physically feel or see. I don't always feel God's arms wrapped around me, but I know for certain He is always here. We couldn't see that Raychel's brain was going through the tough restoration process, but it certainly was. After about that two-year mark, other things started coming alive once more for her. Her smile, her chattiness, being outgoing, it was all steadily coming back. Soon, even her depression was gone.

As a side note, I just want to say that the depression part of opioid addiction is incredibly dark. Coming off the medication, you wake up feeling like there is no hope in sight, and the rest of your day feels the same. You don't want to get out of bed, and all you can see are your failures. If you are choosing to not be on the medication any longer, or don't have access any longer, you may get so low that you can only see one way out. This is one of the most important reasons to have mental health treatment be a part of any recovery. Those coming through recovery need to be reminded, sometimes over and over, that it's just the changes their brain is going through. Life is better than they can see. They need the tools and understanding that mental health specialists provide.

Raychel was also put on medication for hallucinations of voices in her head. They put her on this medication in the treatment facility, and she was on it for over a year and a half. This is also a very common problem for many coming through recovery from what I understand. The medication she was on was for drug-induced schizophrenia. This was super scary for her; she didn't know if the voices and the medication would always be a part of her life. But her brain did heal. It needed to be given time.

Raychel has been sober for seven years now at the time of me writing this memoir. She is audacious. She is beautiful. She is kind. And she is by far the best mama I know. She successfully juggles Kayden's soccer, basketball, honor choir, a full-time job, church, and now a toddler. She found a wonderful and loving husband who treats her like the jewel that she is. No one meeting her today would know the hell of her past. Raychel wanted me to write about her individual journey through addiction to show that recovery is possible, and to say that, if you're struggling, don't give up. Our family is blessed beyond measure because we didn't give up. Understand that everyone's path is different. What works for one might not work for someone else. Medication-assisted treatment, for example, has helped many steer through these dark waters. But it's not right for everyone. There are two things that I will say are important for anyone who is struggling going through recovery: Allow time for your brain to heal, and don't ignore your mental health.

When I speak to groups of high school students, I always ask, "What do you want to be when you grow up?" The answers are usually the same everywhere—a doctor, business owner, school teacher, and so on.

"I want to be an addict"—says no one.

CHAPTER X

FORGIVENESS

*A calm and undisturbed mind are the life and
health of the body, but envy, jealousy, and
wrath are like rottenness of the bones.*

—*Proverbs 14:30, Amplified Bible*

This is without a doubt the most important chapter of this memoir. It's the most important chapter of my life's story, and it's the most important chapter of my walk with God. I could tell you more about Greyhound bus moves, domestic violence, or sexual abuse, but that's not what this memoir is truly about. It's about hope and becoming the person you want to be. Regardless of where you've come from or what your past looks like. Understanding that God can bring you out. Now, he isn't Santa Claus—he doesn't go around dropping presents on us because we ask. What I have found is that oftentimes, it takes work on our end as well. Why have I been pulled from my pile of ashes—the life I grew up in and the problems I've brought on myself? *Because one of the greatest gifts God has given me is understanding the importance of forgiveness.*

Jesus taught often about love; love conquers all and the greatest commandment is to love your neighbor as yourself. He said we are to love our enemies and pray for those who persecute us. Easier said than done, I know. I have learned, however, that the key to loving all crazy like Jesus does is forgiveness. And forgiveness is a tricky little thing. On the surface, forgiveness seems like it's something you do for someone else. Something *you* are *giving* them—your forgiveness. But that's not actually how it works. Forgiveness is something *you do for yourself.* Proverbs 14:30 says that "envy, jealousy, and wrath" rots the bones. Holding onto that is unforgiveness in a nutshell. And that's not talking about the person who did you wrong—that's *your* bones. When you forgive someone, it is you that gets set free. It is you that finds peace.

At some point in my Christian journey, I started praying for God to allow me to see through his eyes and not my own. I realize our eyes are jaded from our journey. I want to see through God's eyes; he knows the backstory. We all have one— why and how we got to where we are today. I'm absolutely *not* saying this gives a free pass to someone treating others badly. I do think, however, that this type of understanding can help to keep offense from being rooted deeply in our hearts. Just like with my biological daddy, had I decided to stay hurt over one phone conversation in a hospital room, or simply take my mother's point of view about him, I would have missed out on my adult years of having a daddy that took up for me, comforted me, always had a wise and non-judgmental word for me, and was always there when I called. For a child who grew up without a daddy in her life, I was more than blessed by him in my adult years. When you've done without for so long, you're happy with just a piece, any piece, of what you've longed for. Because of this, once I had Daddy steady in my life, it wasn't a problem for me to allow him to be who he was, not who I had imagined was the perfect father in my mind. The outcome of me just being happy with whatever I could get from him was that I got the perfect daddy for me. I was much more like him than I had ever realized, and I can never thank God enough for the years he gave me with him.

Stick with me for a bit longer while I take you through a few of my *aha* moments that helped me move past some huge hurdles in my life.

MAMA

Mama may have always been the villain in my mind, but she was always there, and without a question, we knew she loved us. I was an adult before I realized all that her past tainted her with. Once she was diagnosed with Huntington's, I think I allowed her more room for mistakes. Just the knowledge of it helped me in the way that my heart responded to her. God also allowed me to see how the abuses that she went through growing up affected who she became as an adult. As I started understanding more and more, my heart started tearing down some of the walls that I had built.

The anger and frustration that I had toward her because of how she let men run over her and abuse her dwindled when I realized that her self-worth had been utterly distorted and destroyed at such a young age. The betrayal I felt from her taking the money from the accident when I was pregnant and needed help started fading when I realized she never had hope for a better financial situation. She had landed on flat broke so many times that this was her survival instinct. I also realized Mama had no idea that leaving Dallas in the middle of the night would cause the life that we ended up in. For me to assign blame was very immature of me, in a Christian sense. As I've grown wiser and more knowledgeable through God's word, I've realized that I seemed to have empathy for others quite easily. It was time that I gave Mama some of that grace as well.

Most people with Huntington's grow angry and impossible to be around the more the disease progresses. You are losing your mental capacity and it gets harder and harder to communicate. But Mama didn't. She became so sweet. So calm. Her anxiousness was gone. I've often wondered if that was because my little sister moved Mama into her home and cared for her. Lisa cooked for her, hung out with her, and loved on her daily. She worked from home, so she had the ability to take care of Mama while raising a little one as well. I handled all of Mama's finances during that time. I honestly think it must have been the first time in Mama's life that she had complete assurance that she was 100 percent cared for, without owing anyone anything for their kindness.

No matter how hurt I was, I never shut Mama out. I am thankful for that. I always loved her, but to feel like she would pick man after man before us girls, along with all the other painful memories...I mean, I had some major things to let go of. I'm so thankful God allowed me to see her through His eyes before she passed. To truly have His understanding and to release the pain that I had locked down so deep in my soul. Forgiveness allowed me years of being able to love her without all the other junk between us. Never once, since letting it all go, have I ever laid in bed with an angry heart or troubled mind thinking about how we were raised. Not once. That is a supernatural peace that can only come from true forgiveness.

PAPA

Papa was my rock and my safe place. After Grandma passed, he was the only person I could count on and trust. When he sexually abused me, it not only ripped my heart out, it also opened my eyes to what a cold and messed-up world we live in. It was unconscionable to realize that somehow, someway, generations of our family had purposefully ignored, hidden, or maybe even been accepting of this type of behavior. Trust me, I did not have forgiveness in my heart overnight. The beautiful thing is that God didn't leave me there—hurting and angry deep in my bones, like the "rottenness" the Proverb speaks of. He nudged me along and the blessings that I have received from being willing to be nudged are immeasurable.

Looking back at how it all unfolded, I see that God used the fact that I've never been one to shirk my responsibilities. When Papa came asking for help, there was no way that I could have refused. I still loved him, even though I didn't like him, and I sure didn't trust him. However, I knew that if I didn't help, no one else was going to. In my mind, it was mine to do.

I hadn't been around Papa much since he had hurt me. He apologized several times right after it happened, but as I've said many times, words don't mean much to me. The Bible says you will know a tree by its fruit, good or corrupt. I learned early on that it's a person's actions that tell who they are, and his actions were horrific.

I don't hold grudges and I don't hate people. I've never had that in me. I will, however, wall you off in my heart and mind in a New York minute if you hurt me badly enough. That's where my Papa was—walled off. If you would have asked me around that time in my life if I had forgiven him, I'm sure I would have said yes. I didn't harbor ill will on him. I didn't have bad thoughts about him. I just didn't think about him at all. To me, that was forgiveness: being able to move on and forget. What I have found since then is that there's an ocean-size difference between that, and the restoration, peace, and freedom that true forgiveness brings. But like I've said before, God doesn't just drop it on us because we ask him to. Often, there is work to do on our end.

God's "Nudging"

Papa's need for my help started off gradually, like only asking me to go with him to his appointment in Memphis. He was afraid and didn't want to hear the news alone. I couldn't imagine allowing him to go by himself, especially since he broke down and asked for my help. He was a proud man who never asked for anything. Once we got the news, he had to stay in the hospital for his treatments. The treatments were difficult and I thought about how lonely he would feel being sick and facing death with only strangers around. So, I drove back and forth to Memphis visiting him while he went through them. Next came bringing him home and getting him set up with all that he needed.

Every task we completed for which I had made the decision to stay through, another one was just waiting around the corner. Another need that required even more of my help. Before I knew it, I was tending to him three times a day and making sure all of his meals and medication were taken properly. It started from the time I got up in the morning until I was climbing into bed at night. It was a slow and gradual process and before I knew it, I was no longer reminded of how he hurt me. God chipped away slowly at the pain and anger I had locked up in my bones. None of that would have been possible if I would have refused to help because of my unforgiveness.

Papa got better for a short time after his treatments, but then started going downhill pretty fast. We knew from the doctors that his condition wasn't going to get better, so Johnny, Raychel, and I moved in with him. He had become so frail that I was worried about him being alone all night. I found a friend that could do in-home nursing care while I was at work. Papa could afford to pay for it, and I wasn't about to give him baths; personal hygiene is where I draw the line. *So ewww*. No way could I have been a nurse.

What I didn't realize was that my heart needed that time with Papa. As I said earlier, words don't matter to me; actions do. His actions during this time told me daily how much he appreciated me. His actions told me daily how sorry he was for hurting me. He loved me. Before I started caring for him,

I'm not sure I could have said that with such profound confidence. I needed him as a little girl. I mean I *really* needed him. He not only hurt me, but he let me down in a way that no one else could have. My love for him was untouchable; he was my only normal and my only lasting connection to my grandma. Losing all of that left a canyon-size hole. Never knowing how truly sorry he was would have been one of my greatest disappointments. But God gave me a chance. A chance to feel the power of true forgiveness—I am so thankful I took Him up on it.

In the last few weeks of Papa's life, he couldn't get out of bed, so people started visiting the house more. Mama even visited quite a bit too and I'm thankful that she did. Papa had stopped talking and mainly slept through those final days, but I would sit and hold his hand like I had my grandma's all those years before. Same bedroom, same bed, same stool I would drag in to sit close. Aunt Jan came to visit one day after he had stopped responding to us and she sat and sang to him. Her voice was low and raspy; I always loved to hear her sing. Mama and some of the others had been in and out of Papa's room all day but no response. He was resting peacefully, but it had been days since he had been coherent. Mama and the others were in the kitchen visiting so I went into Papa's room to hold his hand and listen to Aunt Jan sing "Amazing Grace." Her voice was like an angel's.

When she finished the song, Papa opened his eyes and looked at me.

Surprised, but not sure if he was actually awake, I gave him a little smile, "Hey, Papa," I said quietly with a little hand squeeze, knowing he wasn't going to be with me much longer.

Papa's gaze stayed on mine. He struggled like he was trying to say something. Aunt Jan and I knew he was alert because he stayed focused on my face the entire time. He had something he wanted to say to me.

Squeezing my hand back softly, he kept moving his lips and clearing his voice. Finally, a gentle "I love you, Holly," came out in a whisper, his gaze still fixed on mine. Then he gave my hand two quick, gentle squeezes.

"I sure love you too, Papa," I softly replied.

Papa stared at me a few seconds longer before he relaxed back into his pillow and closed his eyes again.

With tears rolling down her face, Aunt Jan patted my leg and said, "He woke just to make sure you knew he loved you, baby."

With my whole heart, I knew he did. I had known it as a child, then had my world shattered by the only man I trusted. Through Papa's illness, God had given us both a second chance. Love had healed my heart and allowed me to forgive. Papa had gotten the chance to show me how sorry he was. Because of these things, I got to feel Papa's great love for me once again, and I knew that I was special to him.

Let's break for a minute for me to explain that none of my love, or forgiveness, made what he did acceptable. First, if he wasn't truly repentant for his actions, he would be taking that up with God. Secondly, vengeance is God's. The Bible has a lot of scriptures about seeking revenge. Basically, if we do, we are stepping into God's role, and I don't have to tell you what a bad idea that is.

Finally, we don't get to choose who our family is. When we are abused by someone that we love greatly, in any way, we don't get to turn that love off like it's a water spigot. That's not how love or humanity works. Many of us that are abused by those we love, have such turmoil in our souls. As time starts to heal our wounds, it's impossible to reconcile the pain of what happened, with still feeling love for that person. It just doesn't make sense to us and it's impossible to explain.

Hopefully, my actions immediately following Papa abusing me kept it from happening to anyone else. No longer allowing his abuses to hide in the shadows needed to happen. But what my heavenly Father wanted *me* to have, His child who was harmed, was *His* peace. The peace that surpasses all understanding. Without a shadow of a doubt, I have that.

"I love you, Holly" were Papa's last words before going to live with our heavenly Father. Hours later, as I lay asleep in my bed across the hall from him, I woke suddenly around midnight. I felt a heaviness in my heart, and I knew. Walking into Papa's room, I saw that he was laying peacefully, his body was still warm, but his breathing had stopped. I called the coroner, just as he had instructed me to do. When they arrived, they confirmed he had just passed. I think he woke me on his way out of this world.

LUCIFER

Watching your mama go through so much at the hands of a madman, well, I can tell you that does a lot to a person. It's interesting to look back all these years later and see how easily we fell into such an abusive cycle. Mama really focused on trying to "behave" to keep the horror at bay. To be pleasing to Winston so he wouldn't get upset. Regardless, there is no reason on the planet for a person to abuse another.

But why did she stay? They hadn't been married to him for years, they didn't have children together, and we had walked away with nothing before. It just didn't make sense to me; however, domestic violence seldom does. There's so much manipulation involved, and oftentimes the abuse comes on slowly, almost undetectably. It then grows and grows until you look back and really have no idea how things got so far off the rails.

Years after getting away from Winston, I saw him in Walmart with a little boy that was about five years old. We had the normal pleasantries, cold on my end for sure, but he introduced his little boy to me. I remember looking into that sweet little guy's eyes and just wanting to hold him. I wanted so badly to say, "I know what you're going through and I'm so sorry." I wanted to grab him and run.

After I was elected as state representative, Winston sent me a message on Facebook. It was very complimentary and very kind. He was hoping we could have coffee and catch up soon; he had been serving as a rabbi for years, he said. I closed my Facebook message and went back to it many times before responding. I didn't know how to respond. A part of me wanted to keep him walled off, not even give him a response. But the other part of me wanted to meet with him and say, "Do you still beat your wife?" "Have you realized yet it is a sin?" I wanted to make him face the questions that no one ever asked him.

I eventually responded to him kindly. I thanked him for the nice message and told him I'd reach out soon and we would meet for coffee. Unfortunately, I never got around to it, and he died in a car accident two years later. Many times, over the past thirty-plus years, I've felt in my heart like I have fully forgiven him. Not long after I found out he had passed away, I realized I actually had not.

It's a thirty-minute interstate drive from my home to my business. As I got on the highway from the on-ramp, I noticed a new highway dedication sign on the shoulder of the road. Our department of transportation does these if you match the criteria, pay the cost, and so forth, to get one. They are typically put up in memory of someone at the location on the highway where that person's death occurred. Merging onto the interstate that day, I saw the new sign:

See you in heaven, Winston Wellington.
You will be missed, but not forgotten.

God's got jokes, no doubt about it. Out of all of the miles of highway locations that sign could be placed, it was at my exit. After getting over my shock, I laughed, and cried, all alone in my car for miles. *How about that?* I thought. *I hear you Lord, I hear you; you want me to get on with it.*

On my way back home that day, oh yes, another one. Same mile marker on the northbound shoulder of the road. Our heavenly Father was nudging me along like he had so many times before.

Winston's family had to go through many steps to get those signs put up. My hope is that the little boy in Walmart that day didn't grow up in a house of horror, and that's why his family cared so much to go through the process. I want with all my heart for that to be the truth. What I know for sure, however, is that God isn't allowing me to keep those painful memories pushed into some deep dark hole in my soul like I've done for so many years now: my out-of-sight, out-of-mind attitude. He's showing me that it's time to work through the pain and let it go. I need to forgive. It's not a coincidence that those signs were put at my exit. As you can see, I'm far from perfect and have plenty of work to do myself. I'm thankful He still nudges me along until I get it right.

I have learned in my fifty-plus years now that being human is a mixed bag of pain, love, heartbreaks, and triumphs. We get broken down, we fight to come back, then we heal. The scars from the healing process can make us stronger or, they can break us and make us their victim forever. Genesis 50:20 says that what the devil means for harm, God can use for our good. I believe that, heart and soul. I also know that oftentimes, it doesn't come packaged the way we envision it. God operates from His view—the big picture we usually cannot see.

When Winston got saved and turned Mama onto church, I finally got what I had wanted for so many years. The problem was it didn't come in the neat little church family that I had always dreamed of. I'm sure the devil had a heyday when we figured out Winston hadn't changed, the day that our nightmare returned. But what the devil means for harm, God can change to good. Winston had not changed; that was fact. We witnessed it firsthand, over and over. However, many other things had changed. First, Mama had found Jesus. Regardless of what Winston did, he couldn't take that away from her, from us. When she passed many years later, she was still serving the Lord and heaven bound!

Secondly, even though we had so much hell going on around us during that time, I was being taught by our new church family to pray without ceasing and I was learning the Bible like never before. Having God's word in my heart allowed me to pull from it for direction, strength, and hope. I'm sure the devil only saw a scrawny little broken-down girl with nothing but life's soot covering her face. But just like those cinders I mentioned earlier, God's word had lit a fire inside of me that you couldn't see from the surface. One that could not be blown out by life's ups and downs, because the source was, and is, buried deep inside me. I was in a spiritual training camp and didn't even realize it.

That source, God's Word, has helped me my entire life. The devil didn't see that coming when he was wreaking havoc on my family. The Bible is our training manual for life. Jesus himself used God's word to overcome the devil in the garden of Gethsemane. If Jesus needed to use the Word, you better believe we do! We need to know our weapons and our enemies. Our weapon is the Word. So, know it, and use it. Ephesians 6:12 says, "For we wrestle not against flesh and blood, but against principalities, against powers, against the rulers of the darkness of this world, against a spiritual wickedness in high places." In other words, our enemies are not the people that hurt or wrong us. It's much bigger than that. It's spiritual. We need to fight with our spiritual weapons, the Word of God. Forgiveness comes much easier when we do.

Learn God's Word, forgive those who hurt you, and watch God change your life. If you stay hung up on the bad times, or the unfair things others have put you through, you'll miss out on the beauty of all that God has created, and all that He has created you to be. Seeing that highway sign and remembering Winston so often doesn't bother me, it's a reminder that even on my worst days, He has brought me out of so much more.

RELUCTANT
WARRIOR

Out for dinner with friends one evening, we wandered into a local art show at a downtown gallery. I was raised with an appreciation for the arts, and I love roaming around local galleries. Walking through alone at my own pace, I came across a charcoal drawing of a woman that gave me immediate pause. I felt drawn to her, like maybe I had seen her years before in one of my dreams. Average size, only about a 16 x 24 framed and matted, she seemed to hold such a powerful presence. As I stared intently, everything about this drawing spoke to the deepest parts of me. As I moved closer to study this incredible piece of art, I overheard some around me making misogynistic comments about her. She was drawn naked, and I knew all too well that their joking was only par for the course for her. Irritated, I walked on with the intention of coming back alone to view her in stillness.

Unfortunately, the next few days were unbelievably busy, and before I realized, the show had closed. Not knowing how to locate the artist or how to find out if the drawing had been purchased, I chalked it up to disappointment. But I honestly couldn't get this drawing out of my head.

A couple of years went by. Still thinking about her often, I decided it wouldn't hurt to dig a little. I reached out to a friend who has had art showings of her own at the same gallery and enlisted her help. If there was any way that I could still find this drawing, I needed to try. I explained in detail what I remembered about her; she was only shown from her back, and she was naked with her head hanging down. She held a sword behind her that she seemed to have in a resting position...but somehow, you knew it was ready for battle.

Surprisingly, it didn't take my friend long to find her. No one had purchased her, so she had gone back home with her creator, artist Terry Godwin. Now hanging on my bedroom wall, I think she was waiting for me. We are all born with a purpose, I feel she embodies mine. I'll explain...

- Her head seems hung in obedience to God. "Not my will, but thine be done." —Luke 22:42. This sentiment is my heart.

- Her sword is resting, but she stands ready for battle, as if hoping it won't be necessary— this time. I don't look for fights, but I won't shy away from them either. I strive to do the things God has placed on my heart. To fight for those who cannot fight for themselves. If my obedience to God turns into a struggle with others, then so be it.

- She stands naked. Brutally honest about my life, I hope to use the struggles that God has brought me out of to help others. Many times, however, I feel completely exposed—naked— to a sometimes judgmental and cold world. But for the one person who sees my battle scars and is helped, it is worth it. God has done too much for me to ever hide His light.

Mr. Godwin named her "Samurai," but to me, she is my Reluctant Warrior.

God has made me to be someone who can handle the judgement and ridicule of others. There's nothing about it that I like, but I know who I am in God's eyes, so I do not fear what others might think of me. I don't back down, even though I certainly prefer peace. I believe these are the reasons He has me in the position that I am in now, a state senator, and why this drawing speaks so loudly to my soul. I am a voice for my people. The people who grew up like me, in a culture that doesn't allow much room for them to realize, or rise, to their potential. Not many of us make it to a place where we have the ability to effect change on a large scale. To help open the eyes of others by speaking to issues that many simply cannot or will not. Issues like poverty, addiction, mental illness, and domestic violence.

To help people understand the true power and meaning of *"until you've walked a mile in their moccasins..."*

Charcoal drawing by artist Terry Godwin

ACKNOWLEDGMENTS

I couldn't have completed this without the editing help and direction from my son, Christian M. Rehder, who has been a beautiful writer since he was in the 3rd grade. I'm so grateful for you, my Kissy Kissy. You sure make your Mama's heart smile.

To my Pastors, David and Harriet Craig, who have taught me and trained me up in the word of God since I was nineteen years old. I love you both more than words can say. Thank you for never letting go.